Theorising Noncitizenship

'Noncitizenship', if it is considered at all, is generally seen only as the negation or deprivation of citizenship. It is rarely examined in its own right, whether in relation to States, to noncitizens, or citizens. This means that it is difficult to examine successfully the status of noncitizens, obligations towards them, and the nature of their role in political systems. As a result, not only are there theoretical black holes, but also the real world difficulties created as a result of noncitizenship are not currently successfully addressed. In response, *Theorising Noncitizenship* seeks to define the theoretical challenge that noncitizenship presents and to consider why it should be seen as a foundational concept in social science. The contributions, from leading scholars in the field and across disciplinary backgrounds, capture a diversity of perspectives on the meaning, position and lived experience of noncitizenship. They demonstrate that we need to look beyond citizenship in order to take noncitizenship seriously and to capture fully the lived realities of the contemporary State system.

This book was previously published as a special issue of *Citizenship Studies*.

Katherine Tonkiss is a Lecturer in Sociology and Policy at the School of Languages and Social Sciences, Aston University, UK. She is interested in the ethics of migration, immigration policy, and post-national theories of citizenship.

Tendayi Bloom is a Lecturer in Politics and International Studies at the Open University. Her work examines the nature of the relationships of noncitizens and stateless persons with States.

Theorising Noncitizenship

Concepts, debates and challenges

Edited by
Katherine Tonkiss and Tendayi Bloom

Routledge
Taylor & Francis Group
LONDON AND NEW YORK

First published 2017 by Routledge

2 Park Square, Milton Park, Abingdon, Oxfordshire OX14 4RN
711 Third Avenue, New York, NY 10017

Routledge is an imprint of the Taylor & Francis Group, an informa business

First issued in paperback 2018

British Library Cataloguing in Publication Data
A catalogue record for this book is available from the British Library

ISBN 13: 978-1-138-21052-3 (hbk)
ISBN 13: 978-0-367-03008-7 (pbk)

Typeset in Minion Pro
by RefineCatch Limited, Bungay, Suffolk

Publisher's Note
The publisher accepts responsibility for any inconsistencies that may have arisen during the conversion of this book from journal articles to book chapters, namely the possible inclusion of journal terminology.

Contents

Citation Information vii
Notes on Contributors ix

1. Theorising noncitizenship: concepts, debates and challenges 1
Katherine Tonkiss and Tendayi Bloom

2. Assembling noncitizenship through the work of conditionality 17
Patricia Landolt and Luin Goldring

3. Unequal access to human rights: the categories of noncitizenship 34
David Weissbrodt and Michael Divine

4. The business of noncitizenship 56
Tendayi Bloom

5. Rooted displacement: the paradox of belonging among stateless people 71
Kristy A. Belton

6. Citizenship and inclusion: rethinking the analytical category of noncitizenship 86
Paulina Tambakaki

7. Contractualization, depoliticization and the limits of solidarity: noncitizens in contemporary Australia 100
Shanthi Robertson

8. These fine lines: locating noncitizenship in political protest in Europe 115
Heather L. Johnson

Index 131

Citation Information

The chapters in this book were originally published in *Citizenship Studies*, volume 19, issue 8 (December 2015). When citing this material, please use the original page numbering for each article, as follows:

Chapter 1
Theorising noncitizenship: concepts, debates and challenges
Katherine Tonkiss and Tendayi Bloom
Citizenship Studies, volume 19, issue 8 (December 2015), pp. 837–852

Chapter 2
Assembling noncitizenship through the work of conditionality
Patricia Landolt and Luin Goldring
Citizenship Studies, volume 19, issue 8 (December 2015), pp. 853–869

Chapter 3
Unequal access to human rights: the categories of noncitizenship
David Weissbrodt and Michael Divine
Citizenship Studies, volume 19, issue 8 (December 2015), pp. 870–891

Chapter 4
The business of noncitizenship
Tendayi Bloom
Citizenship Studies, volume 19, issue 8 (December 2015), pp. 892–906

Chapter 5
Rooted displacement: the paradox of belonging among stateless people
Kristy A. Belton
Citizenship Studies, volume 19, issue 8 (December 2015), pp. 907–921

Chapter 6
Citizenship and inclusion: rethinking the analytical category of noncitizenship
Paulina Tambakaki
Citizenship Studies, volume 19, issue 8 (December 2015), pp. 922–935

Chapter 7

Contractualization, depoliticization and the limits of solidarity: noncitizens in contemporary Australia
Shanthi Robertson
Citizenship Studies, volume 19, issue 8 (December 2015), pp. 936–950

Chapter 8

These fine lines: locating noncitizenship in political protest in Europe
Heather L. Johnson
Citizenship Studies, volume 19, issue 8 (December 2015), pp. 951–965

Notes on Contributors

Kristy A. Belton is Post-Doctoral Fellow at the Human Rights Center, University of Dayton, USA. Her work explores the politics of belonging, migration, human rights, and global justice.

Tendayi Bloom is a Lecturer in Politics and International Studies at the Open University. Her work examines the nature of the relationships of noncitizens and stateless persons with States.

Michael Divine is Founding Attorney at Divine Law Group, LLC, St. Paul, USA. He attended the University of Minnesota, USA, for both his undergraduate and legal education.

Luin Goldring is Professor and CERLAC Fellow in the Department of Sociology, York University, Canada. His research interests include immigration, sociology, citizenship and non-citizenship, precarious work, and transnational migration.

Heather L. Johnson is Lecturer in the School of Politics, International Studies and Philosophy, Queen's University, Northern Ireland. Her current research project examines issues of ethics, security, and the governance of mobility.

Patricia Landolt is Associate Professor and Department Chair in the Department of Sociology, University of Toronto, Canada. Her research examines systems of social exclusion and inequality linked with global migrations.

Shanthi Robertson is Senior Research Fellow at the Institute for Culture and Society, Western Sydney University, Australia. Her work explores the social and cultural consequences of globalisation.

Paulina Tambakaki is Senior Lecturer in Political Theory at the Centre for the Study of Democracy, University of Westminster, UK. Her research focuses on citizenship, agonism, and radical democracy. She is author of the Routledge book series, *Advances in Democratic Theory*.

Katherine Tonkiss is a Lecturer in Sociology and Policy at the School of Languages and Social Sciences, Aston University, UK. She is interested in the ethics of migration, immigration policy, and post-national theories of citizenship.

David Weissbrodt is Professor in the School of Law, University of Minnesota, USA. He teaches international human rights law, administrative law, immigration law, and torts.

Theorising noncitizenship: concepts, debates and challenges

Katherine Tonkiss[a] and Tendayi Bloom[b]

[a]Sociology and Policy Group, School of Languages and Social Sciences, Aston University, Birmingham, UK; [b]Global Justice Program, Yale University, New Haven, CT, USA

ABSTRACT
Existing political theory, particularly which deals with justice and/or rights, has long assumed citizenship as a core concept. Noncitizenship, if it is considered at all, is generally defined merely as the negation or deprivation of citizenship. As such, it is difficult to examine successfully the status of noncitizens, obligations towards them, and the nature of their role in political systems. This article addresses this critical gap by defining the theoretical problem that noncitizenship presents and demonstrating why it is an urgent concern. It surveys the contributions to the special issue for which the article is an introduction, drawing on cross-cutting themes and debates to highlight the importance of theorising noncitizenship due to both the problematic gap that exists in the theoretical literature, and the real world problems created as a result of noncitizenship which are not currently successfully addressed. Finally, the article discusses key future directions for the theorisation of noncitizenship.

Introduction

'Noncitizenship' is a surprisingly elusive term. While it might simply be defined as the absence of citizenship, such a definition fails to capture the complexities of practices and constructions of noncitizenship, many of what challenge traditional understandings of what it means to be included within a political community or society. Emerging sociological and cultural studies have begun to embrace the challenge of understanding what it is to be a noncitizen and the role of noncitizenship in contemporary societies as a topic in itself, not contingent on citizenship (e.g. Golding and Landolt 2013; Nair 2012; Rigby and Schlembach 2013; Sigona 2015); however, this development has not been mirrored in political theory. As a result, normative theorising – and particularly that which is concerned with justice and rights – tends to be dominated by (a) the core concept of citizenship, and (b) a definition of noncitizenship as simply the negation of citizenship.

This special issue, in response to this gap, explores how liberal political theory can begin to address directly the question of noncitizenship. Bringing together scholars from legal, theoretical, sociological and applied perspectives, the special issue considers the theoretical problem that noncitizenship presents and how this problem can begin to be addressed with reference to how noncitizenship is conceptualised and the lived experience of noncitizenship. In this introductory paper, we present an examination of the absence of a detailed and accurate conceptualisation of noncitizenship within political theory and the kinds of questions which must be addressed to build the noncitizen into normative theorising effectively. We advance a claim for a more sophisticated approach to the theorisation of noncitizenship and, through our presentation of the papers which comprise the special issue, offer an original and interdisciplinary perspective on the relationship between membership and rights in contemporary societies.

The paper is structured as follows. After first locating the noncitizen in current literatures on citizenship, justice and rights, we highlight the problems inherent in treating noncitizenship as merely the negation of citizenship and the critical omissions from scholarly work that this has driven. We then utilise insights drawn from the papers featured in the special issue to set out the value of recognising a richer definition of noncitizenship within liberal political theory, before finally setting out an agenda for future work on the theorisation of noncitizenship, one which can also drive the inclusion of noncitizenship in policy considerations. In particular, we advocate a normative theoretical approach which embraces rich real world studies of the evolving nature of noncitizenship and its multiple forms in different geographical regions, as well as its intersections with cross-cutting social divisions such as gender and race.

The citizen–noncitizen binary

It is trivial, from an etymological perspective, to state that citizenship and noncitizenship are related concepts. And indeed, we do not deny that they are interrelated. It is our argument in this section, however, that the relationship between the two concepts is far more complex than political theory has tended to presume. Primarily, we reject the idea that noncitizenship needs to be derivative, theoretically, from citizenship, instead viewing them both as foundational concepts.

Scholars typically draw attention to three interrelated attributes of citizenship (Bloemraad, Korteweg, and Yurdakul 2008; Cohen 1999). The first aspect of this is legal, that citizenship is a status which grants rights to the holder while expecting her to meet obligations to the State in return. According to this dimension, citizenship status confers the 'right to have rights' in Hannah Arendt's famous words (1968), with the status of citizenship acting as a gateway to a range of civil, political and social rights (Marshall [1950] 1992). The second attribute is political – that citizenship denotes active participation in the governance of the State in which the individual holds the status. This is the classical Greek definition of citizenship, and indeed also reflects a republican notion of political membership in contrast to being a subject of a sovereign (e.g. Dagger 1997). The third is identity-based – that citizenship confers on an individual the identity of membership in the citizenry (Joppke 2007).

While the western conceptualisation of citizenship was constructed prior to the emergence of the nation-state system, with traditions of citizenship rooted in Ancient Greek and Roman societies, in the modern world the two have become so deeply linked that 'national citizenship', as citizenship of the nation-state, is a virtually hegemonic idea, challenged only by emerging transnational citizenship regimes such as the European Union (Habermas 1995; Isin and Turner 2007). However, scholars are increasingly questioning the national citizenship compound given that (a) international migration has increased and intensified, and (b) an international human rights regime has emerged (Abizadeh 2002; Habermas 1998; Soysal 1994). These dynamics have meant that, while still a very significant factor, membership of a national group is playing a less pronounced role than it once did in determining place of residence and access to core rights. As a result, these developments have altered the ability of a State to control membership of its community through the projection of membership criteria based on national membership (Joppke 2007; Kofman 2005). The contemporary politics of migration control are shaped by this erosion of nation-state control and national identity in an increasingly globalised and interconnected world.

This questioning of the national model of citizenship has led to something of a decentring of traditional theories of citizenship. The Marshallian vision of citizenship has come under increasing critique as a result of the decreasing relevance of homogeneous national identity to citizenship (cf. Bloemraad, Korteweg, and Yurdakul 2008; Isin and Turner 2007; Turner 2001). Citizenships are viewed as co-existing in multiple forms and at multiple levels of political integration, and as intersecting with different forms of social division such as gender, class and race (Lister 2007; Yuval-Davis 2007). As a result, citizenship is recognised as a practice (or an 'act') in addition to a status (Isin 2008), and citizenships beyond the State are increasingly explored as a result of the apparent paradox between nation-state citizenship and the more post-national, transnational and cosmopolitan realities of international migration practices and multi-national and diasporic communities (Kaldor 2003; Müller 2007; Soysal 1994; Tonkiss 2013).

These developments have led to the emergence of works of normative political theory which challenge traditional understandings of the scope of justice – or to what extent and to whom justice and/or rights should apply. In response to John Rawls' presumption of the limits of the State as the limits of justice, where it is only relationships between co-citizens, or indeed heads of households, of the same State which are relevant in considerations of justice (1971, 1999), theorists have sought to explore the extension of Rawlsian principles of justice beyond the State, and thus to extend the argument beyond co-citizens (Beitz 1979; Pogge 1989, 2002), while others have proposed more radical options such as the construction of global institutions and a global citizenship regime (Cabrera 2004, 2010; Held 2004). Still others have argued that the rights typically associated with citizenship apply more widely than this specific category (Weissbrodt 2009) and have explored how the rights of citizenship could be extended beyond traditional models, offering justifications for liberal migration rights and more open access to citizenship for those born outside the State (Benhabib 2004; Carens 2013). This shift includes, crucially, the development of critiques of the persistence of citizenship based on 'birthright', challenging dominant models (Nyers 2006; Shachar 2009).

These theorists seem to be primarily concerned with noncitizenship, inasmuch as noncitizenship is defined as the absence of citizenship. In a more mobile and interconnected world where citizenship is increasingly deterritorialised and memberships recognised as multiple and overlapping, these theorists ask: how should we conceive of the rights of those without access to citizenship, and how should citizenship be transformed as a result? Their answers support the extension of citizenship beyond its traditional limits, and propose more inclusive and fluid forms of citizenship; or at the other extreme, lament the challenges of increasing transnationalism for constructing the robust binding sentiment of national identity which, it is suggested by these critics, is necessary for a robust and active citizenship to emerge (Miller 2000; Tamir 1993; Walzer 1983).

While it is vital to critique to existing limits of citizenship, in these approaches it seems that the theorisation of justice and rights affecting noncitizens is only thought about in relation to the conceptualisation of citizenship and *its* relationship with justice and rights, a problem which is also compounded by the privileged position of political theorists who themselves hold citizenship of affluent States (noted by Cole 2014). Noncitizenship is defined as an absence, which is prima facie logical, but we would contend that this is too simplistic and that noncitizenship is a membership category in its own right. The decentring of citizenship has revealed its contingent and constructed nature, as well as its intersections with other social divisions, and has led to much critique of the status quo. Yet this decentring has not been extended to noncitizenship, and this is problematic. Moreover, noncitizenship should not be seen as a migratory category. Many instances of noncitizenship arise from migration, as is reflected in much of the literature pertaining to noncitizenship, and indeed the formal recognition of noncitizenship as a positive status beyond the simple absence of citizenship, which is for the most part tied to a form of migration (giving rise to statuses such as: economic migrant, asylum seeker, undocumented migrant and so forth). Yet in fact the category is wider, including persons who participate in a noncitizenship relation in a State without crossing international borders. Indeed, this is brought out in some of the contributions to this volume (discussed below).

Noncitizens also have diverse experiences and belongings, which are shaped by intersections with other social divisions. A definition of noncitizenship as the negation of citizenship overlooks these critical dynamics. Exploring these in detail before reconstructing noncitizenship presents the potential for a conceptualisation of noncitizenship as a category of membership which is capable of shaping theorising about membership and rights in contemporary societies. In other words, before we can effectively theorise how justice and rights should be extended to noncitizens, we need a full, robust and accurate conceptualisation of noncitizenship.

Some traditional ways of understanding noncitizenship, in the form of 'denizen', 'resident' and 'dhimmi' are noteworthy for their use in imagining statuses beyond that of citizen. However, these do not quite achieve what is intended by the term noncitizenship in this paper. Denizen, from the medieval French for 'inhabitant', was a legal status something like 'resident' in medieval Britain.[1] Its recent uses have been more problematic, when members of certain groups were considered ineligible for full citizenship, and so were given the status of denizen. As such, residency and denizenship can be seen as intermediaries or stand-in statuses where there should properly be citizenship, rather than a way of understanding noncitizenship. While the experience of persons given this sort of status may be a form of noncitizenship, such a status cannot encapsulate the noncitizenship described here. *Dhimmi*, though etymologically different (deriving from the status of conquered peoples in relation to their conquerors), has had similar uses to denizen in Islamic political theory and practice (e.g. Shoukri 2011 from 58) and as such, it also does not provide the notion of noncitizenship being sought here.

The task of constructing a full and accurate conceptualisation of noncitizenship is critically important for two reasons. Firstly, the lack of attention to, and inadequate conceptualisation of, noncitizenship has given rise to a problematic gap in liberal political theory. It is not possible to develop comprehensive political theory when the concerns of a significant proportion of persons are excluded from these considerations (e.g. discussed in Cole 2000). We argue that theorists have been unable so far to respond to this difficulty because the theoretical tools available for talking about membership and rights are inherently dependent on citizenship, and our ability to appreciate what the paradox between national citizenship regimes and globalised memberships should mean for the scope of rights and justice is limited by a reliance on the conceptual boundaries of citizenship. This lack of appropriate means of analysis is evident in the traditional hyphenated terminology of 'non-citizenship', a hyphenation which we reject in this special issue.

Secondly, the weak conceptualisation of noncitizenship means that contemporary political theories are less able to speak to the kinds of real world issues that noncitizens face. In particular, those with non-national memberships, persons in diasporas, temporary workers, those seeking protection, and members of nomadic groups will remain beyond the scope of the work of political theorists unless they are to work with a more rigorous understanding of noncitizenship beyond its definition as the negation of citizenship rights. In many cases, taking a binary approach to the definition of noncitizenship is problematic in what it omits. Theorists focus on the absence of the legal status of citizenship and its attendant rights without considering the highly differentiated experiences of noncitizenship and the complex ways in which the three dimensions of citizenship (legal, political and identity) interact to construct the exclusion of different categories of noncitizens. Work is needed to examine the relationship between rights and belonging when there are multiple sources of identity and membership (Quiroz Becerra 2014; Tonkiss 2013; Yuval-Davis 2007), and multiple forms of political participation unrelated to citizenship (Nair 2012; Rigby and Schlembach 2013; Sigona 2015).

The kinds of real world challenges presented by noncitizenship which existing political theory struggles to address are seen most keenly in the case of statelessness. The literature on statelessness is still underdeveloped; however, some writers offer theorisations of the status and lack of status of statelessness, and relate this theorisation to real world problems and modes of change. The focus on citizenship as the core form of relationship with the State means that, as Arendt points out, the removal of citizenship can apparently legitimise the exclusion from basic rights of members of certain groups (Arendt 1968, 167; see also Sassen 1999). Indeed, in the case of stateless persons, the lack of any State as a default for rights protection makes clear the danger of noncitizenship seen only as the negation of citizenship at its most extreme (Caballero-Antony et al. 2013, 161). The international legal and theoretical frameworks are not yet able to ensure the rights of these persons, who are noncitizens everywhere (Batchelor 1998; Blitz 2009). We argue that this is entrenched by the upholding of citizenship as the only relevant core relationship with a State, even when international agreements allow otherwise (Weissbrodt 2009).

Indeed, the colloquial treatment of stateless persons and irregular migrants is also particularly telling, as their relationship with the State can often be defined according to a lack. Consider, for example, persons referred to as 'sin papeles' ('without papers') in Spain, and as 'sans papiers' ('without papers') in France, as well as the 'bidoon' (short for 'bidoon jinsiya', or 'without nationality') in the States of the Arab Gulf. This colloquial way of referring to persons solely by their lack of a formal relationship with the State has the effect of reinforcing the idea that there is no relationship and enabling their exclusion from even core rights protections. Yet, as the papers in this volume attest, this is not an accurate picture. This is seen most clearly when noncitizenship is theorised as a positive relationship with a State, as is presented here.

It is our purpose in this special issue to begin the process of building the notion of noncitizenship as a distinct perspective into political theory, by bringing together an interdisciplinary collection of papers offering insights into the theoretical problem that noncitizenship presents and how to develop a more robust conceptualisation of this term. As noted, we use the term 'noncitizenship' rather than 'non-citizenship' in order to move beyond the binary definition described, embracing a diversity of experiences while drawing out cross-cutting practices and exclusions affecting these multiple forms of noncitizenships. We will shortly introduce this conceptualisation of noncitizenship as a basis for liberal political theory with reference to the contributions of the special issue. Before we do so, however, we briefly survey the insights offered by some recent interventions on the subject and their relationship with the ideas presented in this volume.

Emerging noncitizenship studies

At the time of writing, two other important volumes about noncitizenship have recently been published, contributing to serious and developed study in this area. This current volume must be seen as taking a crucial next step. January 2014 saw the publication, in the *Critical Review of International Social and Political Philosophy (CRISPP)*, of a Special Issue under the title 'Domination, migration and non-citizens', edited by Iseult Honahan and Marit Hovdal-Moan. Then, months later, in September 2014, another Special Issue appeared, this time in *Politics and Society*, with the title 'The rights of noncitizens', edited by David Plotke. The close timing of the publication of these three works demonstrates the urgent need to address these issues. These volumes are critically important for the emergence of a rich literature on noncitizenship, and while the papers presented in the current volume take a distinctly different perspective, they do build on these recent studies in key ways.

Honohan and Hovdal-Moan's Special Issue focuses on the notion of 'domination' in discussion of migration and citizenship (2014), defining domination 'in terms of the subjection to the threat of arbitrary interference' (Honohan and Hovdal-Moan 2014, 2). The (usually republican) domination perspective is an important one. Yet the writers in the *CRISPP* collection analyse noncitizenship primarily as a result of migration. They explore the domination of migrants and noncitizens almost interchangeably (some refer to denizenship to describe territorially present noncitizens – e.g. Benton 2014). While their presentation of vulnerability in the form of domination is important and interesting, particularly in terms of the emphasis on the arbitrary domination of those with different statuses (e.g. Hovdal-Moan 2014), we worry that it may also reinforce the idea that there are easily distinguishable mutually exclusive categories of citizens and noncitizens. The insertion of the alternative category of denizen could, *prima facie*, allow for a more fluid understanding of memberships. However, as argued above, it instead acts as an interim between noncitizenship (as an external category) and citizenship and, as such, reinforces this binary distinction.

Bertram (2014), in this important domination-focused special issue, analyses what he calls 'perimeter fence' and 'social boundary' forms of exclusion, arguing that both carry problems – and this is something that our volume builds upon, though with an analysis of the relationship between the State and those engaging with each of the barriers that he describes. Indeed, this relationship with the State is a crucial aspect of understanding the situation for noncitizens. This is emphasised by Sarah Fine who refers to Hannah Arendt's comment that man 'can lose all so-called Rights of Man without losing his essential quality as man, his human dignity' (Arendt 1951, 297, quoted in Fine 2014, 14). She notes how, without citizenship, in the world of States, a man can be denied those human rights that are in fact tied to citizenship. Echoing (but not referring to) Bentham's suggestion that the notion of human rights is 'nonsense on stilts' (Bentham 1843) in the 'absence of a state willing (or another agent able) to protect and enforce them' (Fine 2014, 14). This is particularly interesting when seen in contrast to David Owen's contribution to the same issue (Owen 2014). Owen argues that a migration status may involve an arbitrary exercise of power over the status-bearer; and that it may arise out of an arbitrary exercise of power over that person (Owen 2014, 91). He argues that a legitimate migration status must not impose domination in either of these forms over those subject to that State's rule.

The emphasis throughout the Honohan and Hovdal-Moan volume is on access to citizenship and this precludes the development of a solid notion of noncitizenship. The analysis of domination in cases of migration and noncitizenship is useful and important. However, from our perspective, this leaves out a key means of resolving the difficulties raised. Several of the problematics presented in articles in the Honohan and Hovdal-Moan volume could be usefully addressed through a recognition of a notion of noncitizenship, with an understanding of noncitizenship as a particular sort of relationship with a State, giving rise to the potential for particular forms of domination – forms which the authors instead address using various migratory statuses.

The crucial matter of 'The rights of noncitizens' examined in the September Special Issue edited by Plotke reaffirms the importance of this topic. The papers raise again the problem that noncitizens may be excluded from rights regimes often intended primarily for citizens. The examples presented in the papers in the *Politics and Society* volume join us in challenging the idea that there is a clear divide between citizenship and noncitizenship and as such they provide critically important reading within this emerging discipline. However, the solutions offered tend to relate back to citizenship, and to an understanding of citizenship still as the foundational concept. We argue that challenging the foundationalism of citizenship is necessary in order to conceptualise a situation in which noncitizens have access to rights, not as a magnanimous gesture and not through the issuing of citizenship, but instead through an appreciation of the rights of noncitizens themselves.

For example, de Graauw (2014) reinforces Pogge's notion of a form of variegated membership structure (e.g. see Pogge 2002) by locating cities as sites of belonging. Indeed, if persons can effectively be citizens of cities, without having that status on the national level, this enables a more complex understanding of citizenship. However, this notion of city membership continues to function on the idea that there are citizens, who are insiders, and noncitizens who are outsiders, though at different levels. The border between citizen and noncitizen is also challenged by others in the Plotke volume, looking at how noncitizen engagement in communal activities implies a communal membership without official status (Quiroz Becerra 2014); at the implications of migration in situations where the State is not acting as the focal point for legal rights so that communal memberships in fact become more important (Landau 2014); where intertwined histories of colonialism and conflict mean that memberships and State obligations are more complex than evidenced solely in citizenship (Smith 2014); or when a shared victimhood among citizens and noncitizens creates a membership even when it is not officially recognised (Délano and Nienass 2014).

The papers in the *Politics and Society* collection aim to 'address difficult questions about how the boundaries of citizenship are drawn (and should be drawn) in countries with large numbers of noncitizen residents' (Plotke 2014, 289). The current volume goes one step further. It asks whether it is helpful to focus on boundary-drawing at all, and advocates instead starting with noncitizenship as itself a foundational concept, and indeed itself representative of a special relationship with the State. The aim, then, for us, is not to 'reconcile citizenship, membership, and presence in decent political regimes' (Plotke 2014, 290), so much as to revisit the case and to note that noncitizens have rights in virtue of *their* relationship with a State.

Plotke warns against an approach that would be directed at toppling citizenship (Plotke 2014, 291) and this is not the aim here either. However, a proper understanding of noncitizenship will certainly lead to a better understanding of the practice of citizenship in contemporary societies and, as such, will contribute to a steadying also of the notion of citizenship.

Interdisciplinary approaches to theorising noncitizenship

The papers in this volume do two things. First, they present why it is crucial to develop a way to theorise noncitizenship without assuming citizenship as a foundational concept, moving beyond the notion of noncitizenship as simply a lack, or showing why neither term, or the distinction between the terms have diminished in their usefulness. Second, they offer their own distinct perspectives on how to move forward. The papers in this Special Issue do not all agree. Instead, they raise a debate that is long overdue, looking at ways to reformulate the notion of noncitizenship. Overall, however, they agree that citizenship should not be seen as the only foundational concept, and that noncitizenship should not only be seen as an absence or a lack, with the rights of noncitizens as an add-on or an approximation to something relating to citizenship. In turn, this theoretical debate will help theorists and policy-makers respond to changing landscapes, in which it is becoming increasingly important to address directly the needs of noncitizens, and in which new frameworks will be needed in order to acknowledge and actualise them.

The project of finding a new way to theorise noncitizenship needs to be multidisciplinary, interweaving theory and practice in new ways. Luin Goldring and Patricia Landolt (this volume) demonstrate this by showing how noncitizenship is heterogeneous and complex, in ways which are overlooked by the definition of noncitizenship as mere negation and by the ways in which noncitizens have been 'siloed' into specific categories for the purposes of academic study. They argue that noncitizenship is socially constituted by the ways in which individuals and institutions navigate laws, policies and procedures in multiple settings, by the ways in which noncitizenship is discursively framed in those settings, and by both noncitizen agency and the actions of individuals and institutions who may help or hinder access to rights. As a result, the rights of noncitizens may be realised differently in different social contexts, something which the authors demonstrate through the presentation of four diverse cases which show how noncitizenship is conditional and crucially tied to agency, an analysis that is supported by the cases provided by Heather Johnson (this volume) and Shanthi Robertson (again, this volume). As such, the complexity they highlight becomes crucial for understanding the societies in which individuals come to be noncitizens, and the relations between citizenship and residency.

Goldring and Landolt develop a diverse and complex notion of noncitizenship, one which can be understood by 'assemblage' and which can be seen through the multiple engagements of noncitizens, including also protest and rights-claiming as well as sociability and labour, themes that are picked up throughout this Special Issue. They draw attention to both formal and informal aspects of noncitizenship and the ways in which these interact, in ways that are dynamic and unequal. The way in which the following papers develop these themes both complement the framework developed by Goldring and Landolt and contest it, setting the stage for what we hope will be ongoing debate in this area.

In order to provide the legal framework within which the volume is functioning, David Weissbrodt and Michael Divine (also this volume) present the friction that currently exists between international arrangements of human rights and the assumption of citizenship. They present noncitizenship as a diverse category and detail the ways in which this affects real-world legal rights-claiming. Understanding this will be key to the subsequent contributors' analyses of informal claims and forms of agency. Weissbordt and Divine challenge the traditional legal binary between citizens and noncitizens, arguing that, while in international law, citizens and noncitizens may in theory be equally eligible for human rights, noncitizens may find themselves excluded from their entitlements. Once again, the authors present the nature of noncitizenship, and the associated rights of noncitizens, even in its apparently legal formulation, as contingent on the nature of the social context in which it is enacted and constructed. As such, the current tendency to defer to a social and political construction of noncitizenship as a negation of citizenship introduces a form of privation that contradicts already existing international legal systems.

This power of political and social context, and a range of actors, to affect the substance of legal constructions of noncitizenship reinforces the importance of examining the informal developments discussed in subsequent papers alongside the associated legal constructs. Together, Goldring and Landolt, and Weissbrodt and Divine set the stage for a new way to theorise noncitizenship as a situation of conditionality and contingency, but also one which helps us to understand the meanings of membership, rights and the State.

The role of the private sector in noncitizenship construction has been little theorised. This is addressed by Tendayi Bloom's piece (this volume). While the migration industry is huge and growing, Bloom provides an analysis of privatised migration control specifically, as a crucial part of the larger industry, and deeply tied to migration facilitation. She presents how the private sector acts within the frameworks presented by the first two papers to create another, often unseen, layer to the construction and experience of noncitizenship. Bloom's taxonomy of the migration control industry offers a new way of understanding the roles of non-State actors in migration control and as a result, the new modes of noncitizenship construction taking place in the private sector. Bloom presents the private sector as an often unnoticed mediator of State migration control, and in fact therefore a constructor of noncitizenship. She argues that the very involvement of the private sector in some cases creates problems for the legitimacy of noncitizen-exclusion measures and alters the noncitizen-State relationship as well as the way in which legal frameworks are implemented.

Analysis of noncitizenship can sometimes imply that it is essentially tied to migration; yet, as argued above, this is inaccurate. Kristy Belton's article (this volume) serves to demonstrate the importance of recognising the non-migrant status of many noncitizens when conceptualising noncitizenship. She describes how situations of statelessness (noncitizenship everywhere) are created *in situ* in the Caribbean context, indeed hampering people's ability to move. Drawing from the particularities of her case studies of the Bahamas and the Dominican Republic, Belton argues that a system in which there is either (specifically national) citizenship or noncitizenship, persons who are excluded from citizenship are seen as without relationship of obligation with the State and put into situations of extreme vulnerability both in terms of physical protection and in terms of personal membership identity. This happens where a person is unable to be a citizen of either Haiti (their country of heritage) or Bahamas or the Dominican Republic (the country where they live). The binary notion of citizen/noncitizen, whereby a person must be one or the other, and citizenship is the only foundational form of relationship with a State is what makes such individuals particularly vulnerable. It puts them into a situation of having no recognised relationship with any State, despite being at the same time unable to leave the State that has constructed them as noncitizens and in fact engaging with that State.

For Belton, this constructed noncitizen 'immobility' is crucial to understanding the situation, and she argues that in the absence of a more complex theoretical and legal concept of noncitizenship, people can be stranded in unfavourable socioeconomic or geographic situations with a lack of personal agency. As such, Belton contributes both a crucial facet to the conceptualisation of noncitizenship as not intrinsically a matter of migration, and highlights that critical real world problems cannot be addressed without a new, more complete and accurate language of noncitizenship.

While the first four papers of this collection have focused primarily on the construction of noncitizenship by others – by the State, the society, the lawmakers and the private sector – and the problems this may cause, Paulina Tambakaki looks at the ways in which noncitizens construct noncitizenship themselves (this volume). Coming from the perspective of radical democracy theory, in which she re-examines what it is to be a democratic subject, Tambakaki introduces the idea of 'subversive politicisation' which, she argues, avoids the traditional construction of a citizen/noncitizen binary where 'noncitizenship is reduced to a journey to citizenship'. Rather, viewing noncitizenship through the lens of politicisation enables Tambakaki to theorise noncitizenship as practice, and specifically the political practice of questioning and challenging the rights regimes from which noncitizens are excluded. By analysing the nature of noncitizenship and how it functions within a system of what she refers to as 'citizenisation', she advocates either an expansive and inclusive understanding of citizenship or, better, a rejection of both the citizen and the noncitizen concepts all together.

To build upon these more general and theoretical approaches, it is useful to hone in on some theorised case studies. In particular, Shanthi Robertson (this volume) and Heather Johnson (also this volume), separately, look at the *noncitizen* construction of noncitizenship through case studies. Importantly, their findings both complement and challenge each other. In Robertson's Australia, it is the State that constructs a new form of noncitizenship as a temporary condition before citizenship, and she examines how noncitizens engage within this framework. She shows that within this context, noncitizenship comes to be seen as a non-status, not recognised even by noncitizens themselves as important, who instead are forced to look towards forms of formal status acquisition in order to put themselves in a position from which to claim rights.

Robertson argues that the solidarity movements that exist in Australia exist as networks of co-workers, or co-ethnics, not explicitly drawing on a shared noncitizenship. As such, she argues that noncitizens themselves also construct noncitizenship, not as a status in its own right, but in opposition to the rights of citizenship. However, this does not mean that noncitizenship for Robertson is the mere negation of citizenship. As in earlier papers, Robertson demonstrates the complex ways in which noncitizenship is constituted in situated contexts and highlights, somewhat contrarily to other contributions, that noncitizenship is in the Australian context experienced as part of a journey to citizenship. However, Robertson makes a further, subtle step. In Tambakaki's paper, protest was presented as removing the relevance of the citizen/noncitizen categories altogether. Robertson agrees, contesting not the citizen/noncitizen binary, but its relevance too. In describing networks of co-workers and co-ethnics, she also highlights the blurring of boundaries between the categories of citizen and noncitizen, where solidarities and sources of collective identification exist across these memberships and highlights the ways in which noncitizens enact membership of groups and communities despite their formal exclusion from citizenship.

Heather Johnson's approach is the reverse to this position, in many ways. She examines precisely a noncitizen solidarity movement, this time in Austria. She argues that in the case she studies, the members of the movement mobilise around the notion of noncitizenship, sometimes referred to as 'refugees' (not necessarily in the sense of the legal definition of refugee, but to denote what we are referring to in this volume as 'noncitizens'). Linking the protest to other protests in Europe, Johnson argues that it is precisely the mobilisation of noncitizenship as a status in itself, collectively and individually vulnerable to the State, which drives the movement, as a 'self-organised struggle'. In some ways Johnson's subjects reinforce the notion of a noncitizenship necessarily constructed in opposition to citizenship. They explicitly present their rights-claiming as a noncitizen or 'refugee' movement which does not require or want the interference of citizens.

However, this is to oversimplify. Johnson shows how noncitizen groups in Austria and elsewhere are engaging in a form of rights-claiming that is a specifically noncitizen one. It is not derivative to or approximating to citizenship. The actors she presents argue not for the protections of citizenship, but for rights as noncitizens who may be integrated into 'collective life', irrespective of any citizenship or citizenship-like status (some are convention refugees, some are not, for example). As such, while Robertson finds that in the Australian context there is not space for solidarity *on the basis of* noncitizenship alone, Johnson sees a European situation in which noncitizens in fact mobilise on the basis of their shared claims. It is important to take these two sets of cases together. They reinforce the presentation by Landolt and Goldring that the noncitizenship landscape is complex and changing. They also show how, in practice, the legal vagaries presented by Weissbrodt and Divine lead to very different noncitizenship experiences and expressions. Both Robertson and Tambakaki demonstrate how in practice, individuals around the world, in different and localised ways, are challenging the traditional presentation of a simplistic dichotomy between citizenship and noncitizenship and are assuming a noncitizenship that represents a relationship with the State in its own right.

A future agenda for theorising noncitizenship

The contributors to this Special Issue, then, provide the stepping-off point for a new multi-disciplinary agenda in the theorisation of noncitizenship. They have demonstrated how the traditional approach of characterising noncitizenship simplistically as the opposite of citizenship needs to be revisited. Their rich insights highlight some particularly central features which should be drawn on in theorising noncitizenship as a foundational concept in political theory, which it is hoped can contribute also to developing policy which can properly ensure the protection of the rights of noncitizens.

The first key point is that noncitizenship is heterogeneous and complex. It is not a single, neat category but rather an amalgamation of different categories according to status, both official and not, and cutting across different social divisions and relationships. Critically, the papers in this volume illustrate that noncitizenship is constituted by the social, political and legal contexts through which noncitizens navigate. Rather than conceptualising noncitizenship simply as the negation of citizenship, identifying this complexity implicit within noncitizenship serves to decentre the concept and as a result enables us to theorise the complex and contingent nature of membership in contemporary societies. Moreover, as has been seen in different ways throughout the Special Issue, these social, political and legal contexts may involve different forms of noncitizenship and citizenship which themselves interact. This multi-layered complexity makes it impossible to understand noncitizenship as a mere opposite of citizenship, since noncitizenships and citizenships may be variously experienced by the same individual across the social, political and legal contexts in which they interact and construct themselves. This leads to the second point.

The second key point is that noncitizenship is constructed by multiple actors, in different places and through different modes. State actors, non-State actors and individual noncitizens themselves all play a role in constructing the noncitizenship category. In particular, the papers have emphasised the importance to political theory of recognising and exploring the relationship between noncitizens and the State within whose territory they reside, rather than assuming that without citizenship there is no relationship with this State. The papers also emphasise noncitizen agency as a critical factor in how noncitizenship is enacted – as politicisation, and as forms of solidarity which challenge conceptual boundaries between different forms of membership. Although it has not been considered in this volume, it is likely also that individual citizens play a role in constructing noncitizenship, a topic touched upon elsewhere (e.g. Tonkiss forthcoming). This characterisation of noncitizenship as heterogeneous, complex and constructed by multiple actors is critical to developing a rich and rigorous understanding of noncitizenship. Indeed, the ways in which noncitizenship is constructed and by whom, and how it intersects with other social divisions, shape the nature of the inclusions and exclusions from society which are experienced by noncitizens.

We are keenly aware that, in the space of this Special Issue, it has not been possible to consider all of the key complexities which shape noncitizenship. This includes the construction of noncitizenship in contexts beyond those geographic regions mentioned here (particularly African, Asian and Latin American contexts are missing here); as well as the ways in which noncitizenship is mediated through other social locations such as race, class, gender, sexuality and disability. A full theorisation of noncitizenship would need to embrace these additional diversities of the noncitizen experience. However, we hope that in conceptualising noncitizenship as heterogeneous and complex we have at least been able to emphasise the critical importance of these features to producing a robust theory of noncitizenship and to indicate how these other factors could be incorporated. The third key point to take away from the papers is that the relationship between noncitizenship and citizenship is also complex and multi-faceted, rather than dichotomous. The heterogeneous nature of noncitizenship means that there are many different points at which noncitizen and citizen categories intersect with diverse consequences. This supports our assertion that noncitizenship is far more than the binary opposite of citizenship but rather itself is a relationship between a noncitizen and a State in its own right, and highlights the complex, overlapping and fragmented nature of memberships in contemporary societies. The study of intersections between noncitizenship and citizenship has also been beyond the scope of the featured papers, but examining noncitizenship and citizenship at their transition points could add valuable insights to further break down the simplistic assumptions associated with the relationship between the two categories.

The fourth and final key point from the papers is that noncitizenship is associated with vulnerability and powerlessness. This might be the vulnerability which results from a lack of basic human rights, the vulnerability of lacking permanence in the country of residence, or the vulnerability of the individual against State and non-State actors. Yet it also might lead us to examine instances challenging the vulnerability of noncitizens through counter-movements and protests (such as that seen in Johnson, this volume), which in itself suggests the value of conceptualising noncitizenship as vulnerability for speaking to real world concerns and problems. While noncitizenship is often thought of as exclusion – exclusion from the citizenry, exclusion from rights – focusing instead on the idea of vulnerability provides a way of theorising rights and justice as they affect noncitizens without recourse to the binary definition of noncitizenship which, as noted, does not reflect how noncitizenship exists in the real world.

As a result, the papers in this Special Issue have emphasised that noncitizenship is far more than a lack of citizenship status, and that in this sense it is active – an individual is a noncitizen, rather than not-a-citizen. Noncitizenship as a heterogeneous category of social membership in its own right which has a fluid and multi-faceted relationship with citizenship, and which is characterised by the experience of vulnerability, presents a useful starting point for theorising rights and justice, embracing the fractured and multiple nature of membership in contemporary societies and positioning the noncitizen in relation to justice and rights. Coming from a diverse range of disciplines and presenting studies from a range of geographical contexts, the papers in this Special Issue present the urgent need for a new theory of noncitizenship that can ground a new understanding of the contemporary realities of noncitizenship as a relationship with a State. Policy frameworks based on the outmoded notion of citizenship as the only foundational relationship with the State have been shown to be inadequate in ensuring recognition and supporting rights-claiming of noncitizens. This Special Issue offers part of the first step in a move towards a better theoretical and policy landscape in this area.

This introductory paper is not intended as a cohesive theory of noncitizenship, but rather as a means to begin to address the absence of a robust conceptualisation of noncitizenship which could underpin a political theory which takes noncitizenship as a starting point, rather than assuming the centrality of citizenship. Our intention was not to present a complete political theory of noncitizenship, but rather to demonstrate the value of conceptualising noncitizenship as a concept in its own right. In doing so we have illustrated the central importance of an approach which embraces interdisciplinarity in order to draw on research into the real world experiences of noncitizens as well as the operation of noncitizenship through institutions in the real world, and an approach which combines rigorous theorising with rich insights from empirical research.

As a result, we are able to identify some key features of a future research agenda focused on theorising noncitizenship. This agenda has two inter-related aspects, the first of which is conceptualising noncitizenship. This collection has brought together a number of different approaches to this, and we suggest that building on these to further refine the conceptualisation, particularly with regards to the operation of noncitizenship in contexts beyond the developed world and to its experience in relation to other social divisions, is pressing. The second feature of our research agenda is the production of political theories which are grounded in noncitizenship as a foundational concept, drawing on and justifying one or more of these conceptualisations to offer new accounts of the relationship between membership, justice and rights in contemporary societies. For both of these aspects, we support an approach which combines theory with insights from the real world and looks towards supporting the development of policy that properly acknowledges the relationship of noncitizenship and the need for protection, as the best means for addressing both the gap in theory surrounding noncitizenship and the inability of theory, at present, to speak to the real world concerns of noncitizens.

Note

1. 'denizen, n. and adj.' OED Online. December 2014. Oxford University Press. http://www.oed.com/view/Entry/49985?rskey=VTvOqo&result=1 (accessed February 20, 2015).

Acknowledgements

The editors would like to thank Peter Nyers for his enthusiastic support for, and assistance in the production of, this Special Issue. They would also like to thank some individuals who helped to make this volume possible, in alphabetical order: Megha Amrith, Luis Cabrera, Theodora Christou, Zaid Clor, Phillip Cole, Maria Ferreira, Demelza Jones, Lindsey Kingston, Diletta Lauro, Pedro F Marcelino, Maria Luisa Sánchez Barrueco, Ninna Nyberg Sørensen, Julia Mourão Permoser, Nando Sigona and Annette Zimmermann. The editors are also grateful to participants at the 'Theorising Noncitizenship' MANCEPT Political Theory Workshop in September 2013, and at the 'Theorising Noncitizenship' panel at the ECPR Conference in September 2014, both of which offered important moments of critical reflection and discussion in the process of bringing this collection to publication. Finally, Bloom would like to acknowledge the support of the Institute on Globalization, Culture and Mobility at the United Nations University, where she was a research fellow at the beginning of this project.

Disclosure statement

No potential conflict of interest was reported by the authors.

References

Abizadeh, Arash. 2002. "Does Liberal Democracy Presuppose a Cultural Nation? Four Arguments." *American Political Science Review* 96 (3): 495–509.

Arendt, Hannah. 1968. *The Origins of Totalitarianism*. San Diego, CA: Harvest Harcourt.

Batchelor, Carol. 1998. "Statelessness and the Problem of Resolving Nationality Status." *International Journal of Refugee Law* 10: 156–182.

Beitz, Charles. 1979. *Political Theory and International Relations*. Princeton: Princeton University Press.

Benhabib, Seyla. 2004. *The Rights of Others: Aliens, Residents and Citizens*. Cambridge: Cambridge University Press.

Bentham, Jeremy. 1843. "Anarchical Fallacies; Being an Examination of the Declaration of rights Issued During the French Revolution." In *The Works of Jeremy Bentham Volume II (Judicial Procedure, Anarchical Fallacies, works on Taxation)*, edited by John Bowring, 489–543. Edinburgh: William Tait. http://oll.libertyfund.org/titles/1921

Benton, Meghan. 2014. "The Problem of Denizenship: A Non-Domination Framework." *Critical Review of International Social and Political Philosophy* 17 (1): 49–69.
Bertram, Christopher. 2014. "Competing Methods of Territorial Control, Migration and Justice." *Critical Review of International Social and Political Philosophy* 17 (1): 129–143.
Blitz, Brad. 2009. *Statelessness, Protection and Equality, Forced Migration Policy Briefing 3*. Refugee Studies Centre, University of Oxford.
Bloemraad, Irene, Anna Korteweg, and Gökçe Yurdakul. 2008. "Citizenship and Immigration: Multiculturalism, Assimilation and Challenges to the Nation-State." *Annual Review of Sociology* 34: 153–179.
Caballero-Antony, Mely, Alistair DB Cook, Priyanka Bhalla, and Pau Khan Khup Hangzo. 2013. "Forced Migration." In *Non-Traditional Security in Asia: Issues, Challenges and Framework for Action, Institute of SEA Studies*, edited by Mely Caballero-Antony and Alistair DB Cook, 158–201. Singapore: Institute for South-East Asian Studies.
Cabrera, Luis. 2004. *Political Theory of Global Justice*. London: Routledge.
Cabrera, Luis. 2010. *The Practice of Global Citizenship*. Cambridge: Cambridge University Press.
Carens, Joseph. 2013. *The Ethics of Immigration*. Oxford: Oxford University Press.
Cohen, Jean L. 1999. "Changing Paradigms of Citizenship and the Exclusiveness of the Demos." *International Sociology* 14 (3): 245–268.
Cole, Phillip. 2014. "Beyond Reason: The Philosophy and Politics of Immigration." *Critical Review of International Social and Political Philosophy* 17 (5): 503–520.
Cole, Phillip. 2000. *Philosophies of Exclusion*. Edinburgh: Edinburgh University Press.
Dagger, Richard. 1997. *Civic Virtues: Rights, Citizenship and Republican Liberalism*. Oxford: Oxford University Press.
Délano, Alexandra, and Benjamin Nienass. 2014. "Invisible Victims: Undocumented Migrants and the Aftermath of September 11." *Politics & Society* 42 (3): 399–421.
Fine, Sarah. 2014. "Non-domination and the Ethics of Migration." *Critical Review of International Social and Political Philosophy* 17 (1): 10–30.
Golding, Luin, and Patricia Landolt. 2013. *Producing and Negotiating Non-Citizenship: Precarious Legal Status in Canada*. Toronto: University of Toronto Press.
de Graauw, Els. 2014. "Municipal ID Cards for Undocumented Immigrants: Local Bureaucratic Membership in a Federal System." *Politics & Society* 42 (3): 309–330.
Habermas, Jürgen. 1995. "Citizenship and National Identity: Some Reflections on the Future of Europe." In *Theorising Citizenship*, edited by Ronald Beiner, 255–282. Albany: SUNY Press.
Habermas, Jürgen. 1998. *The Inclusion of the Other*. Cambridge: Polity.
Held, David. 2004. *Global Covenant: The Social Democratic Alternative to the Washington Consensus*. Cambridge: Polity.
Honohan, Iseult, and Marit Hovdal-Moan. 2014. "Introduction: Domination, Migration and Non-Citizens." *Critical Review of International Social and Political Philosophy* 17 (1): 1–9.
Hovdal-Moan, Marit. 2014. "Unequal Residence Statuses and the Ideal of Non-domination." *Critical Review of International Social and Political Philosophy* 17 (1): 70–89.
Isin, Engin. 2008. "Theorising Acts of Citizenship." In *Acts of Citizenship*, edited by Engin Isin and Greg M. Nielsen, 15–43. London: Zed.
Isin, Engin, and Bryan S. Turner. 2007. "Investigating Citizenship: An Agenda for Citizenship Studies." *Citizenship Studies* 11 (1): 5–17.
Joppke, Christian. 2007. "Transformation of Citizenship: Status, Rights, Identity." *Citizenship Studies* 11 (1): 37–48.
Kaldor, Mary. 2003. "The Idea of Global Civil Society." *International Affairs* 79 (3): 583–593.
Kofman, Eleonore. 2005. "Citizenship, Migration and the Reassertion of National Identity." *Citizenship Studies* 9 (5): 453–467.
Landau, Loren B. 2014. "Conviviality, Rights, and Conflict in Africa's Urban Estuaries." *Politics & Society* 42 (3): 359–380.
Lister, Ruth. 2007. "Inclusive Citizenship: Realizing the Potential1." *Citizenship Studies* 11 (1): 49–61.
Marshall, Thomas H. [1950] 1992. *Citizenship and Social Class*. London: Pluto Press.
Miller, David. 2000. *Citizenship and National Identity*. Cambridge: Polity.

Müller, Jan-Werner. 2007. *Constitutional Patriotism*. Princeton: Princeton University Press.
Nair, Parvati. 2012. "The Body Politic of Dissent: The Paperless and the Indignant." *Citizenship Studies* 16 (5–6): 783–792.
Nyers, Peter. 2006. "The Accidental Citizen: Acts of Sovereignty and (Un)Making Citizenship." *Economy and Society* 35 (1): 22–41.
Owen, David. 2014. "Republicanism and the Constitution of Migrant Statuses." *Critical Review of International Social and Political Philosophy* 17 (1): 90–110.
Plotke, David. 2014. "The Rights of Noncitizens: Introduction." *Politics and Society* 42 (3): 287–291.
Pogge, Thomas. 1989. *Realising Rawls*. Ithaca: Cornell University Press.
Pogge, Thomas. 2002. *World Poverty and Human Rights: Cosmopolitan Responsibilities and Reforms*. Cambridge: Polity Press.
Quiroz Becerra, M. Victoria. 2014. "Performing Belonging in Public Space: Mexican Migrants in New York City." *Politics & Society* 42 (3): 331–357.
Rawls, John. 1971. *A Theory of Justice*. Oxford: Oxford University Press.
Rawls, John. 1999. *A Theory of Justice*. Cambridge, MA: Harvard University Press.
Rigby, Joe, and Raphael Schlembach. 2013. "Impossible Protest: Noborders in Calais." *Citizenship Studies* 17 (2): 157–172.
Sassen, Saskia. 1999. *Guests and Aliens*. New York: The New Press.
Shachar, Ayelet. 2009. *The Birthright Lottery: Citizenship and Global Inequality*. Cambridge, MA: Harvard University Press.
Shoukri Arafat Madi. 2011. *Refugee Status in Islam: Concepts of Protection in Islamic Tradition and International Law*. London: I.B. Taurus.
Sigona, Nando. 2015. "Campzenship: Reimagining the Camp as a Social and Political Space." *Citizenship Studies* 19 (1): 1–15.
Smith, Rogers M. 2014. "National Obligations and Noncitizens: Special Rights, Human Rights, and Immigration." *Politics & Society* 42 (3): 381–398.
Soysal, Yasemin. 1994. *Limits of Citizenship: Migrants and Postnational Membership in Europe*. Chicago, IL: University of Chicago Press.
Tamir, Yael. 1993. *Liberal Nationalism*. Princeton: Princeton University Press.
Tonkiss, Katherine. Forthcoming. "Experiencing Transnationalism at Home: Open Borders and the Everyday Narratives of Non-Migrants." *Politics*.
Tonkiss, Katherine. 2013. *Migration and Identity in a Post-National World*. Basingstoke: Palgrave Macmillan.
Turner, Bryan S. 2001. "The Erosion of Citizenship." *British Journal of Sociology* 52 (2): 189–209.
Walzer, Michael. 1983. *Spheres of Justice*. New York: Basic Books.
Weissbrodt, David. 2009. *The Human Rights of Non-Citizens*. Oxford: Oxford University Press.
Yuval-Davis, Nira. 2007. "Intersectionality, Citizenship and Contemporary Politics of Belonging." *Critical Review of International Social and Political Philosophy* 10 (4): 561–574.

Assembling noncitizenship through the work of conditionality

Patricia Landolt[a] and Luin Goldring[b]

[a]Department of Sociology, University of Toronto, Toronto, Canada; [b]Department of Sociology, York University, Toronto, Canada

ABSTRACT

We develop a framework for understanding noncitizenship that combines attention to systemic processes with interest in contingency and indeterminacy in the production and substantive practices associated with noncitizen legal status categories and trajectories. We argue that noncitizenship is a dynamic, multi-scalar assemblage that brings together disparate elements in patterned and changing ways. Individuals and institutions generate the formal and substantive systems that confer or deny noncitizens the formal and substantive right to be present in a country and/or to access entitlements. Noncitizens exercise agency in choosing to make claims (or choosing to not make claims) to substantive rights, and the individuals and institutions with which they interact may facilitate or hinder such claims-making. In this process, social actors are enacting conditionality; they are working to meet the conditions required to maintain presence and access. Discretion, migrant agency, unequal social interactions, and social learning unfold over time and can generate a range of experiences of noncitizenship and legal status trajectories. These do not necessarily conform to expected pathways and timelines, and may combine access to various resources and public goods in variable and contingent ways. We illustrate the framework with data from research conducted in Toronto.

Introduction

Dramatic shifts in the volume and character of global migration are rewriting the content, boundaries, and pathways between citizenship and noncitizenship. States and international institutions engaged in migration management have responded with restrictive policies of noncitizen exclusion and persecution, while noncitizens themselves and civil society actors have sometimes run counter to this global lockdown, through claims-making and by enacting substantive citizenship. These processes are occurring at different scales, animated by diverse institutional actors, and framed by competing understandings of membership; they point to the increasing significance of noncitizenship, and legal status more generally, both as a dimension of global social inequality and of global political struggle.

This paper presents a conceptual framework for understanding noncitizenship that combines attention to systemic processes, such as the socio-legal production of diverse and changing noncitizen categories and their formal and practical interconnections, with interest in contingency and indeterminacy in the production of and substantive practices associated with these legal status categories and trajectories. We argue that noncitizenship is relational and assembled dynamically by individuals and institutions that negotiate and navigate the formal and substantive systems that confer or deny rights to remain present in a country, and to access entitlements. Noncitizens exercise agency in choosing to make claims (or choosing to not make claims) to substantive rights; the individuals and institutions with which they interact may facilitate or hinder such claims making. In this process, social actors enact conditionality: they work to meet the material and discursive conditions required to exercise formal or substantive rights to presence and access. Discretion, migrant agency, and social learning shape experiences and trajectories in variable ways. Consequently, formal and substantive experiences of noncitizenship do not necessarily conform to expected pathways and timelines. Thus, we conceptualize noncitizenship as a dynamic multi-scalar assemblage that brings together disparate elements – social actors, relations of power, regulations, discursive frames, bureaucracies, sectors, etc. – in patterned and changing ways.

As discrete legal status categories, citizenship and noncitizenship stand as mirror opposites; the former denotes rights and responsibilities and the latter their absence (Bosniak 1994). While citizenship status confers formal rights and membership in a political community (Marshall 1950), noncitizenship assures neither. Noncitizen legal status categories specify the formal bases regulating how long a person can remain and under what conditions (*presence*), conditions regarding *access* to labor markets, and regulations establishing *access* to social citizenship, particularly public goods and services. These categories also establish the possibility and pathways to eventual citizenship, or lack thereof.

Substantively, both citizenship *and* noncitizenship are relational, dynamic, uneven and unequal in practice, experience and outcomes (Stasiulis and Bakan 1997; Yuval-Davis 1997; Bosniak 2000; Rhus and Anderson 2010; Kubal 2013). There is variation within the categories of citizen and of noncitizen, and the boundaries between them are dynamic and porous. The socio-legal production of citizenship and noncitizenship through law, regulations, and social practices makes the exercise and experience of citizenship and noncitizenship by individuals and groups uneven (Sharma 2006; Walia 2010). These intersect with social location (Omi and Winant 1989; Yuval-Davis 1997), temporality, spatiality and scale (Painter and Philo 1995), and regulatory frameworks and enforcement (Stasiulis and Bakan 2005; Fudge and MacPhail 2009). Experiences of noncitizenship and citizenship are thus both patterned and contingent. Both hold the possibility for changes in security and precarity that have long-term implications for individuals and broader social inequality. We present empirical data from our research in Toronto to illustrate our theoretical framework and arguments.

Conceptualizing noncitizenship

Existing scholarship takes three broad approaches to the way that noncitizenship is assembled, to its meanings and to its relationship to citizenship. The first approach argues that the socio-legal production of noncitizenship and citizenship is embedded in transnational efforts to control migration and access to residence and entitlements, and to govern mobile populations deemed dangerous, non-deserving, or otherwise unfit (Puar and Rai 2002;

Morris 2003; De Genova 2007; De Genova and Peutz 2010; Rygiel 2010; Mountz 2011). Research on the production of migrant 'illegalization' and deportability is a cornerstone of this literature (Calavita 1998; De Genova 2002; Ngai 2004; De Genova and Peutz 2010; Basok, Bélanger, and Rivas 2013; Menjívar and Kanstroom 2014; Heyman 2014). States use detention, deportability and deportation in tandem with immigration policies that include probationary residence and selective inclusion through 'legalization' (Makaremi 2009; Moffette 2014) to generate differential inclusion for noncitizens in a variety of administrative categories (e.g. undocumented, irregular, and temporary). Assessments of conduct and deservingness are key mechanisms of selective removal as well as inclusion (Pratt 2005; Vasta 2011; Chauvin and Garcés-Mascareñas 2012; Villegas 2012a; Dobrowolsky 2013; Moffette 2014; Schweitzer 2014).

A second approach focuses on noncitizen agency, subjectivity, and 'acts of citizenship' as well as broader mobilizations. This scholarship challenges conceptions of undocumented and other noncitizens as abject subjects, non-agents permanently relegated to (silent) suffering (Lowry and Nyers 2003; Wright 2003; Isin 2008; Basok 2009; Abji 2013; Pallares 2015).[1] It also captures a range of strategies to mitigate fear of living with forms of precarious status, including non-status. These include avoiding certain public places and developing strategies to cope with illegality and deportability (Willen 2007; Gonzales 2011); forging new or borrowed identities and gaining access to employment and resources through strategic and/or extra-legal 'papering' processes (Vasta 2011); situational 'passing' as legal (Young 2005); 'learning to be illegal' (Gonzales 2011; Bloch, Sigona, and Zetter 2014); 'ordinary' or routine practices of citizenship by noncitizens and citizens (Staeheli et al. 2012); negotiating substantive access to services (Landolt, Villegas, and Villegas 2012; Kisson 2013); and establishing records of employment and deservingness that might be used in future claims-making, even though such strategies may run counter to efforts to govern migrants (Chauvin and Garcés-Mascareñas 2014, 2012).

A third area of scholarship focuses on boundary negotiations as enacted by institutional actors. This work argues that legal status boundaries are not fixed, sharp, or impermeable (Calavita 1998; Coutin 2000; Lamont and Molnár 2002; Bosniak 2006, 1994, 2000), and that social actors (including a range of gatekeepers and noncitizen migrants) play a role in negotiating boundaries within categories of noncitizenship and between these and citizenship. That is, social actors play roles in regulating entry to a territory and legal status category; generating and claiming access to public services; in movement between legal status boundaries; and in shaping ongoing presence as well as practices of detention or removal (Makaremi 2009; Landolt, Villegas, and Villegas 2012; Alpes and Spire 2014; Satzewich 2014). Migrant legal status trajectories are an example of boundary crossing, and may have contingent outcomes leading to greater status security, including citizenship, legally produced illegalization; or churning through various forms of noncitizen precarious legal status (Calavita 1998; Martínez Veiga 2007; McKay et al. 2009; Goldring and Landolt 2011; Goldring and Landolt 2013; Landolt and Goldring 2013; Tandian and Bergh 2014; Vickstrom 2014). These trajectories can be shaped by gatekeeper practices and migrant's strategic agency. Researchers show that agency, discretion, and deservingness play crucial roles in organizing boundary negotiations for noncitizens. Discretion and deservingness inform negotiations and claims about access to resources such as work or housing, and to both formal entitlements and those that are accessed substantively, regardless of entitlement (Landolt, Villegas, and Villegas 2012; Willen 2012; Chauvin, Garcés-Mascareñas, and Kraler

2013; Chauvin and Garcés-Mascareñas 2014). Discretion and deservingness intersect with local-level jurisdictional dynamics, histories, and mobilizations to generate differentiation and contingency (Varsanyi 2005; Gleeson 2012; Villegas 2013; Pallares 2015).

These approaches have three limitations. The first approach offers a critical perspective on noncitizenship and citizenship as entwined technologies of governmentality (Rygiel 2010), but offers limited tools for understanding contingency and variation across or within national jurisdictions and tends towards perhaps unintentional structural determinism. A second limitation crosscuts the three approaches and involves the tendency to produce siloed analyses. Researchers consider the production of or negotiations surrounding specific categories of noncitizenship, particularly illegality and specific temporary worker categories, without adequately addressing their systemic interconnections and their intersections with citizenship (Goldring and Landolt 2013). Analyses of legal status trajectories and illegalization offer a corrective, but focus on unidirectional pathways of irregularization and illegalization (De Genova 2002; Villegas 2012b; Vickstrom 2014), legalization (Hagan 1994), *or* churning through forms of noncitizenship (McKay et al. 2009).

Another set of limitations revolves around agency, temporality, and scale. The literature on acts of citizenship or noncitizen mobilizations highlights visible and even spectacular forms of noncitizen agency while downplaying other, less visible, and more routine forms of strategic agency. It notes gatekeeper discretion, migrant practices, and frames of deservingness, but is unclear about the pathways and trajectories emerging from accumulated interactions over time.

To address these limitations, we call attention to systemic contingency and present a framework that takes a systemic approach to analyzing the production of multiple, connected, yet changing legal status categories, each with potentially distinct configurations of social benefits, which may also change over time. This framework also takes into account the multi- and inter-scalar processes involved in navigating and negotiating potentially indeterminate and multidirectional trajectories of legal status, and the social learning implicated in evolving patterns of formal and substantive claims-making with regard to presence and access to services which may at the same time be contoured by shifting policies, configurations of entitlements, and frames of deservingness.

Noncitizenship as assemblage

The idea of assemblage provides a useful conceptual and methodological metaphor for understanding the social production and organization of noncitizenship (Ong and Collier 2005; Sassen 2006; Villegas 2012a, 2012b; Villegas 2015). Following Deleuze's usage, the assemblage metaphor challenges understandings of social life as rooted in fixed, stable, and predictable ontologies and relationships, proposing instead a vision of social life constituted dynamically and contingently by complex configurations that assemble or come together in particular social formations (Little 2012). It offers an alternative way of seeing and understanding, one that captures multi-scalar, dynamic, contingent, institutional arrangements involving configurations of disparate elements, including variously situated social actors, relations of power, institutions, regulations, policies, organizations, etc., that come together in patterned but changing ways to constitute noncitizenship. An understanding of noncitizenship as an assemblage intentionally moves away from a focus on precarity or a narrow concern with specific categories of noncitizenship and instead highlights relations across categories of noncitizenship and between these and citizenship, and how they are dynamically constituted and assembled.

Key elements in the noncitizenship assemblage include laws, policies, and procedures that are generated and implemented at various scales, by citizen and noncitizen actors, in multiple settings. Inter-scalar tensions are revealed when laws, policies, and procedures are explicitly contradictory or are unevenly applied. Discursive frames of deservingness are another important element. These frames may vary across scale and institutional settings, and across groups and identities, and change over time. Social location also generates distinct experiences of noncitizen assemblages. Migrant agency and gatekeeper discretion are also important, and temporality and scale represent additional cross-cutting elements. This approach means paying attention to policies, but also to how they are implemented and negotiated, by noncitizens and citizens, in various localities and institutional settings and at various scales.

Assemblages of noncitizen conditionality

Noncitizenship assemblages are enacted through the conditionality of presence and access. Conditionality denotes the material and discursive conditions that must be met to acquire and exercise the formal or substantive right to remain present within a national territory and/or to access entitlements and social goods, including the labor market. Conditionality is framed by regulations, policies, and procedures that take hold through social relations, interactions, and negotiations. Conditionality is embedded in moral frameworks of deservingness, of who deserves to remain present and to gain access to resources and under what terms (van Oorschot 2000; Fassin 2005). While conditionality recognizes the imposed discipline and self-regulation that may be involved in meeting conditions, there is also room for non-routine and counter claims-making. Thus, conditionality always involves *work* for establishing, negotiating, and evaluating claims to presence and access (Cf. Villegas 2012a). This work occurs across multiple scales and within different and potentially overlapping institutional arenas, such as labor markets, health care, education, newcomer settlement services, and social welfare. The work of conditionality is characterized by unequal relations of power that are visible in macro-level processes and micro-level interactions.

Migrant agency, conduct, and the discretionary power of institutional actors to grant or deny presence and access organize the micro-level work of conditionality and help explain contingent and potentially variable outcomes at different points in time and over time (Spire 2008; Lipsky 2010; Landolt, Villegas, and Villegas 2012). Everyday micro-interactions, such as those between noncitizens and front-line workers, are constituted in the context of interpersonal interactions, frames, and claims of deservingness, and organizational cultures. They are also shaped by state and local policies and procedures, which establish the formal parameters of presence and access. Agency occurs as people navigate the institutional landscape of noncitizenship, gaining and claiming presence and access. Over time, through the work of conditionality, the boundaries between citizenship and noncitizenship, and between categories of noncitizenship, can be contested, breached, negotiated, and otherwise altered, more or less durably and at different scales (Iacovetta 2006; Goldring 2010; Landolt, Villegas, and Villegas 2012; Villegas 2012a). This *work* may reconfigure access to resources and goods, creating a dynamic patchwork of formal and substantive access, with variable long-term implications regarding the security of presence, legal status, and social inequality.[2] Varying levels of accumulated experience and *social learning* result in variation in the kinds of *work* that noncitizens undertake to ensure ongoing presence and improved access.

Migration narratives and the work of conditionality

We profile four migration stories to demonstrate the work of conditionality and model the Canadian assemblage of noncitizenship. The cases show the degrees to which migrants experience, meet, navigate, and try – or not – to change their formal or substantive conditions of presence and access over time. This occurs through social interactions with friends, family, and other actors situated across different institutional arenas. The trajectories and the similarities and differences across the four cases illuminate how the boundaries between formal and substantive claims to presence and access undergo transformation. They also capture the importance of migrant agency and social learning and the role of gatekeeper discretion.

We selected the four case studies from a mixed-methods survey conducted in 2006 with Caribbean and Latin American immigrants living and working in the City of Toronto in Canada. In this project, we developed a multi-step random sampling design to generate a study population of 300 respondents. We asked respondents questions on a number of themes, including reasons for migration and early settlement experiences; approaches for dealing with employment challenges and opportunities; and patterns of contact with institutions and organizations that constitute Toronto's settlement infrastructure. We also asked about their legal status and the jobs they held at four points in time and changes in both.[3] Toronto has two settlement infrastructures that differ based on funding and clients. Recognized immigrants and refugees secure access to services through formal settlement service provider organizations that are funded to serve them. Settlement services are also accessed substantively in agencies that receive funding from other sources by noncitizens who are de facto residents but not recognized as immigrants. In some cases, the same organization may serve both populations (Goldring and Landolt 2012).

Case 1: In 2002, 26-year-old Raul, a university trained computer engineer, travelled from Colombia to the US–Canada land border where he made an inland claim for asylum. He was driven to Toronto and housed in a refugee shelter, where he lived for three months. The shelter-based social worker helped Raul complete paperwork for social assistance, a temporary work permit, and state-funded health coverage. She also encouraged him to do volunteer work in order to receive additional social assistance payments and explained his eligibility for free English as a Second Language (ESL) classes. Raul was provided a legal aid voucher and a list of lawyers available to help prepare and present his asylum case before the Immigration and Refugee Board of Canada. For 12 months, Raul made full use of the entitlements granted to refugee claimants. He lived on social assistance, attended English classes, and volunteered at a community center. He learned important survival skills and received invaluable support from fellow ESL students and advice from the volunteer coordinator at the community agency where he did his volunteer hours. In 2003, Raul was granted asylum and immediately looked for work in his field. In less than a month, he was hired on a one-month probationary contract as a software engineer. After this, a 16-month delay in Raul's permanent residence meant that he remained on probation at work and was not eligible for extended health benefits. His employer did help Raul with the multiple renewals of his temporary work permit. Once he had permanent resident status, Raul made plans to return to school to upgrade his skills and apply for Canadian citizenship.

Case 2: In 2002, Janet, her husband Pedro, and their two young children fled Argentina for Toronto where Pedro's father and brother lived. A few days after arriving, they made an inland refugee claim. Both Janet and Pedro were educated white-collar workers with years of professional experience. On the advice of Pedro's brother, who believed that accepting social assistance reduced the chances of a positive refugee determination, the family did not apply for welfare but instead worked a series of low-end and low-paying jobs. Janet started out doing unpaid child minding and housecleaning for her brother and sister-in-law. Later and on the suggestion of a neighbor in her building, she babysat for other families, which also allowed her to take care of her own children. Eventually and again with the encouragement of other immigrant mothers in her building, she got a part-time job stocking shelves in a health food store, where she had a fixed schedule and was paid minimum wage. Pedro started out working with his brother in construction and snow removal. After a few months during which he was often underpaid or his wages were withheld, he moved on to a cleaning job.

Because they did not to apply for welfare, the couple did not receive a day care subsidy for their children and had no time for ESL classes. Unaware that their refugee claim made them eligible to receive basic health coverage and under pressure from Pedro's brother, they also purchased private health insurance from one of his friends. They also failed to make use of their legal aid voucher. Instead, they worked on their asylum case with a lawyer who charged them approximately $3000 and failed to disclose their entitlement to subsidized legal counsel. In 2003, the couple was granted asylum and they received their permanent residence papers in 2004. They distanced themselves from Pedro's brother. At the time of the interview in 2006, their English was still rudimentary and they continued to be precariously employed in low-wage jobs.

Case 3: In 1998, 22-year-old Rachel came to Toronto from St. Vincent to join her aunt. She had a high school education and hoped to continue her schooling in Canada. Rachel did not need a visa to enter and was not certain how long she would stay. Although she did not have a work permit, Rachel registered with a temporary employment agency and quickly found work as a live-out nanny. During her first year in Canada, she worked Monday through Friday for $1000 a month and sometimes cleaned houses for cash on weekends. She was socially isolated, had no contact with community agencies, and was largely at the mercy of her employers. Over time, Rachel did build a social network through work. She developed friendships with other 'illegal nannies' from the Caribbean. They would tell her many things about where to go, and what to do about her papers, but often the information would be inaccurate. Looking back she realized the other nannies were misinformed. However, four years and two employers after arriving, her nanny friends told her about an organization that provided employment and legal status-related services and support for caregivers. The staff there encouraged Rachel to work with her employer so that she could enter the federal government's Live-in Caregiver Program (LCP).

Over the years, Rachel had spent a lot of time and money trying to regularize her status. After a couple of years working without a work permit or authorization to be in Canada, she contacted a lawyer to apply for permanent residence based on Humanitarian and Compassionate grounds (H&C). The lawyer took $400 and disappeared. Then she thought about marrying someone to stay. Regularization and permanent residence came through employer sponsorship and the LCP. Eight years after arriving in Canada, Rachel got her permanent residence. At the time of the interview, she continued to work as a caregiver, volunteered for work experience in her field, and was going to school part-time.

Case 4: In 1999, Ana joined her husband in Toronto. He had made an inland refugee claim in 1998 and was awaiting a decision. Ana was originally from Peru but had spent a number of years working as a nurse in Argentina before moving to Canada. Shortly after her arrival, Ana's husband became abusive. In 2002, facing a possible miscarriage of her second child and with the support of women in her English language classes, Ana left her husband and moved to a women's shelter. This triggered a family sponsorship breakdown, and thus her irregularization. She was out of status, without health care coverage, a valid work permit, or the right to presence in Canada.

At the same time, Ana's move into a women's shelter granted her substantive access to an extensive and diverse network of community agency resources. She received health care from a community health clinic, part of a system of clinics with some funds for primary care for the uninsured. She and her daughter were referred to a psychologist for free counseling. The shelter also connected her with a legal clinic that helped her file for permanent residence on H&C.[4] Because an H&C application does not grant provincial health coverage, a work permit or protection from deportation, Ana continued to access resources under the radar. Although the acceptance rate on H&Cs is under 10% and processing times are very slow, Ana was granted permanent residence four years later, seven years after arriving in Canada.

Before receiving her permanent residence, Ana held a variety of low-end jobs. She had a valid work permit for two years and a temporary Social Insurance Number; the latter authorized the payment of taxes but not employment unless it was paired with a work permit. In an effort to stay in her professional field, she often worked as a personal support worker. She also worked as a cleaner and waitress. She always volunteered and had begun to take courses with the hope that she would be able to eventually revalidate her nursing degree.

Discussion: assembling noncitizenship through the work of conditionality

Taken together, these cases exemplify the relational quality of noncitizenship as it is assembled and organized through the work of conditionality. They confirm the range and diversity of the institutional arenas in which conditionality plays out, as well as the multi-scalar socio-legal bases of conditionality. The cases reveal the formal and substantive infrastructures of social service provision and access, and the work of conditionality in which migrants and other actors engage, generating variable and dynamic configurations and trajectories of presence and access. They also highlight the benefits of social learning and the consequences of social scarring that may occur over time. These have direct implications for understanding the ways in which noncitizenship deepens the fault lines of social inequality and indefinitely prolongs the prospects for legal status security and occupational mobility.

The first case details the experience of a Colombian refugee claimant; a university-educated man without children or a spouse, from a country the Canadian Government had designated as refugee producing. It profiles the robust package of entitlements associated with Canada's refugee determination system in 2006 and the possibilities it generated when accessed to its fullest.[5] The case represents an instance where an educated and unattached migrant is unambiguously able to exercise his formal entitlements and where the formal refugee settlement infrastructure recognizes him as deserving of presence and access. The second case stands in sharp contrast with the first. It tells the story of a middle-class professional couple with children who, like Raul, also made an inland refugee claim. The couple was formally entitled to, but did not access the public goods associated with the refugee determination process. In this case, the couple's extended family played a central role in their decision to opt out of these entitlements based on their notions of how to construct deservingness. The case highlights how social networks and scripts of moral deservingness work together to mediate the exercise of formal entitlements in ways that have unpredictable yet significant and lasting impacts on incorporation; it also points to the range of actors that mediate these processes, including predatory legal consultants.

The third case shifts the focus away from the refugee determination system toward Canada's burgeoning temporary migrant worker system. It presents the case of a young, unattached Caribbean woman who entered Canada as a tourist, worked for years without legal status or a work permit, and eventually gained permanent residence through one of Canada's oldest migrant worker programs, the LCP. Her case illustrates the role of information of variable quality, including another predatory lawyer, and the accumulation of social learning. The case captures how friendship networks and the infrastructure of substantive settlement constitute the terrain of conditionality, and the potential multidirectionality of legal status trajectories. Finally, the fourth case captures the interface between federal policy and local advocacy for and with precarious noncitizens. It presents the case of a Peruvian health professional that entered Canada as a dependent on a refugee application, was illegalized when she left her abusive spouse, and then accessed public goods and eventually acquired permanent residence through the professional networks and advocacy of a women's shelter. Through these multiple transitions, her family situation, friendship networks, and a complex infrastructure of organizations overlapped to mediate her legal status trajectory and access to formal and substantive entitlements.

The cases offer an empirical basis for mapping the elements of the assemblage of noncitizenship and highlighting how they are connected dynamically and at times contingently through the work of conditionality. The Canadian regulatory and policy framework sets a baseline of possibilities for relations with noncitizens and experiences of noncitizenship. The four cases are a window into the possibilities set by Canada's refugee determination system, the LCP, and the application for permanent residence based on H&C. Through immigration targets, funding, rules for eligibility, application fees, and processing times, the federal government shapes the parameters for legal status trajectories and formal entitlements associated with categories and programs. Federal and provincial policy and funding also impact the design and delivery of services for migrants entering under these legal status entrance categories.

The cases also reveal the range of settlement and social services available for migrant noncitizens, and capture the formal and substantive logics of conditionality and frames of deservingness that are woven together throughout. Formal programs include those that connect noncitizens to the housing shelter system, the provincial social assistance program, community agencies that accept volunteers, settlement service organizations, and local school boards that deliver English language classes. Also of relevance is a substantive settlement service infrastructure that includes community health clinics, women's shelters, and advocacy groups, among others serving specific populations regardless of legal status. In Toronto, the substantive settlement infrastructure has grown exponentially over the last 10 years as organizations respond creatively to the de facto settlement of noncitizens (Community Social Planning Council-Toronto 2007; Bhuyan 2012). A Sanctuary City policy enacted in 2013 expanded the possibilities for substantive access to city services (Keung 2013).

Discretion by institutional actors operates across *de jure*, substantive and mixed socio-legal arenas and is informed by frames of deservingness and probationary policies. Frontline workers may interpret regulations narrowly or generously, and may carry out their duties actively or passively regardless of the formal grounds on which a noncitizen claims presence and access. While not developed in the case studies, frames of deservingness and associated forms of discretion may be a product of personal biographies, political culture of a specific workplace, the funding environment at a given point in time, and so forth. Frames of deservingness are also shaped by the broader political climate and media moment. This adds a multi-scalar perspective to discretion. It also points to a key source of systemic contingency in assemblages of noncitizenship.

The cases illustrate the roles that other social and institutional actors may play in legal status trajectories and the work of conditionality. While legal consultants and lawyers can play inclusionary roles, in the second and third cases they act as resource drains and offer no help. Their discretionary power in the assemblage of noncitizenship is clear, as is the fact that they can contribute to moving people in different and contingent directions over time. Elsewhere, we develop this line of analysis by referring to the chutes and ladders of immigration and legal status trajectories (Goldring and Landolt 2013; Landolt and Goldring 2013).

The cases also demonstrate the central role of migrant agency, in varied and changing modalities, as another source of dynamism and complexity in the work of conditionality. Practices of access and social learning are captured throughout. The case of Rachel is particularly instructive. Initially, she focused on the everyday task of wage work. Later, as she explained, she networked with other nannies and began to think about her situation and weigh her options. Rachel dedicated time and resources to reducing the precarity of her legal and work status, connecting with different actors along the way: other nannies who provided unclear information that led her to postpone her efforts to regularize, a lawyer who took her money but provided no help, and eventually an advocacy organization that told her to partner with her employer to help her enter the LCP. In this case, the slow transition from less to more purposeful action occurred as Rachel deciphered information gained through social networks and began to connect with different institutional actors. Interactions with different social and institutional actors generated learning that involved reflection and evaluation of past experiences to adjust present and future action.

Over time, migrant noncitizens with varying degrees of security make claims to presence, which are logically connected to practices of access. Migrants do so through interactions with other migrants and non-migrants in specific places and institutional arenas. The relationship between claims of presence and access can be inconsistent and contradictory. Ana exits an abusive relationship and enters a women's shelter. In so doing, she claims access to protection from violence but jeopardizes her claim to authorized presence. The shelter system offers substantive access to legal assistance, which allows her to reclaim authorized presence and achieve permanent residence. The cases also confirm that legal status trajectories can easily diverge from those expected and prescribed by policy. Directions and timelines may deviate and be indeterminate. Thus, Rachel churned through multiple legal status categories before eventually receiving her Permanent Residency through the LCP. Raul, the epitome of a best-case scenario of successful refugee determination, experienced a delay in obtaining his Permanent Residence after being granted asylum, which postponed his transition to a permanent position at work. Systemic contingency is produced through policy enforcement, gatekeeping, discretion, migrant action, and social learning, which are at play through iterative interactions within different, sometimes isolated and other times overlapping institutional actors and arenas. In turn, these processes are likely to generate a dynamic hodge-podge configuration of socio-legal bases for presence and access, across institutional arenas.

The cases capture the consequences of prolonged experiences of precarious noncitizenship for social inequality. Raul's case, which is emblematic of the prescribed refugee claimant trajectory, is the only case of a transition to secure status accompanied by positive improvements in employment. His labor market trajectory reflects his class-based resources and the importance of the settlement service infrastructure that he accessed as someone recognized as a deserving refugee claimant. In contrast, in the other three cases, people remained in the same labor market situation they found themselves in when they arrived in Canada. After varying lengths of time (from 4 to 8 years), they achieved the security of permanent residence, but were still in low-wage precarious employment. Over the course of their trajectories they dealt with poor information, predatory actors, relationship breakdowns, and other challenges. These experiences drained resources they may have been able to use for other purposes, and limited their opportunities to translate experience into improved labor market incorporation. However, their situations at the time of the interview were not uniformly negative. Ana and Rachel had accumulated experience that allowed them to look forward to pursuing educational objectives that might improve their employment. Janet and Pedro felt more independent and capable of improving their lives after cutting ties with his brother. In spite of these changes, they were precariously employed with limited prospects for social mobility or finding decent work. This also demonstrates the lasting impacts of noncitizenship on broader patterns of social inequality.

Conclusion

How we understand social life matters. Frameworks shape our understanding of how processes become institutionalized and normalized; how disparate elements are related to each other at particular moments; how they contribute to causal ordering, patterned practices, and durable social structures and inequalities; and how they are linked to agency by a range of differently situated actors. How we understand noncitizenship also matters. The metaphor of assemblage enables us to make sense of both systemic processes and contingent and heterogeneous patterns – in our case, legal status trajectories that take diverse courses in terms of timing, direction, and outcomes. As shown in the cases we profiled, refugee claimants may not have uniform experiences, the long arm of migration control does not uniformly or inexorably illegalize, and people's access to resources (including employment) and services changes and combines formal and substantive access that may vary by institutional arena (e.g. health, education), over time, and without necessarily fitting prescribed patterns of access. Our research on noncitizen migrants in Toronto finds that interactions with frontline workers in refugee and women's shelters, with relatives, friends and acquaintances, neighbors, legal consultants, and other institutional actors, organize trajectories that go in various directions, along disparate timelines, with some variation in outcomes. At the same time, navigating and negotiating noncitizenship has clear implications for social location and stratification, as it contributes to getting stuck in low-wage employment.

Understanding noncitizenship as assemblage provides a conceptual and methodological framework for analyzing how distinct elements, each with their own logics, come together to generate a systemic yet contingent social formation. The assemblage includes disparate policy and regulatory frameworks that touch on migrants' lives, in ways that vary over time and place. Key elements of the assemblage of noncitizenship include, but are not limited to: national and transnational policies and regulations that govern migrants, refugees, populations in transit, etc.; settlement and integration policies; social welfare and service provision, including health and education systems; service delivery organizations; multiple levels of government; etc. They also include variable modalities of agency on the part of a wide range of institutional and social actors. Social relations and agency are mediated by discretion and variable and dynamic frames of deservingness. These elements are constituted at multiple scales, over time, and may change as a result of processes that take place at multiple levels. How the global assemblage of noncitizenship is grounded in specific contexts will vary.

The metaphor of assemblage invites an inductive examination of how noncitizenship is constituted and negotiated. In the Canadian case, a country with a long tradition of immigrant reception and state-funded social policies and programs, elements of the assemblage include refugee and immigration hearings, labor markets, health care, schools and other educational systems, refugee advocacy organizations, women's shelters, immigrant settlement service organizations, welfare offices, unions and other worker's rights organizations, etc. Interactions include those with frontline workers, but also a wider range of actors, from teachers and lawyers to relatives and acquaintances. Many of these arenas and actors have a history of being implicated in the production of citizenship and noncitizenship; others have been drawn into co-producing noncitizenship more recently.

We operationalize the assemblage of noncitizenship through the concept of conditionality, which refers to the multi-actor and multi-scalar work involved in securing presence and access. Practices of conditionality assemble and organize noncitizenship in specific contexts and jurisdictions, in ways that may be contradictory and do not necessarily follow prescribed or consistent noncitizen legal status trajectories. The evidence presented in the four cases demonstrates the work of securing presence and gaining access to employment, immigrant settlement services, and other public services such as health and education. This work of conditionality is shaped not only by legal status categories and social location, but also through contact with different types of organizations. Analyzing the work of conditionality with regard to presence and access helps make sense of the dynamic hodge-podge of formal and substantive bases of access to resources and services in different arenas. Discretion and deservingness may not operate evenly across these arenas, as actors in distinct institutional settings and organizations work to grant or limit access. At the same time, migrants learn from their interactions and encounters, and this social learning informs decisions about subsequent practices and claims. These interactions, particularly ones that act as turning points in trajectories, shape pathways and patterns of access.

Understanding noncitizenship through the metaphor of assemblage and the concept of conditionality offers a way to account for contingency and systemic processes. Variable arenas and elements, all come together to assemble noncitizenship. Globally, noncitizenship is associated with extreme forms of vulnerability and exploitation that may have cumulative negative impacts for individuals and also shape social inequality. However, there is variation and contingency in legal status trajectories and experiences of prolonged noncitizenship. This variation is generated through the work of conditionality, through unequal social relations in a variety of institutional arenas, and through agency and social learning. Examining how noncitizenship is assembled through the work of conditionality can enhance our understanding of noncitizenship and its relationship to citizenship, and inform strategic interventions to address the long-term negative consequences of noncitizenship.

Notes

1. This is not meant to minimize the scarring and traumatic impacts of illegalization, raids, and surveillance. Literature eloquently addresses the fear and stigma that illegalized noncitizens in particular must deal with, and the impacts of fear on emotion and subjectivity (Chavez 1998; Abrego 2011; Saad 2013).
2. Because this *work* takes time and resources, migrants who are eventually successful in gaining secure legal status may feel they have to 'start all over' in an effort to gain occupational recognition and mobility. In turn, service providers in a setting that does not support inclusionary practices may experience burnout, attempt to change organizational practice, organize through movements with shared affinities and goals, and/or continue to practice inclusion on their own. At a systemic level, this is consistent with selective inclusion.
3. The research was funded by a grant from the Social Sciences and Humanities Research Council of Canada. For details and materials see: http://www.yorku.ca/ine/.
4. The H&C process is the one of the only options for a direct transition from being non-status (illegalized) to permanent residence. It involves establishing a rationale for permanent status based on humanitarian or compassionate grounds, both of which are subject to discretion and frames of deservingness, and demonstrating good conduct (more deservingness) and community participation (substantive membership).
5. Canada's refugee determination system, including the formal package of entitlements granted to refugee claimants has undergone cutbacks over the last decade. In some provinces, services were partially restored after significant mobilizations.

Disclosure statement

No potential conflict of interest was reported by the authors.

References

Abji, Salina. 2013. "Post-Nationalism Re-Considered: A Case Study of the 'No One is Illegal' Movement in Canada." *Citizenship Studies* 17 (3–4): 322–338.

Abrego, Leysi J. 2011. "Legal Consciousness of Undocumented Latinos: Fear and Stigma as Barriers to Claims-Making for First- and 1.5-Generation Immigrants." *Law and Society Review* 45 (2): 337–370.

Alpes, Maybritt Jill, and Alexis Spire. 2014. "Dealing with Law in Migration Control: The Powers of Street-Level Bureaucrats at French Consulates." *Social & Legal Studies* 23 (2): 261–274.

Basok, Tanya. 2009. "Counter-Hegemonic Human Rights Discourses and Migrant Rights Activism in the US and Canada." *International Journal of Comparative Sociology* 50 (2): 183–205.

Basok, Tanya, Danièle Bélanger, and Eloy Rivas. 2013. "Reproducing Deportability: Migrant Agricultural Workers in South-Western Ontario." *Journal of Ethnic and Migration Studies* 40 (9): 1394–1413.

Bhuyan, Rupaleem. 2012. "Negotiating Citizenship on the Frontlines: How the Devolution of Canadian Immigration Policy Shapes Services Delivery to Women Fleeing Abuse." *Law and Policy* 3 (2): 211–236.

Bloch, Alice, Nando Sigona, and Roger Zetter. 2014. *Sans Papiers: The Social and Economic Lives of Young Undocumented Migrants*. London: Pluto Press.

Bosniak, Linda. 1994. "Membership, Equality, and the Difference That Alienage Makes." *New York University Law Review* 69 (6): 1047–1149.

Bosniak, Linda. 2000. "Universal Citizenship and the Problem of Alienage." *Northwestern University Law Review* 94 (3): 963–982.

Bosniak, Linda. 2006. *The Citizen and the Alien*. Princeton: Princeton University Press.
Calavita, Kitty. 1998. "Immigration, Law, and Marginalization in a Global Economy: Notes from Spain." *Law and Society Review* 32 (3): 529–566.
Chauvin, Sébastien, and Blanca Garcés-Mascareñas. 2012. "Beyond Informal Citizenship: The New Moral Economy of Migrant Illegality." *International Political Sociology* 6: 241–259. doi:10.1111/j.1749-5687.2012.00162.x.
Chauvin, Sébastien, and Blanca Garcés-Mascareñas. 2014. "Becoming Less Illegal: Deservingness Frames and Undocumented Migrant Incorporation." *Sociology Compass* 8: 422–432. doi:10.1111/soc4.12145.
Chauvin, Sébastien, Blanca Garcés-Mascareñas, and Albert Kraler. 2013. "Employment and Migrant Deservingness." *International Migration* 51 (6): 80–85. doi:10.1111/imig.12123.
Chavez, Leo. 1998. *Shadowed Lives: Undocumented Immigrants in American Society*. Fort Worth, TX: Harcourt Brace College Publishers.
Community Social Planning Council-Toronto. 2007. *Toronto Community Service Resource Guide for Non-Status Immigrants*. Toronto: Community Social Planning Council-Toronto and Davenport Perth Neighbourhood Centre.
Coutin, Susan Bibler. 2000. *Legalizing Moves: Salvadoran Immigrants' Struggle for U.S. Residency*. Michigan: University of Michigan Press.
De Genova, Nicholas. 2002. "Migrant 'Illegality' and Deportability in Everyday Life." *Annual Review of Anthropology* 31: 419–447.
De Genova, Nicholas. 2007. "The Production of Culprits: From Deportability to Detainability in the Aftermath of 'Homeland Security'." *Citizenship Studies* 11 (5): 421–448. doi:10.1080/13621020701605735.
De Genova, Nicholas, and Nathalie Peutz. 2010. *The Deportation Regime: Sovereignty, Space, and the Freedom of Movement*. Durham, NC: Duke University Press.
Dobrowolsky, Alexandra. 2013. "Nuancing Neoliberalism: Lessons Learned from a Failed Immigration Experiment." *Journal of International Migration and Integration* 14: 197–218.
Fassin, Didier. 2005. "Compassion and Repression: The Moral Economy of Immigration Policies in France." *Current Anthropology* 20 (3): 362–387.
Fudge, Judy, and Fiona MacPhail. 2009. "The Temporary Foreign Worker Program in Canada: Low-Skilled Workers as an Extreme Form of Flexible Labor." *Comparative Labor Law and Policy Journal* 31: 5–45.
Gleeson, Shannon. 2012. *Conflicting Commitments: The Politics of Enforcing Immigrant Worker Rights in San Jose and Houston*. Ithaca, NY: Cornell University Press.
Goldring, Luin. 2014. "Resituating Temporariness as the Precarity and Conditionality of Non-citizenship." In *Liberating Temporariness: Migration, Work, and Citizenship in an Age of Insecurity in Canada*, edited by Leah F. Vosko, Valerie Preston, and Robert Latham, 218–254. Kingston and Montreal: McGill-Queen's University Press.
Goldring, Luin, and Patricia Landolt. 2011. "Caught in the Work-Citizenship Matrix: The Lasting Effects of Precarious Legal Status on Work for Toronto Immigrants." *Globalizations* 8 (3): 325–341.
Goldring, Luin, and Patricia Landolt. 2012. "The Impact of Legal Status on Immigrants' Economic Outcomes." IRPP report No. 35. Ottawa: Institute for Research on Public Policy.
Goldring, Luin, and Patricia Landolt. 2013. "Introduction. The Conditionality of Legal Status and Rights: Conceptualizing Precarious Non-Citizenship in Canada." In *Producing and Negotiating Non-Citizenship: Precarious Legal Status in Canada*, edited by Luin Goldring and Patricia Landolt, 3–27. Toronto: University of Toronto Press.
Gonzales, Roberto. 2011. "Learning to Be Illegal: Undocumented Youth and Shifting Legal Contexts in the Transition to Adulthood." *American Sociological Review* 76 (4): 602–619.
Hagan, Jacqueline Maria. 1994. *Deciding to Be Legal: A Maya Community in Houston*. Philadelphia, PA: Temple University Press.
Heyman, Josiah M. 2014. "'Illegality' and the U.S.-Mexico Border: How It is Produced and Resisted." In *Constructing Illegality in America: Immigrant Experiences, Critiques, and Responses*, edited by Cecilia Menjivar and Daniel Kanstroom, 111–135. New York: Cambridge University Press.
Iacovetta, Franca. 2006. *Gatekeepers: Reshaping Immigrant Lives in Cold War Canada*. Toronto: Between The Lines.

Isin, Engin. 2008. "Theorizing Acts of Citizenship." In *Acts of Citizenship*, edited by Engin Isin and Greg M. Nielsen, 15–43. London: Zed Books.
Keung, Nicholas. 2013. "Toronto Declared Sanctuary City to Non-Status Migrants." *The Toronto Star*, February 21. http://www.thestar.com/news/gta/2013/02/21/cisanctuarycity21.html
Kisson, Priya. 2013. "Precarious Immigration Status and Precarious Housing Pathways: Refugee Claimant Homelessness in Toronto and Vancouver." In *Producing and Negotiating Non-Citizenship: Precarious Legal Status in Canada*, edited by Luin Goldring and Patricia Landolt, 195–217. Toronto: University of Toronto Press.
Kubal, Agnieska. 2013. "Conceptualizing Semi-Legality in Migration Research." *Law and Society Review* 47 (3): 555–587.
Lamont, Michèle, and Virág Molnár. 2002. "The Study of Boundaries in the Social Sciences." *Annual Review of Sociology* 28: 167–195.
Landolt, Patricia, and Luin Goldring. 2013. "The Social Production of Non-Citizenship: The Consequences of Intersecting Trajectories of Precarious Legal Status and Precarious Work." In *Producing and Negotiating Non-Citizenship: Precarious Legal Status in Canada*, edited by Luin Goldring and Patricia Landolt, 154–174. Toronto: University of Toronto Press.
Landolt, Patricia, Paloma E. Villegas, and Francisco Villegas. 2012. *Patchworks of Access: Education and Healthcare for Immigrants with Precarious Legal Status*. CERIS, The Ontario Metropolis Centre Research Summary. Toronto: CERIS.
Lipsky, Michael. 2010. *Street-Level Bureaucracy: Dilemmas of the Individual in Public Service*. 30th Anniversary Expanded Edition ed. New York: Russel Sage Foundation.
Little, Daniel. 2012. "Assemblage Theory." In *Understanding Society: Innovative Thinking about Agency and Structure in a Global World*. Accessed May 12, 2015. http://understandingsociety.blogspot.ca/2012/11/assemblage-theory.html
Lowry, Michelle, and Peter Nyers. 2003. "'No One is Illegal': The Fight for Refugee and Migrant Rights in Canada." *Refuge* 21 (3): 66–72.
Makaremi, Chowra. 2009. "Governing Borders in France: From Extraterritorial to Humanitarian Confinement." *Canadian Journal of Law and Society* 24 (3): 411–432.
Marshall, T. H. 1950. *Citizenship and Social Class*. Cambridge: Cambridge University Press.
Martínez Veiga, Ubaldo. 2007. "Irregular Migration, Informal Labour and Poverty in the Agricultural Sector in Spain." In *Irregular Migration, Informal Labour and Community: A Challenge for Europe*, edited by Erik Berggren, Branka Likic-Brboric, Gülay Toköz and Nicos Trimikliniotis, 199–214. Maastricht: Shaker Publishing VB.
McKay, Sonia, Eugenia Markova, Anna Paraskevopoulou, and Tessa Wright. 2009. *The Relationship between Migration Status and Employment Outcomes*. London: Working Lives Research Institute, London Metropolitan University.
Menjívar, Cecilia, and Daniel Kanstroom. 2014. *Constructing Immigrant 'Illegality': Critiques, Experiences, and Responses*. New York: Cambridge University Press.
Moffette, David. 2014. "Governing Immigration through Probation: The Displacement of Borderwork and the Assessment of Desirability in Spain." *Security Dialogue* 45 (3): 262–278.
Morris, Lydia. 2003. "Managing Contradiction: Civic Stratification and Migrants' Rights." *International Migration Review* 37 (1): 74–100.
Mountz, Alison. 2011. "The Enforcement Archipelago: Detention, Haunting, and Asylum on Islands." *Political Geography* 30: 118–128.
Ngai, Mae. 2004. *Impossible Subjects: Illegal Aliens and the Making of Modern America*. Princeton: Princeton University Press.
Omi, Michael, and Howard Winant. 1989. *Racial Formation in the United States: From the 1960s to the 1980s*. New York: Routledge.
Ong, Aihwa, and Stephen J. Collier, ed. 2005. *Global Assemblages: Tehnology, Politics, and Ethics as Anthropological Problems*. Malden, MA: Blackwell.
van Oorschot, Wim. 2000. "Who Should Get What, and Why? On Deservingess Criteria and the Conditionality of Solidarity among the Public." *Policy & Politics* 28 (1): 33–48.
Painter, Joe, and Chris Philo. 1995. "Spaces of Citizenship: An Introduction." *Political Geography* 14 (2): 107–120.

Pallares, Amalia. 2015. *Family Activism: Immigrant Struggles and the Politics of Noncitizenship*. New Brunswick, NJ: Rutgers University Press.

Pratt, Anna. 2005. *Securing Borders: Detention and Deportation in Canada*. Vancouver: UBC Press.

Puar, Jasbir K., and Amit Rai. 2002. "Monster, Terrorist, Fag: The War on Terrorism and the Production of Docile Patriots." *Social Text* 20 (3): 117–148.

Rhus, Martin, and Bridget Anderson. 2010. "Semi-Compliance and Illegality in Migrant Labour Markets: An Analysis of Migrants, Employers and the State in the UK." *Population, Space and Place* 16 (3): 195–211. doi:10.1002/psp.588.

Rygiel, Kim. 2010. *Globalizing Citizenship*. Vancouver: UBC Press.

Saad, Samia. 2013. "The Cost of Invisibility: The Psychosocial Impact of Falling out of Status." In *Producing and Negotiating Non-Citizenship: Precarious Legal Status in Canada*, edited by Luin Goldring and Patricia Landolt, 137–153. Toronto: University of Toronto Press.

Sassen, Saskia. 2006. *Territory, Authority, Rights: From Medieval to Global Assemblages*. Updated edition ed. Princeton: Princeton University Press.

Satzewich, Victor. 2014. "Canadian Visa Officers and the Social Construction of 'Real' Spousal Relationships." *Revue canadienne de sociologie* [Canadian Review of Sociology] 51 (1): 1–21.

Schweitzer, Reinhard. 2014. "The Making and Unmaking of Irregular Migration: Migrant 'Illegality', Regularisation and Deportation in Spain and the UK." *Integrim online papers*, N°4. http://www.integrim.eu/wp-content/uploads/2014/02/Schweitzer-the-making-and-unmaking-of-irregular-migration.pdf

Sharma, Nandita. 2006. *Home Economics: Nationalism and the Making of 'Migrant Workers' in Canada*. Toronto: University of Toronto Press.

Spire, Alexis. 2008. *Accueillir Ou Reconduire: Enquête Sure Les Guichets De L'immigration* [To Welcome or Turn Away: Research on the Front-lines of Immigration]. Paris: Raisons D'Agir.

Stasiulis, Daiva, and Abigail Bakan. 1997. "Negotiating Citizenship: The Case of Foreign Domestic Workers in Canada." *Feminist Review* 57 (1): 112–139.

Stasiulis, Daiva, and Abigail Bakan. 2005. *Negotiating Citizenship: Migrant Women in Canada and the Global System*. Toronto: University of Toronto Press.

Staeheli, L. A., P. Ehrkamp, H. Leitner, and C. R. Nagel. 2012. "Dreaming the Ordinary: Daily Life and the Complex Geographies of Citizenship." *Progress in Human Geography* 36 (5): 628–644. doi:10.1177/0309132511435001.

Tandian, Aly, and Sylvia I. Bergh. 2014. "From Temporary Work in Agriculture to Irregular Status in Domestic Service: The Transition and Experiences of Senegalese Migrant Women in Spain." In *Migration, Gender and Social Justice: Perspectives on Human Insecurity*, edited by Truong Thanh-Dam, Des Gasper, Jeff Handmaker and Sylvia I. Bergh, 47–67. New York: Springer Link.

Varsanyi, Monica W. 2005. "The Paradox of Contemporary Immigrant Political Mobilization: Organized Labor, Undocumented Migrants, and Electoral Participation in Los Angeles." *Antipode* 37 (4): 775–795.

Vasta, Ellie. 2011. "Immigrants and the Paper Market: Borrowing, Renting and Buying Identities." *Ethnic and Racial Studies* 34 (2): 187–206.

Vickstrom, Erik. 2014. "Pathways into Irregular Status among Senegalese Migrants in Europe." *International Migration Review* 48 (4): 1062–1099. doi:10.1111/imre.12154.

Villegas, Francisco. 2013. "Getting to 'Don't Ask Don't Tell' at the Toronto District School Board: Mapping the Competing Discourses of Rights and Membership." In *Producing and Negotiating Non-Citizenship: Precarious Status in Canada*, edited by Luin Goldring and Patricia Landolt, 258–272. Toronto: University of Toronto Press.

Villegas, Paloma E. 2012a. "Assembling a Visa Requirement against the Mexican 'Wave': Migrant Illegalization, Policy and Affective 'Crises' in Canada." *Ethnic and Racial Studies* 36: 1–20. doi:10.1080/01419870.2012.705009.

Villegas, Paloma E. 2012b. *Assembling and Re(Making) Migrant Illegalization: Mexican Migrants with Precarious Status in Canada*. OISE: University of Toronto.

Villegas, Paloma E. 2015. "Fishing for Precarious Status Migrants: Surveillant Assemblages of Migrant Illegalization in Toronto, Canada." *Journal of Law and Society* 42 (2): 230–252.

Walia, Harsha. 2010. "Transient Servitude: Migrant Labour in Canada and the Apartheid of Citizenship." *Race and Class* 52 (1): 71–84.
Willen, Sarah S. 2007. "Toward a Critical Phenomenology of 'Illegality': State Power, Criminalization, and Abjectivity among Undocumented Migrant Workers in Tel Aviv, Israel." *International Migration* 45 (3): 8–38.
Willen, Sarah S. 2012. "How is Health-Related 'Deservingness' Reckoned? Perspectives from Unauthorized Im/Migrants in Tel Aviv." *Social Science & Medicine* 74 (6): 812–821. doi:10.1016/j.socscimed.2011.06.033.
Wright, Cynthia. 2003. "Moments of Emergence: Organizing by and with Undocumented and Non-Citizen People in Canada after September 11." *Refuge* 21 (3): 5–15.
Young, Julie. 2005. "'This is My Life:' Questions of Agency and Belonging among Youth Living with Less than Full Status." Major Research Paper, Ryerson University, Toronto.
Yuval-Davis, Nira. 1997. "Women, Citizenship and Difference." *Feminist Review* 57: 4–27.

Unequal access to human rights: the categories of noncitizenship

David Weissbrodt[a] and Michael Divine[b]

[a]School of Law, University of Minnesota, Minneapolis, MN, USA; [b]Divine Law Group, LLC, St. Paul, MN, USA

ABSTRACT

International human rights law consists of a body of basic rights and principles that States are to enforce with respect to every person within their borders. The unfortunate reality, however, is that many States are incapable of ensuring the rights of everyone, and in some instances simply do not wish to do so. Accordingly, citizenship serves as an acknowledgment by a State that the status holder is entitled to a higher degree of protection. Conversely, noncitizens may enjoy less rights than citizens, and certain categories of noncitizens frequently find themselves outside of the State's protection entirely. This article outlines many of the rights that international law directs should be enjoyed by every human being, the factors that contribute to unequal enjoyment of these rights, and the categories of noncitizen associated with the mediated allocation of basic human rights.

There is an inherent friction in the relationship between international human rights law and citizenship. On the one hand, human rights law is inclusive, and meant to confer rights on every individual without regard to where they were born, their connection to a particular State, their religion, or their ethnic group. On the other hand, citizenship is exclusive, having as its aim the proscription of certain rights, and serving as de facto gate keeper to the enjoyment of other derivative rights. This friction is mediated to a degree by diplomatic, customary, and treaty law, but is also intensified by sociopolitical considerations both local and global in character.

The term 'noncitizen' itself refers to a diverse range of persons including, but not limited to, migrants, foreign students, temporary visitors, permanent residents, refugees, asylum seekers, victims of trafficking, and stateless persons. Each category of noncitizen is subject to different legal regimes, and may in part be defined by the rights enjoyed by persons associated with the particular category. Individuals belonging to all categories of noncitizen, however, experience many similar obstacles in the realization of rights. Noncitizens may face pervasive official and non-official discrimination, resulting in hostile social and practical realities. Noncitizens may also be subjected to racism, xenophobia, lack of political representation, and diminished or nonexistent access to judicial systems.

This text has the ambition of assisting readers to better understand the international legal tools, systems, circumstances, and justifications expanding and retracting the scope of rights enjoyed by various categories of noncitizen. The authors are attorneys, however, not theorists, and acknowledge the boundaries of their expertise. Accordingly, the authors have attempted to focus the subject matter on legal materials.

Section 1 of this article begins with a discussion on the mechanisms of human rights implementation. Section 2 covers the often ignored legal authorities mandating States to enforce human rights without discrimination on grounds of citizenship. Section 3 outlines various categories of noncitizens, specific rights that should be enforced, and the obstacles to their realization. Lastly, Section 4 discusses the particularly difficult experience of migrant workers in receiving even the most basic of protections.

1. Implementation of human rights

Human rights protections are largely dependent upon the legal mechanisms present where a noncitizen resides. Accordingly, the primary actors in human rights implementation are States and their constituent legal systems. Unfortunately, States frequently fail to codify necessary protections, let alone see to their enforcement. At the very highest levels, national constitutions often improperly guarantee certain rights only to citizens, or otherwise distinguish between persons who obtained nationality through birth (*jus soli*), through the nationality of a parent (*jus sanguinis*), or some other means. Even where a nation's laws are largely consistent with international human rights norms, implementation and enforcement at all levels of government – from national to local – may be lacking due to inability, ignorance, or unwillingness of the officials charged with their execution.

In some instances, noncitizens may seek protections from outside of the State where they are presently residing.[1] Indeed, the Vienna Convention on Consular Relations (1963) requires that when a noncitizen is detained, the arresting State must inform the consular officials of the person's home State, which may then act to safeguard the person's rights. The effectiveness of consular intervention, however, depends on the relationship between the noncitizen's home State and the detaining State. Political, military, and economic considerations may therefore limit a detainee's access to meaningful protections (International Law Commission 2006).[2]

The implementation bodies of multilateral human rights treaties may also oversee the protection of rights belonging to noncitizens residing within the borders of States Parties to the respective treaties and their protocols. One such body is the Committee on the Protection of the Rights of All Migrant Workers and Members of their Families, which held its first session in 2004 and generally meets twice a year to review reports from States on the steps taken to implement the International Convention on the Protection of the Rights of All Migrant Workers and Members of Their Families (1990).[3] The Human Rights Committee, which monitors the widely ratified International Covenant on Civil and Political Rights ('Civil Rights Covenant'),[4] has also been known to advocate on behalf of the rights of noncitizens, and may hear complaints from noncitizens residing in States Parties to the First Optional Protocol to the Civil Rights Covenant (1976).[5] The Human Rights Committee issued General Comment No. 15 in 1994,[6] specifically reiterating States Parties obligations to protect the human rights of noncitizens living within their borders.

Lastly, some noncitizens may seek protections from regional human rights bodies, which operate under their own respective multilateral treaties. For example, the European Court of Human Rights accepts applications directly from individuals alleging violation of their rights under the European Convention on Human Rights. The Inter-American Court of Human Rights, which interprets and applies the American Convention on Human Rights, permits individual applicants, though only once a complaint has been deemed admissible by the Inter-American Commission on Human Rights. The African Court of Human and Peoples' Rights, which interprets the African [Banjul] Charter on Human and Peoples' Rights (1986),[7] has jurisdiction over complaints brought against States that have ratified the Protocol to the African Charter on Human and Peoples' Rights on the Establishment of an African Court on Human and Peoples' Rights. Ratifying States, however, may choose whether individual complainants have direct access to the Court.

Where human rights protections are available outside of the State in which a person is residing, access to enforcement mechanisms may be hindered by various considerations. A noncitizen whose rights have been violated may refrain from petitioning an enforcement body due to fears that a complaint may cause retaliation, or other adverse consequences worse than a violation of the right at issue. A common fear is that filing a complaint may result in the revocation of a visa, and/or deportation.[8] Other noncitizens simply do not have access to the resources necessary to petition an enforcement body.

2. Equality and nondiscrimination

Contemporary international human rights law is built upon the foundational premise that every person, by virtue of their existence, is entitled to certain rights and protections. Accordingly, human rights law generally prohibits discriminatory enforcement of rights on any grounds, and specifically forbids discrimination based upon 'race, colour, sex, language, religion, political or other opinion, *national or social origin*, property, birth, or other status' (see, e.g., Universal Declaration of Human Rights 1948). The principle of nondiscrimination permits very few lawful limitations and, with respect to noncitizens, is only permissible in narrow circumstances inherently tied to certain State rights under international law.

States must equally protect and enforce noncitizens' rights to be free from arbitrary killing; arbitrary detention; freedom from cruel, inhuman, or degrading treatment or punishment; to be free from slavery or servitude; to liberty and security of their person; equality before courts and tribunals; freedom from arbitrary or unlawful interference with privacy, family, home, or correspondence; to peaceful assembly; to receive protection as minors; and freedom of thought, conscience, and religion (see, e.g., UN Human Rights Committee 1986). The International Covenant on Civil and Political Rights (1966), one of the core documents comprising the International Bill of Human Rights,[9] however, permits nations to distinguish between citizens and certain categories of noncitizens with respect to political rights explicitly guaranteed to nationals, and freedom of movement. Article 25 of the Civil Rights Covenant requires that States need afford only citizens the rights to 'take part in the conduct of public affairs … to vote … (and to) have access, on general terms of equality, to public service.' The right to liberty of movement and the freedom to choose one's residence are similarly limited by Article 12, to persons 'lawfully within the territory of a State.' Accordingly, a State need not generally guarantee freedom of movement to undocumented and out-of-status migrants ('irregular migrants'), though a State must take care to ensure that other rights are not violated if it chooses to avoid doing so. For example, a State has still violated its obligations under the Civil Rights Covenant if an irregular migrant's inability to move freely results in involuntary servitude, or inability to access judicial systems (International Covenant on Civil and Political Rights 1966). The permissive language in Articles 12 and 25 can never be used to justify a discriminatory derogation of other rights.[10]

The International Covenant on Economic, Social, and Cultural Rights (1966) – the other treaty comprising the International Bill of Human Rights – permits developing nations to limit the extent to which certain economic rights are afforded noncitizens.[11] As with the distinctions permissible under the Civil Rights Covenant, though, discriminatory application of Economic rights must still be construed so as to maintain the overall thrust of the human rights protection.

Despite the existence of an extensive framework for noncitzens' rights, there remains a disparity between prescribed rights and the realities noncitizens must face. The failure of some States to ensure the rights of noncitizens may be due, in part, to economic inability or practical reality. In other instances, geopolitics, nationalism, and/or outright racism contribute to the withholding of protections owed to noncitizens. At the same time, the legal status of noncitizens may preclude them from participation in elections, inhibiting the realization of corrections and meaningful representation through democratic process.

3. Categories of noncitizens

Citizenship is an essential requirement for the practical securing of human rights protections. Although international law requires States generally protect the human rights of all persons – regardless of citizenship – many States only ensure full civil, political, economic, and social rights to their own nationals. Furthermore, stateless persons receive less protection internationally, as they have no home State to intercede on their behalf through diplomatic channels.

3.1. Stateless persons

Statelessness, or the condition of having no legal ('*de jure*')[12] or effective ('de facto') citizenship,[13] has many causes (Office of the United Nations Office High Commissioner for Refugees [UNHCR] 1999).[14] The mechanisms of *de jure* statelessness may be a State's citizenship laws, which are often premised upon the principles of: (1) *jus soli*, basing nationality on place of birth; (2) *jus sanguinis*, basing nationality on familial descent, or; (3) some combination of *jus soli* and *jus sanguinis*. As an example, a migrant leaving a State where nationality requires birth within the State, to live in a State where nationality is conditioned upon having descended from a national of such a State, may produce children with no right to citizenship in either State. A person may also become stateless if their government revokes their citizenship; passes laws changing citizenship criteria; or when a State is dissolved, succeeded, or broken up.

Effective, or de facto, statelessness occurs when a person has citizenship, but is unable to enjoy its associated rights. While *de jure* statelessness may be caused by legal oversights or mistakes, de facto statelessness is more often the result of crime or State discrimination. In the context of slavery and sex trafficking, for example, a person may be effectively deprived of their rights through the confiscation of passports or other documents capable of proving nationality. Without identity documents, it is far more difficult to find jobs, register the birth of children, obtain education, return to a home State, access judicial processes, or even obtain asylum.

Stateless persons are far more susceptible to human rights abuses. Accordingly, Article 15 of the Universal Declaration of Human Rights requires that '[e]veryone has a right to nationality' and 'no one shall be arbitrarily deprived of his nationality' (Universal Declaration of Human Rights 1948). Stateless children are particularly vulnerable, and the Civil Rights Covenant (1966) specifically reiterates that '[e]very child has the right to acquire a nationality.' The Convention on the Rights of the Child (1989) elaborates by providing children 'shall be registered immediately after birth and shall have the right from birth to a name, [and] the right to acquire nationality ... in particular where the child would otherwise be stateless.'[15] States must also ensure that no woman lose her nationality because of marriage to an alien, a spouse changing nationality,[16] or divorce from a national (Convention on the Elimination of All Forms of Discrimination Against Women 1979).

Though ratified by fewer States, the 1961 Convention on the Reduction of Statelessness ('1961 Convention') includes many rules that would assist States in reducing statelessness. The 1961 Convention requires, for example, that States Parties must 'grant nationality to a person born on its territory who would otherwise be stateless'; grant nationality to children not born in its territory if one parent is a national and the child would otherwise be stateless; and must not revoke a person's nationality if doing so would result in statelessness of the person or the person's family (Convention on the Reduction of Statelessness 1961).

In extreme cases, such as Nazi deprivation of Jewish citizenship during World War II, States have used citizenship as a tool to rid themselves of people that it considers undesirable. Hannah Arendt, in her book *Eichmann in Jerusalem* (1963), notes that at the Wannsee Conference,[17] prior to the Nazi's implementation of the 'Final Solution' to the 'Jewish Question', the Nazi government purposefully rendered stateless all Jews in its territory. This measure made it impossible for any country to inquire about the fate of these Jews, and it enabled the State of residency to seize their property (115). Additionally, when the Nazis began deporting Jews from other States, such as Holland and France, the stateless Jews were more vulnerable than Jewish Dutch and French citizens. Indeed, 'deportations [almost always] ... started with stateless Jews' (167) Arendt asserts that 'the Jews had to lose their nationality before they could be exterminated (240).

3.2. Refugees and asylum seekers

The 1951 Geneva Convention Relating to the Status of Refugees ('Refugee Convention') defines a refugee as a person who

> owing to well-founded fear of being persecuted for reasons of race, religion, nationality, membership of a particular social group or political opinion, is outside the country of his nationality and is unable, or owing to such fear, is unwilling to avail himself of the protection of his former habitual residence ... is unable or, owing to such fear, is unwilling to return to it. (art. 1)

Refugees may face many of the same obstacles as stateless persons in the realization of their rights. Like stateless persons, refugees are generally unable to access diplomatic rights protections from a State of origin. Like all migrants, refugees must battle racism, xenophobia, and practical difficulties with assimilating into the receiving State.

The Universal Declaration of Human Rights (1948) records that '[e]veryone has the right to seek and to enjoy in other countries asylum from persecution.' The right to asylum is principally implemented by the Refugee Convention, and its widely ratified Protocol Relating to the Status of Refugees ('1967 Protocol') though it is also articulated in numerous other global and regional legal documents.[18] Eligibility for protection may be based upon the terms of the Refugee Convention or domestic laws, which are frequently in line with the Refugee Convention. A person who meets the criteria outlined in the UNHCR Statute, which is nearly identical to those of the Refugee Convention, may also qualify for protection as a refugee, regardless of whether a host country recognizes them as such (UNHCR 1992). When applying to a State that uses its own eligibility process, the UNHCR may still assist by providing information on country conditions and, in some limited instances, issuing advisory opinions.

In 2001, the Norwegian freighter *MV Tampa* rescued 438 asylum seekers from a sinking wooden ferry off Australia's Christmas Island in the Indian Ocean. The asylum seekers were fleeing Taliban rule in Afghanistan. Although the medical situation of several of the ship's passengers was critical, and the *Tampa*'s crew had sent out distress messages, the Australian government denied the *Tampa* permission to dock at Christmas Island. The asylum seekers on board the *Tampa* suffered from severe diarrhea, scabies, and dysentery and two women in the advanced stages of pregnancy were sheltering under borrowed blankets in the ship's hold. In order to prevent the *Tampa* from docking at Christmas Island, Australian naval ships were sent to the scene. Heavily armed Australian troops from naval ships boarded the *Tampa* and lined its deck to ensure that the asylum seekers did not jump overboard and attempt to swim to the nearby island. John Howard, Australia's Prime Minister who was running for reelection, indicated that Australia took such measures in order to send the message that '[Australia is] not a country of easy destination ...' (Howard 2001). In addition to the Australian government, the Indonesian government also refused to accept the asylum seekers. The Indonesian foreign minister, Hasan Wirayuda, remarked that Indonesia should not take the asylum seekers because '[w]e have enough problems dealing with illegal migrants already here' (BBC News 2001). Wirayuda also remarked that the problem of the asylum seekers should not be transferred to Indonesia, because the asylum seekers 'are under the full protection of a ship which belongs to a rich country ...' (Barkham and Aglionby 2001). Eventually, 150 of the *MV Tampa* asylum seekers were accepted by New Zealand and the remainder were sent the extremely remote Pacific island of Nauru. Since that time, most of the *MV Tampa* passengers left in Nauru were found to be refugees and were resettled in Australia, Canada, Denmark, New Zealand, Norway, and Sweden. Some of the asylum seekers were returned to Afghanistan, however, where at least one is known to have been killed by the Taliban.

While persons who have already been granted refugee or asylee status generally receive and enjoy some form of asylum, the above example illustrates the inaccessibility of the right to *seek* asylum. Indeed, many countries deter 'boat people', stowaway asylum seekers, and other such persons before these persons are given sufficient opportunity to assert their claim to asylum. Because of the high costs associated with hosting asylum seekers and determining refugee or asylee status, many States are motivated to turn asylum seekers away from their asylum systems before they even reach a port of entry.

States with large populations of asylum seekers are increasingly turning to a broad range of policy measures designed to exclude asylum seekers from State asylum systems.

Exclusion from asylum determination procedures was the effect of the United States' policies – implemented in 1994 – that created offshore temporary refuges for Cubans in Panama and Haitians in Guantánamo Bay, Cuba (Fitzpatrick 1994). While these offshore detention centers provided a minimal level of safety, interdiction and detention policies prevented many 'boat people' from accessing the US asylum system and 'illustrate the ease of blocking access to durable asylum ...' (Fitzpatrick 1994, 50). As stated in an overview of the United States Coast Guard's Alien Migrant Interdiction Program, 'interdicting migrants at sea means they can be quickly returned to their countries of origin without the costly processes required if they successfully enter the United States' (Rosenberg 2003). The US Immigration and Naturalization Service reported that 'between 1981 and 1991, more than 25,000 [Haitians] were interdicted, while only six had been 'screened in' for transfer to the United States' (Rosenberg 2003). When one considers the human rights situation in Haiti during this 10-year period, however, the fact that only 6 of approximately 25,000 persons interdicted at sea were considered *potential* refugees suggests that many bona fide refugees were stopped and not allowed adequate opportunity to apply for asylum. The legality of the US Coast Guard's interdiction practices were nonetheless upheld by the US Supreme Court, which ruled in *Sale v Haitian Centers Council* (1993) that Article 33 of the 1951 Refugee Convention, which prohibits *refoulement*, does not apply on the high seas.[19]

The Universal Declaration of Human Rights provides in Article 14 that everyone has the right to both *seek* and *enjoy* asylum. Likewise, the African [Banjul] Charter on Human and Peoples' Rights and the American Convention on Human Rights (1969) similarly provide for the right to seek asylum.[20] It is generally accepted that an asylum seeker is someone who has left a country of origin in order to seek international protection as a refugee or an asylee. It should be noted, however, that the phrase 'asylum seeker' is not used or defined in a single major treaty and the definition of the phrase, therefore, varies with the laws of each country. In some countries, a person must have made a formal application for protection in order to be considered an asylum seeker, while in other countries, the fact that a person has fled their country of origin in order to seek international protection makes them an asylum seeker in and of itself. For example, in Ireland, an asylum seeker is merely someone 'who seeks to be recognised as a refugee under the terms of the 1951 Convention relating to the Status of Refugees' (Citizens Information 2015) whereas in the UK, a person must 'make a formal application for asylum ... [and await] a decision about their status in order to be considered an asylum seeker ...' (BBC News 2005).

In countries such as Ireland and the UK, asylum seekers who apply for protection from inside the receiving country, as well as from abroad, become refugees if authorities determine that they fit the international refugee definition (UNESCO, n.d.). Some countries, however, differentiate between persons who apply for a State's protection inside the proposed country of asylum and persons who leave their country of origin and enter a third State to apply for protection from the country of proposed asylum.[21] Furthermore, it should be noted that while some documents use the terms 'asylum seeker,' 'asylee,' and 'refugee' interchangeably, asylum seekers have generally not been granted protected status while refugees and asylees have been granted such status.

There are many paths to refugee or asylee status. An asylum seeker may enter a potential host country by way of land, sea, or airplane. They may enter a country as part of a mass influx, or be rerouted to a second country for refugee status determination and possible resettlement. Asylum status determination can be done on both an individual basis and/or a group basis. Depending upon the circumstances of arrival and national practices, asylum seekers can be granted protection under national, regional, or international law, and they may be granted refugee status, asylee status, humanitarian leave to remain, or some form of informal, ad hoc, or temporary protection. Indeed, refugee status determination procedures are by no means uniform: they vary greatly in selectivity and methods of determination.

Given that States provide protection to refugees and asylees, States usually determine whether asylum seekers are eligible for refugee or asylee status. The UNHCR, however, often plays a role in determining eligibility for protection and involvement of the UNHCR in asylum decisions – ranging from total engagement in some States, to no formal role in other States. In countries such as Turkey and Cambodia – which are parties to the 1951 Convention as well as the 1967 Protocol Relating to the Status of Refugees but nonetheless do not have their own refugee determination processes – the UNHCR is entirely responsible for refugee status determination. In other countries, such as the USA, the UNHCR has no formal involvement in asylum proceedings. At the request of the asylum applicant the UNHCR may, nonetheless, assist asylum seekers in the USA by providing their 'representatives with information on country conditions … and [issuing] advisory opinions in cases of significant impact' (UNHCR Washington).

Over the last several decades, human rights abuses have persisted while advances in transportation and communications technologies have given refugees increased opportunities to leave their countries of origin in search of asylum. In many States, the resulting increase in the number of asylum seekers has led to enhanced awareness of the burden States must shoulder in receiving asylum seekers as well as the unmet economic needs of citizens and other residents. This awareness is particularly present in European countries, where traditional immigration channels are virtually nonexistent and asylum is seen as one the few remaining 'backdoors' to European immigration. Radical and mainstream politicians alike have sought to exploit public xenophobia for political ends and mobilize voters by framing asylum seekers as 'freeloaders' and blaming economic ills on asylum seekers (Legomsky 1996).

While politicians have sought to leverage public xenophobia, many governments have implemented asylum system reforms in order to respond to increased refugee flows. In many instances, such reforms have created unnecessary barriers to asylum. Of these reforms, safe country of origin and interdiction programs are among the most problematic because they often summarily deny asylum to genuine refugees who face real persecution if they are forced to return to their countries of origin (Legomsky 1996). The situation has only worsened in the aftermath of the September 2001 attacks on the USA. Indeed, asylum reforms have become more widely adopted and more severely applied in the name of public security and several countries have invoked antiterrorism measures to detain indefinitely or otherwise violate the rights of asylum seekers on the basis of unspecified allegations related to terrorism or national security. The government of the USA, for example, has detained and summarily deported thousands of individuals – many of whom are asylum seekers – from Middle Eastern and Asian nations. In short, asylum has become more difficult to obtain despite the fact that human rights abuses are by no means diminishing.

3.3. Noncitizen workers

Noncitizen workers include seasonal agricultural laborers, permanent noncitizen residents of a State, and everything in between. It is not uncommon for seasonal workers to endure squalid temporary housing, abusive employment conditions, and wages far less than provided to a citizen. While permanent residents fare better, they may still experience reduced access to social services and education, racism, and difficulty securing employment on a par with nationals of the State. The perception that noncitizen workers take jobs from citizens may also perpetuate social resentment, contributing to the failure of receiving states to correct inequities.

Under international law, everyone – regardless of citizenship – has the right to work, and governments are obligated to take progressive measures to safeguard this right (International Covenant on Economic, Social and Cultural Rights 1966). Noncitizens who are lawfully present in a State are entitled to treatment equal to that enjoyed by citizens in the realm of employment and work (Taran 2003). Everyone has the right to just and favorable conditions of work, (International Covenant on Economic, Social and Cultural Rights 1966) and international standards that provide protection in treatment and conditions at work in areas such as safety, health, hours of work, and remuneration apply to all workers regardless of citizenship or status (Taran 2003). States must ensure the right of everyone to establish and join trade unions. Noncitizen workers may not be barred from holding trade union office, and their right to strike should not be restricted (Committee on Economic, Social & Cultural Rights 1993).

International Labour Organization (ILO) conventions and recommendations (for example, as to collective bargaining, discrimination, workers' compensation, social security, working conditions and environment, abolition of forced labor and child labor) generally protect the rights of all workers irrespective of citizenship. The eight fundamental ILO conventions,[22] and the recommendations that accompany them, apply to all workers regardless of citizenship (Taran 2003). There are several ILO instruments that specifically protect migrant workers and their families, the most significant of which are Convention 97 concerning migration for employment; Convention 143 concerning working conditions and equal treatment of migrant workers; and Convention 118 concerning equality of treatment in social security. In many instances, the conventions guarantee certain rights, e.g. equal remuneration and minimum wage with respect to past employment and maintenance of social security benefits to noncitizens regardless of the legality of the migrant's presence in the territory (Taran 2003). Other rights are extended only to those persons lawfully within a territory, e.g. rights to equal opportunities and vocational training (ILO Recommendation 151, 1975).

ILO Convention 143 provides specific guidance as to the treatment of irregular migrants and those migrants who are employed unlawfully. In laying out the minimum norms applicable to such persons, Article 1, for example, establishes that States parties must 'respect the basic human rights of all migrant workers' regardless of their migratory status or legal situation (Taran 2003). The Committee of Experts on the Application of Conventions and Recommendations has interpreted these rights to be fundamental human rights as enshrined in the International Bill of Human Rights, the International Convention on the Protection of All Migrant Workers and Members of Their Families, and the ILO Declaration on Fundamental Principles and Rights at Work. (The ILO Declaration on Fundamental Principles and Rights at Work 1988.)[23]

The Inter-American Court of Human Rights has confirmed the applicability of international labor standards to noncitizens, and particularly to those noncitizens in irregular status. In an opinion issued in September 2003, the Court held that nondiscrimination and the right to equality are *jus cogens,* nonderogable, rights that are applicable to all residents regardless of immigration status. Hence, governments cannot use immigration status as a justification for restricting the employment or labor rights of unauthorized workers, such as rights to social security. The Court found that governments do have the right to deport individuals and refuse to offer jobs to people who do not possess employment documents, but held that once an employment relationship has been initiated, unauthorized workers become entitled to all the employment and labor rights that are available to authorized workers (Corte Interamericana de Derechos Humanos 2003).

The International Convention on the Protection of All Migrant Workers and Members of Their Families, of which ILO Conventions 97 and 143 formed the basis, protects all migrant workers and their families, but does not generally include international organization employees, foreign development staff, refugees, stateless persons, students, and trainees (Articles 1, 3). The Convention provides for a number of rights, including:

- Nondiscrimination (Article 7).
- Freedom from torture and ill-treatment (Article 10).
- Freedom from slavery or forced labor (Article 11).
- Freedom from arbitrary or unlawful interference with privacy, family, home, correspondence, or other communications (Article 14).
- Property rights (Article 15).
- Liberty and security of person (Article 16).
- No imprisonment for failure to fulfill a contract (Article 20).
- No destruction of travel or identity documents (Article 21).
- Right to consular or diplomatic assistance (Article 23).
- Right to recognition as a person before the law (Article 24).
- Equality of treatment between nationals and migrant workers as to work conditions and pay (Article 25).
- Right to participate in trade unions (Article 26).

The Committee on the Elimination of Racial Discrimination (CERD) has frequently expressed concern that noncitizens who serve as domestic workers are subjected to debt bondage, other illegal employment practices, passport deprivation, illegal confinement, rape, and physical assault (CERD 1993). States are urged to put an end to the practice of employers who retain the passports of their foreign employees, in particular of domestic workers (CERD 2003a).

3.4. *Victims of trafficking*

Trafficking of noncitizens for the purpose of sexual exploitation or other labor occurs from, to, or through every country in the world. Such a flow that is often discussed in terms of supply and demand. People who are living in poverty, fleeing armed conflict, or migrating illegally across national borders are targeted by criminals, organized crime networks, or corrupt officials who force them into marriage, servitude, or prostitution. While certainly not limited to women, women are particularly vulnerable to sex trafficking because of persistent inequalities that limit their opportunities. Saudi Arabia, for example, is a major destination country for trafficked women because women in that country are denied many political and social rights.

Traffickers offer promises of marriage, employment, educational opportunities, and/or a better life. They control their victims by making their environment unpredictable and their lives unsafe. Traffickers use coercive tactics, such as fraud, intimidation, isolation, physical force, or debt bondage. Rape is commonly used to coerce and control such victims. Trafficked persons frequently suffer serious physical and psychological injuries, including post-traumatic stress disorder, severe depression, damaged reproductive systems, damage from sexual assault and beatings, and sexually transmitted diseases.

International trafficking in women and children intensifies this dynamic of power and control as, isolated from their families and traditional support structures, victim are more dependent upon their abusers. Women and children trafficked across borders may be unfamiliar with the national language of the country to which they are transported and unable to access the criminal justice or social service system. One survey conducted by Amnesty International (2004) found that fewer than 10% of trafficked women in Kosovo had access to healthcare. Trafficked women may live in fear of being exposed to the authorities who, in countries such as Bosnia–Herzegovina and Cambodia, treat the women like criminals (Human Rights Watch 2002). In some countries, government officials actually facilitate trafficking by accepting bribes or ignoring the complaints of trafficked persons, particularly if the trafficked persons are noncitizens.

3.5. Children

Article 2 of the Convention on the Rights of the Child provides that 'States Parties shall respect and ensure the rights set forth in the present Convention to each child within their jurisdiction without discrimination of any kind ...'. The Committee on the Rights of the Child encourages States to continue and strengthen their legislative efforts to integrate the right to nondiscrimination that is enshrined in Article 2 fully in all relevant legislation concerning children, and to ensure that this right is effectively applied in all political, judicial, and administrative decisions and in projects, programs, and services which have an impact on all children, including noncitizen children and children belonging to minority groups (Committee on the Rights of the Child 2003c). The Committee recommends that 'States develop comprehensive and coordinated policies to address the developing phenomenon of immigration, including public information campaigns to promote tolerance; monitor and collect data on racially-motivated acts'; and 'study the situation of noncitizen children, especially in the school system, and the effectiveness of measures taken to facilitate their integration' (Committee on the Rights of the Child 2003a). States should also take effective measures to address discriminatory attitudes or prejudices, in particular toward noncitizen children. Accordingly, States should fully and effectively implement adopted legal measures to prevent discrimination and ensure their legislation is in full compliance with Article 2 of the Convention on the Rights of the Child (Committee on the Rights of the Child 2003d).

Children of noncitizens have the right to a name and the right to acquire a nationality (Convention on the Rights of the Child 1989). Under Article 7 of the Convention on the Rights of the Child, a child 'shall be registered immediately after birth and shall have the right from birth to a name, [and] the right to acquire a nationality ... States Parties shall ensure the implementation of these rights ... in particular where the child would otherwise be stateless.' In view of the nearly universal ratification of the Convention on the Rights of the Child, the principle of *jus soli* (citizenship based on the place of birth) has emerged as the overriding international norm governing the nationality of children born to noncitizen parents.[24] This right must be enforced without discrimination as to the gender of the parent.[25] Article 7 of the Convention also requires transmittal of citizenship from a parent to his or her adopted child.[26] Article 7 should be read in conjunction with Article 8 (preservation of identity, including nationality, name, and family relations), Article 9 (avoiding separation from parents), Article 10 (family reunification), and Article 20 (continuity of upbringing of children deprived of their family environment). Within the holistic approach recommended by the Committee on the Rights of the Child for the interpretation of the Convention, those articles should be understood according to the general principles of the Convention as reflected in Articles 2 (right to nondiscrimination), 3 (principle of the best interests of the child), 6 (right to life and development), and 12 (right to respect for the child's views in all matters affecting the child and opportunity to be heard in any judicial or administrative proceedings affecting the child [Hodgkin and Newell 1998]).

Children of noncitizens are entitled to those measures of protection required by their status as minors. Children of noncitizens without legal status may not be excluded from schools (UN Human Rights Committee 1986)[27] and schools that allow children of noncitizens to be educated in programs designed in their country of origin are welcome (Committee on the Elimination of Racial Discrimination: Saudi Arabia 2003a). Children of noncitizens – including children of asylum seekers and refugees and children who are themselves asylum seekers or refugees – may not be the subject of discrimination in the enjoyment of economic, social, and cultural rights such as access to education, health care, and social services (Committee on the Rights of the Child 2002).[28]

4. Migrant workers

Migrant workers are often treated as criminals or at least characterized as illegal. Migrants make convenient scapegoats for crime, unemployment, disease, and other social ills that usually result from domestic causes, including a lack of adequate government services. As a result, migrants are often subject to situations that force them to endure: housing and employment discrimination; abuse; arbitrary expulsion; and high-risk travel.

4.1. Housing and employment discrimination

Migrant workers often live in conditions that are unsatisfactory, and face serious accommodation deficiencies. Although they contribute to social security programs, migrant workers and their families often do not enjoy the same benefits and access to social services that are enjoyed by citizens of the host country. Migrants and their families are often excluded from education and denied access to health care, including emergency care. They are also subject to discrimination in areas such as housing and employment. In the case of *F. A. v. Norway* (2001), for example, CERD heard the case of a migrant using a housing service in order to find an apartment. The applicant noted that about half of the housing advertisements indicated that persons from certain groups were not desired as tenants. Statements like 'no foreigners desired,' 'whites only,' and 'only Norwegians with permanent jobs' punctuated such housing lists. Discrimination in employment against migrant workers includes exclusions or preferences with regard to types of jobs that are open to migrants, difficulty in gaining access to vocational training, and different standards that are often applied to citizens and migrant workers with regard to job tenure.

4.2. *Abuse*

Migrant workers frequently face outright abuse. Migrant workers employed as domestic servants, for example, have been subjected to debt bondage, illegal employment practices, passport deprivation, illegal confinement, rape, and physical assault. In some cases, the treatment of migrant workers constitutes forced labor. The ILO has identified a number of abuses associated with forced labor, including threats of physical abuse; physical abuse; confinement or restriction of movement; debt bondage; withholding payment or excessive wage reductions; retention of identity documents; or threats of denunciation to authorities (ILO 2005).

Since most countries do not provide legislative protection against labor discrimination of migrants, it is often difficult for migrant workers to obtain legal protection from abuse. Kuwait and Saudi Arabia – two countries with many migrants – exclude all migrant workers from national social and labor laws. It is usually the case that migrant workers cannot assert their rights for fear of retribution and, as noncitizens, have no way of participating in the political process so as to assure legal protection. Further, migrants may be unfamiliar with the national language, laws, and practices, and thus have little knowledge regarding their rights. As a result, they are often left without the effective means to challenge, or seek remedies for, violations of their human rights.

4.3. *Arbitrary detention and expulsion*

A major problem that noncitizens continue to face is arbitrary detention, i.e. detention without any due process or judicial proceeding to determine whether a law has been violated. Although arbitrary detention is prohibited by the International Covenant on Civil and Political Rights, noncitizens – especially asylum seekers, undocumented immigrants, and victims of trafficking – continue to be placed in detention (European Commission Against Racism and Intolerance 1999)[29] for indefinite periods (Human Rights Watch 1998). These persons, who have often been traumatized by experiences of persecution or abuse, are detained side-by-side with criminals in prison facilities which are frequently overcrowded and unhygienic. They are often denied contact with their families, access to legal assistance, (Human Rights Watch 1998) and the opportunity to challenge their detention. Even unaccompanied children and families are placed in arbitrary detention (ECRI 2001). In the case of families, children may be separated from their parents and taken to other facilities (UN Committee on the Rights of the Child 2002). Detained children are too often deprived of the special care they generally require, (Committee of the Rights of the Child: Czech Republic 2003b, 56) and specifically deprived of the right to education (Committee on the Rights of the Child 2003b).

This situation has worsened since September 2001 as several countries have invoked antiterrorism measures to detain indefinitely or otherwise violate the rights of noncitizens on the basis of unspecified allegations related to terrorism or national security (UN Submission

2003). The government of the USA, for example, has detained and summarily deported thousands of immigrants and nonimmigrants from certain Middle Eastern and Asian nations (Human Rights Watch 2004).

In virtually every country, migrant workers have been captured and confined in deportation jails. Many migrants detained in deportation jails describe severe overcrowding, inadequate sanitation facilities, and corporal punishment. In the USA, the Department of Homeland Security has handed over more than 60 percent of migrant detainees to local sheriffs and other jail officials. These migrant detainees are held in jails inappropriate to their noncriminal status where they may be mixed with accused and convicted criminal inmates, and where they are sometimes subjected to physical ill-treatment and inadequate conditions of confinement.

Local jails profit from Homeland Security detainees. For example, jails charge the federal government between $35 and $100 per day, per detainee. Migrant detainees are often unable to contact their families or obtain legal representation. In some cases, migrant detainees cannot be deported because they are stateless, or because neither their own country nor any third country will accept them, a situation which itself may amount to de facto statelessness. In these cases, the detainee is sometimes held indefinitely and does not know when, if ever, they will be released (Human Rights Watch 1998).

In addition to indefinite detention and deportation, migrant workers may be subjected to arbitrary expulsion. When noncitizens face expulsion orders, they may be denied the right to challenge those orders in court (UN Sub-Commission on the Promotion and Protection of Human Rights 2003). They may also be faced with expulsion to their country of origin ('refoulment' [Convention Relating to the Status of Refugees 1951]),[30] which is particularly problematic in the case of asylum seekers fleeing persecution or abuse (HRC 2002). In 2003, for example, Thai authorities expelled as many as 10,000 Burmese migrants per month on the grounds that they were illegal workers. Some of these deportees were transported directly to holding centers in Burma that were operated by the Burmese military. The Burmese authorities did not allow NGOs or other monitors to ensure that the deportees were treated properly, adding to concern that the returned Burmese migrants – and particularly those of certain ethnic minorities – may have been targeted for ill-treatment (Human Rights Watch 2004).

4.4. *Irregular movement and high-risk travel*

At the time, this article was being written the authors' nation of residence, the USA, was engaged in a heated internal debate over whether domestic laws should be amended to provide undocumented and out-of-status migrants an easier path for obtaining citizenship. In 2013, US Senate Democrats proposed a bill that would have provided a 'pathway to cit izenship' for certain irregular migrants, albeit only after many requirements were first met. Republicans in the US House of Representatives responded with their own proposal, a set of immigration guidelines that conceded protection from deportation for irregular migrants, but stopped short of permitting citizenship outright (Kim and Sherman 2014). Late in 2014 the President of the USA also proposed a provisional limitation on the deportation of the millions of parents of US citizen children.

Various reasons have been offered for and against providing a pathway to citizenship for irregular migrants presently in the USA. Opponents, for example, suggest that providing citizenship to irregular migrants would reward breaking the law, and thus undermine established immigration procedures, which can be expensive for applicants and may take many years to complete. Both sides have also offered economic arguments illustrating why their position should be preferred. Suggesting even moderate changes, however, resulted in severe political repercussions for some high-ranking legislators (Kim 2014) and, consequently, other would-be reformers are now reluctant to champion the cause.

Hundreds of thousands of men and women leave their homes each year in search of opportunities to earn wages and also improve the economic status of their families. As migration flows have increased, many governments have responded by tightening legal controls and fortifying geographical borders. Studies and experience demonstrate, however, that efforts to obstruct or deter migration have had negative consequences. Tighter border controls have only partially curbed the flow of migrants, and these controls have frequently made migrants more vulnerable to irregular and life-threatening forms of transport.

Undocumented migrant workers and persons who have been victims of human smuggling or trafficking are particularly vulnerable to deaths that result from border control practices and policies. Migrants are 'irregular' if they have entered illegally by avoiding border controls or by using false documents; by posing as a student or tourist while intending to work; or by continuing to work after the termination of an employment contract. Undocumented/irregular migrants may live under substandard conditions, face raids on their homes and workplaces, and interrogations in which they may be subjected to abuse, inhuman, or degrading treatment, and violations of the right to privacy. Their encounters with the police may not be noticed because they have no relatives to raise questions about their detention or even death. Even when they suffer violations of their human rights, they may not seek judicial remedies due to their fear of deportation. Undocumented migrants' lack of legal status in the host State may compel them to accept terrible working and living conditions. Hence, if undocumented workers can find work, they are often employed in the informal economy, in which employers can exploit their fear of being reported to the authorities and may subject them to conditions that resemble slavery. Without documentation, they also cannot obtain basic government services like health care and education (Bogusz et al. 2004).

4.5. The plight of women migrants

Over the last four decades, women have accounted for nearly half of all international migrants. As of 2000, women's share of total international migration was 49 percent, up from 46% in 1960 (Zlotnik 2003). While many women migrate to accompany or join family members, increasing numbers of female migrants travel on their own and are the principal breadwinners for themselves and their families. Most move voluntarily for economic reasons, but a significant number are forced migrants who have been trafficked or are fleeing conflict, natural disasters, or persecution (Forbes Martin 2004).

While migration can empower women with new economic opportunities and increased independence, many migrant women face serious discrimination and abuse in their host countries. Migrant women face discrimination and abuse due to their status as both women and migrants. Employment opportunities are often limited to occupations that are stereotypically female-dominated, and women migrants frequently have no option but to take work as domestic workers, cleaners, sweatshop laborers, sales girls, or sex workers. Many of these jobs are in the informal economy and are either not covered, or only partially covered, by the host country's labor code and social security provisions. In addition, many migrant women lack the legal status or information necessary to challenge abusive practices by employers, supervisors, spouses, or co-workers (ILO Gender Promotion Program 2003, 4).

The experience of migrant women as domestic workers illustrates the challenges many migrant women face. Domestic work is the single largest employment category for women migrants (ILO Gender Promotion Program 2003, 1).[31] Working conditions for domestic workers can vary widely: some women are treated as members of their employer's family, while others are exploited and subjected to conditions amounting to slavery or forced labor (Report of the International Labour Conference 2004). In many States, domestic work is expressly excluded from part or all of the host State's labor code, resulting in excessive hours with no rest days or holidays. Some immigration and labor laws foster dependence by not allowing women to change employers or requiring their visas be sponsored by a national.[32] Furthermore, domestic workers are commonly exposed to sexual harassment, violence, and other forms of abuse. In some cases, domestic workers are physically or legally restrained from leaving the employer's home by means of threats, violence, or the withholding of pay or identity documents (ILO Gender Promotion Program 2003, 4).

5. Conclusion

As shown above, there are many treaties obligating States to protect the human rights of noncitizens, not the least of which is the United Nations Charter. The principle of territorial sovereignty necessitates that States hold primary responsibility for the protection of these rights with regard to all persons within their borders. Categorizations such as 'citizen,' 'noncitizen,' and 'illegal immigrant,' however, are regularly used to justify the provision of these rights. In failing to pass and implement laws enabling protections for irregular migrants, and by permitting the stratified protection of rights for other categories of noncitizens, States violate various obligations under international law. Though diplomatic mechanisms and treaty bodies exist to assist in the protection of human rights in instances when States are unwilling or unable, sovereignty, politics, and economics combine in a manner that causes large gaps in rights enforcement.

An important aim of international human rights law is to place every person under the umbrella of certain basic protections. A function of domestic citizenship law, however, is to remove selected persons from that very same guardianship. The conventions referred to in the previous sections are the product of the ongoing negotiation between these two conflicting ambitions, and represent the give and take between States wishing to retain autonomy over the treatment of people within their borders, and human rights advocates seeking protections for particularly vulnerable persons. While narrower views of citizenship serve as a barrier to the realization of these protections, the various categories of noncitizenship permit States and human rights advocates a useful, albeit imperfect, medium for compromise.

Notes

1. In the USA, an arresting authority must inform the nearest US Attorney whenever a noncitizen is arrested. The US Attorney is then obligated to contact the relevant consulate. 28 C.F.R. § 50.5 (2014).
2. In 2006, the International Law Commission – the organization charged under the UN Charter with making recommendations for codifying and progressively developing international law – published its Draft articles on Diplomatic Protection. The Draft articles identify a series of principles, including, for example, States' right to exercise diplomatic protection (art. 2), diplomatic protection of stateless persons and refugees (art. 8), and recommended practices (art. 19). The draft articles are binding upon States to the extent they codify international law.
3. International Convention on the Protection of the Rights of All Migrant Workers and Members of Their Families (hereinafter Migrant Worker Convention). Though broad in scope, the Migrant Worker Convention is still in the early stages of gaining wide adoption. As of January 2015, the Migrant Worker Convention has only 38 signatories, and 47 States Parties. The USA has not signed or ratified the Convention.
4. International Covenant on Civil and Political Rights (hereinafter Civil Rights Covenant).
5. Optional Protocol to the International Covenant on Civil and Political Rights.
6. Human Rights Committee, General Comment 15: The Position of Aliens Under the Covenant, Compilation of General Comments and General Recommendations Adopted by Human Rights Treaty Bodies (hereinafter H.R.C. General Comment 15).
7. African [Banjul] Charter on Human and Peoples' Rights (hereinafter African Charter).
8. Article 13 of the Civil Rights Covenant requires that the expulsion of a noncitizen lawfully within a territory may only be accomplished 'in pursuance of a decision reached in accordance with law,' permitting the noncitizen 'except where compelling reasons of national security otherwise require ... to submit the reasons against his expulsion and to have his case reviewed by, and represented for the purpose before, the competent authority or a person or persons especially designated by the competent authority'.
9. Together, the Universal Declaration of Human Rights; the International Covenant on Civil and Political Rights; and the International Covenant on Economic, Social and Cultural Rights comprise the International Bill of Human Rights. Articles 55 and 56 of the United Nations Charter require that members must take actions toward the 'achievement of universal respect for, and observance of, human rights and fundamental freedoms for all.' The Universal Declaration of Human Rights serves to define the human rights guaranteed under the Charter, and reiterates their importance. The International Covenant on Civil and Political Rights and the International Covenant on Economic, Social and Cultural Rights expand upon the protections, and also contain clauses requiring States Parties to guarantee rights to all persons within their jurisdiction – not just citizens.
10. Article 4 of the Civil Rights Covenant permits derogation from the Covenant's obligations to the extent absolutely necessary to address a 'public emergency which threatens the life of the nation.' Civil Rights Covenant. States, however, must take care to ensure that a derogating act is a proportionate and narrowly tailored response that does not encroach upon other human rights; and which does not involve discrimination 'solely on the ground of race, colour, sex, language, religion or social origin'. Rights that may *never* be derogated from – under any circumstance – include, but are not limited to, the rights: to life (art. 6); to be free from torture, cruel, inhuman, or degrading treatment or punishment (art. 7); to be free from slavery and servitude (art. 8); to be free from imprisonment for breach of contract (art. 11); to recognition as a person under the law (art. 16); and to freedom of thought, conscience, and religion (art.18).
11. International Covenant on Economic, Social and Cultural Rights (hereinafter International Covenant on Economic, Social and Cultural Rights).
12. Article 1 of the Convention Relating to the Status of Stateless Persons defines a stateless person as 'a person who is not considered as a national by any State under the operation of its law.'.

13. The terms 'citizenship' and 'nationality' will be used interchangeably for the purposes of this article.
14. The Office of the UNHCR lists among the reasons for statelessness: (1) conflict of laws; (2) transfer of territory; (3) laws related to marriage: (4) administrative practices; (5) discrimination; (6) laws related to registration of births; (7) *jus sanguinis*; (8) denationalization; (9) renunciation of citizenship; and (10) automatic loss of citizenship by operation of law. UNHCR, *Information and Accession Package: The* 1954 *Convention Relating to the Status of Stateless Persons and the 1961 Convention on the Reduction of Statelessness*, January 1999, *available at* http://www.refworld.org/docid/3ae6b3350.html.
15. See also David Weissbrodt, Final Report on the Rights of Non-Citizens, par. 9 (indicating that *jus soli* principle of citizenship has emerged as the international legal norm, and that the rights under the Convention on the Rights of the Child must be enforced without discrimination as to the gender of the parent).
16. See also Convention on the Nationality of Married Women, Art. 2.
17. The Wannsee Conference (20 January 1942) was a 'meeting of Nazi officials in the Berlin suburb of Grossen-Wannsee for the purpose of planning the 'final solution' (Endlösung) of the 'Jewish question.' *New Encyclopedia Britannica*, 489 (15th ed. 1989).
18. See e.g. African Charter note 10; Charter of Fundamental Rights of the European Union; Specific Aspects of Refugee Problems in Africa; Cartagena Declaration on Refugees.
19. The UNHCR stated that the Supreme Court's decision was 'contrary to the views of UNHCR's Executive Committee that refugees should not be refused entry to a country where they are seeking asylum, and that asylum seekers rescued at sea should always be admitted, at least on a temporary basis ....' Press Release, Office of the High Commissioner for Refugees, Office of the High Commissioner concerned by Supreme Court Haitian Decision (22 June 1993). In addition, the UNHCR emphasized that the *Sale* decision was 'a setback to modern international refugee law which has been developing for more than forty years'.
20. The Charter of Fundamental Rights of the European Union also declares that '[t]he right to asylum shall be guaranteed with due respect for the rules of the Geneva Convention of 28 July 1951 and the Protocol of 31 January 1967 relating to the status of refugees ....' Charter of Fundamental Rights of the European Union. The [European] Convention for the Protection of Human Rights and Fundamental Freedoms, however, does not provide for the right to asylum.
21. For example, in the USA, persons who arrive on US soil and apply for protection are considered 'asylum seekers'; if their asylum applications are accepted, they become 'asylees'. If a person leaves their home country, enters a second country, and seeks protected status in the USA, however, they are considered refugees, not asylees, if their application in successful.
22. Convention on Forced Labour, (ILO No. 29); Convention on Freedom of Association and the Right to Organise (ILO No. 87); Convention on the Right to Organise and Collective Bargaining (ILO No. 98); Equal Remuneration Convention (ILO No. 100); Abolition of Forced Labour Convention (ILO No. 105); Discrimination (Employment and Occupation) Convention (ILO No. 111); Convention on Minimum Age (ILO No. 138); Convention Concerning the Prohibition and Immediate Action for the Elimination of the Worst Forms of Child Labour (ILO No. 182).
23. The ILO Declaration on Fundamental Principles and Rights at Work, 86th Session, Geneva, June 1988, establishes that all member States of the ILO have an obligation arising from the very fact of their membership 'to respect, to promote and to realize' the principles of human rights enunciated in the eight fundamental conventions even if they have not yet been ratified by those States.
24. See Asbjørn Eide, Citizenship and international law with specific reference to human rights law: status, evolution and challenges; Asbjørn Eide, Working paper on citizenship and the minority rights of noncitizens; see also Concluding Observations of the Committee on the Rights of the Child: Latvia; Concluding Observations of the Committee on the Rights of the Child: Lithuania. Efforts by States to end discrimination in their nationality laws between children born in and out of wedlock are welcome. Concluding Observations of the Committee on the Rights of the Child: United Kingdom of Great Britain and Northern Ireland.

25. See Concluding Observation of the Committee on the Elimination of Racial Discrimination: Egypt; Concluding Observations of the Committee on the Elimination of Discrimination Against Women: Singapore, UN; Concluding Observations of the Committee on the Elimination of Discrimination Against Women: Guinea, UN; Concluding Observations of the Committee on the Rights of the Child: Monaco; Concluding Observations of the Committee on the Rights of the Child: Lebanon.
26. See e.g. Concluding Observations of the Committee on the Rights of the Child: Palau; Inter-country adoptions must allow adopting parents to transfer their nationality to adopted children, who must be allowed to own or inherit land or benefit from health, education, and social service subsidies.
27. See also Concluding Observations of the Committee on the Rights of the Child: Iceland.
28. Concluding Observations of the Committee on the Rights of the Child: Israel); Concluding Observations of the Committee on the Rights of the Child: United Kingdom of Great Britain and Northern Ireland. See Concluding Observations of the Committee on the Rights of the Child: Italy; Concluding Observations of the Committee on the Rights of the Child: Israel.
29. See e.g. ECRI, Second Report on Croatia.
30. See e.g. Convention Relating to the Status of Refugees; Protocol Relating to the Status of Refugees; Convention Against Torture, and Other Cruel, Inhuman, or Degrading Treatment or Punishment; International Covenant on Civil and Political Rights; European Convention on Human Rights.
31. ILO Gender Promotion Program, *Preventing Discrimination, Exploitation and Abuse of Women Migrant Workers: An Information Guide, Booklet 1*, ILO Website, available at http://www.ilo.org/public/english/employment/gems/download/mbook1.pdf.
32. For example, the United Arab Emirates requires every foreign laborer to have a national sponsor to keep their status. See R. Sabban, United Arab Emirates: Migrant Women in the United Arab Emirates the Case of Female Domestic Workers.

Acknowledgements

The authors thank Anna Gusaas for her assistance in preparing this article. Portions of this article also draw on the authors' earlier works, *The Human Rights of Migrants*, Foundations of International Migration Law (Cambridge University) (2012); The Human Rights of Non-citizens, (Oxford, 2008); Office of the United Nations High Comm'n. for Human Rights, *The Rights of Non-Citizens*, U.N. Doc. HR/PUB/06/11 (2006). Thanks are given to Zaid Clor for his work formatting the references for this piece.

Disclosure statement

No potential conflict of interest was reported by the authors.

References

African Charter on Human and Peoples' Rights. 1986. UNTS Vol. 1520, No. 26363, October 21. Nairobi. https://treaties.un.org/pages/showDetails.aspx?objid=08000002800cb09f.

American Convention on Human Rights. 1969. UNTS Vol. 1144, No. 17955, November 22. San José. https://treaties.un.org/pages/showDetails.aspx?objid=08000002800f10e1.

Amnesty International. 2004. *Does That Mean I Have Rights?: Protecting the Human Rights of Women and Girls Trafficked for Forced Prostitutions in Kosovo*. London: EUR 70/010/2004. http://www.un-ngls.org/orf/Amnesty-EUR7001004.pdf.

Arendt, Hannah. 1963. *Eichmann in Jerusalem*. New York: Penguin.

Barkham, Patrick, and John Aglionby. 2001. "Stranded Refugees Start Hunger Strike." *The Guardian*. http://www.theguardian.com/world/2001/aug/29/johnaglionby.patrickbarkham.

BBC News. 2001. "UN Pressure over Refugee Ship." http://news.bbc.co.uk/1/hi/world/asia-pacific/1512725.stm.

BBC News. 2005. "Asylum Seekers and Immigrants Who's Who?" http://news.bbc.co.uk/cbbcnews/hi/newsid_3080000/newsid_3086400/3086429.stm.

Bogusz, B., R. Cholewinski, A. Cygan and E. Szyszczak., eds. 2004. *Irregular Migration and Human Rights: Theoretical, European and International Perspectives.* Martinus Nijhoff. http://www.brill.com/irregular-migration-and-human-rights-theoretical-european-and-international-perspectives.

CERD (Committee on the Elimination of Racial Discrimination). 1993. *Concluding Observations of the Committee on the Elimination of Racial Discrimination: Kuwait.* U.N. Doc. A/48/18. par359-81, September 15. http://www.unhchr.ch/tbs/doc.nsf/(Symbol)/31f0b399ca3d57938025655d005375be?Opendocument.

CERD (Committee on the Elimination of Racial Discrimination). 2003a. *Concluding Observations of the Committee on the Elimination of Racial Discrimination: Saudi Arabia.* U.N. Doc. CERD/C/62/CO/8, par. 6, March 21. http://www.unhchr.ch/tbs/doc.nsf/(Symbol)/CERD.C.62.CO.8.En?Opendocument.

CERD (Committee on the Elimination of Racial Discrimination). 2003b. *Concluding Observations of the Committee on the Elimination of Racial Discrimination: Czech Republic.* U.N. Doc. CRC/C/15/Add.201, December 10. http://www.refworld.org/publisher,CERD,,CZE,403e0ed04,0.html.

Citizens Information. 2015. "Coming to Ireland as an Asylum Seeker or Refugee." http://www.citizensinformation.ie/en/moving_country/asylum_seekers_and_refugees/the_asylum_process_in_ireland/refugees_asylum_seekers_introduction.html.

Committee on Economic, Social & Cultural Rights. 1993. *Response to the Periodic Report of Senegal.* U.N. Doc E/C/12/1993/18.

Committee on the Rights of the Child. 2002. *Concluding Observations of the Committee on the Rights of the Child: Israel.* U.N. Doc. CRC/C/15/Add.195, para. 26.

Committee on the Rights of the Child. 2003a. *Concluding Observations of the Committee on the Rights of the Child: Iceland.* U.N. Doc. CRC/C/15/Add.203, par. 23, January 31. http://www.refworld.org/cgi-bin/texis/vtx/rwmain?page=search&docid=3f25910b2&skip=0&query=concluding%20observations%20&coi=ISL&searchin=title&sort=date.

Committee on the Rights of the Child. 2003b. *Concluding Observations of the Committee on the Rights of the Child: Italy.* U.N. Doc. CRC/C/15/Add.198, March 18. http://www.refworld.org/docid/3f2594d04.html.

Committee on the Rights of the Child. 2003c. *Concluding Observations of the Committee on the Rights of the Child: Czech Republic.* U.N. Doc. CRC/C/15/Add.201, para. 29.

Committee on the Rights of the Child. 2003d. *Concluding Observations of the Committee on the Rights of the Child: Romania.* U.N. Doc. CRC/C/15/Add.199, para. 26.

ILO 29, Convention Concerning Forced or Compulsory Labour. 1930. 39 UNTS 55, June 28. http://www.ilo.org/dyn/normlex/en/f?p=1000:12100:0::NO::P12100_ILO_CODE:C029.

ILO 143, Convention Concerning Migrations in Abusive Conditions and the Promotion of Equality of Opportunity and Treatment of Migrant Workers. 1975. June, 24. Geneva. http://www.ilo.org/ilolex/cgi-lex/convde.pl?C143.

ILO 87, Convention on Freedom of Association and the Right to Organise. 1948. UNTS Vol. 68, No. 881, July 9. San Francisco, CA. https://treaties.un.org/pages/showDetails.aspx?objid=080000028015a947.

Convention on the Elimination of All Forms of Discrimination against Women. 1979. UNTS Vol. 1249, No. 20378, December 18. New York. https://treaties.un.org/pages/showDetails.aspx?objid=080000028000309d.

Convention on the Reduction of Statelessness. 1961. UNTS Vol. 989, No. 14458, August 30. New York. https://treaties.un.org/pages/showDetails.aspx?objid=0800000280035afb

ILO 98, Convention on the Right to Organise and Collective Bargaining. 1981. UNTS Vol. 1331, No. 22344, September 19. Geneva. https://treaties.un.org/pages/showDetails.aspx?objid=08000002800dc08e.

Convention on the Rights of the Child. 1989. UNTS Vol. 1577, No. 27531, November 20. New York, NY. https://treaties.un.org/pages/showDetails.aspx?objid=08000002800007fe.

Convention Relating to the Status of Refugees. 1951. UNTS Vol. 189, No. 2545, July 28. Geneva. https://treaties.un.org/pages/showDetails.aspx?objid=080000028003002e.

Convention Relating to the Status of Stateless Persons. 1954. UNTS Vol. 360, No. 5158, September 28. New York, NY. https://treaties.un.org/pages/showDetails.aspx?objid=0800000280032b94.
Corte Interamericana de Derechos Humanos [Inter-American Court of Human Rights]. 2003. *Condicion Juridica Y Derechos De Los Migrantes Indocumentados* [Juridical Condition and Rights of Undocumented Migrants]. Opinion Consultiva OC-08/03. solicitada por los Estados Unidos Mexicanos [Advisory Opinion OC-18/03. Requested by the United Mexican States], September 17.
ECRI (European Commission Against Racism and Intolerance). 1999. *Second Report on Belgium*, June 18. http://hudoc.ecri.coe.int/XMLEcri/ENGLISH/Cycle_02/02_CbC_eng/02-cbc-belgium-eng.pdf.
ECRI (European Commission Against Racism and Intolerance). 2001. *Second Report on Malta*, December 14. http://hudoc.ecri.coe.int/XMLEcri/ENGLISH/Cycle_02/02_CbC_eng/02-cbc-malta-eng.pdf.
ILO 100, *Equal Remuneration* Convention. 1951. June 29. Geneva. http://www.ilo.org/dyn/normlex/en/f?p=NORMLEXPUB:12100:0::NO:12100:P12100_ILO_CODE:C100
ILO 118, Equality of Treatment (Social Security) Convention. 1964. April 25. Geneva. http://www.ilo.org/ilolex/cgi-lex/convde.pl?C118.
European Convention for the Protection of Human Rights and Fundamental Freedoms. 1950. UNTS Vol. 213, No. 2889. https://treaties.un.org/pages/showDetails.aspx?objid=080000028014a40b.
F.A. v. Norway. 2001. Communication No. 18/2000. U.N. Doc. CERD/C/58/D/18/2000.
Fitzpatrick, Joan. 1994. *Flight from Asylum: Trends toward Temporary 'Refuge' and Local Responses to Forced Migrations*. 35VA J of Int'l L. 13.
Forbes Martin, Susan. 2004. *Women and Migration 12*. http://www.un.org/womenwatch/daw/meetings/consult/CM-Dec03-WP1.pdf.
Hodgkin, Rachel, and Peter Newell. 1998. *Implementation Handbook for the Convention on the Rights of the Child 97*. http://www.unicef.org/publications/files/Implementation_Handbook_for_the_Convention_on_the_Rights_of_the_Child.pdf.
Howard, John. 2001. *Transcript of the Prime Minister the Honorable John Howard*. September 2.
Human Rights Watch. 1998. *Locked Away: Immigration Detainees in Jail in the United States*. September. http://www.hrw.org/reports98/us-immig.
Human Rights Watch. 2002. *Hopes Betrayed: Trafficking of Women and Girls to Post-Conflict Bosnia and Herzegovina for Forced Prostitution*. November. http://www.hrw.org/reports/2002/bosnia/.
Human Rights Watch. 2004. *Out of Sight, out of Mind: Thai Policy toward Burmese Refugees and Migrants*. 16 Hum. Rts. http://www.hrw.org/sites/default/files/reports/thailand0204.pdf.
ILO Declaration on Fundamental Principles and Rights at Work. 1988. June 18. Geneva. http://www.ilo.org/declaration/thedeclaration/textdeclaration/lang–en/index.htm.
ILO Recommendation 151. 1975. *Recommendation concerning Migrant Worker*. June 24. Geneva. http://www.ilo.org/dyn/normlex/en/f?p=NORMLEXPUB:12100:0::NO:12100:P12100_INSTRUMENT_ID:312489:NO.
International Convention on the Protection of the Rights of All Migrant Workers and Memers of Their Families. 1990. UNTS Vol. 2220, par. 3, December 18. New York. https://treaties.un.org/Pages/ViewDetails.aspx?src=TREATY&mtdsg_no=IV-13&chapter=4&lang=en.
International Covenant on Civil and Political Rights. 1966. United Nations, Treaty Series Vol. 999, No. 14668, December 16. http://www.refworld.org/docid/3ae6b3aa0.html.
International Covenant on Economic, Social and Cultural Rights. 1966. UNTS Vol. 993, No. 14531, December 16. New York. https://treaties.un.org/pages/showDetails.aspx?objid=080000028002b6ed.
International Labor Organization. 2005. *A Global Alliance against Forced Labour. Global Report under the Follow-up to the ILO Declaration on Fundamental Principles and Rights at Work. 93rd Session*. http://www.ilo.org/wcmsp5/groups/public/@ed_norm/@declaration/documents/publication/wcms_081882.pdf.
International Labour Conference. 2004. *Towards a Fair Deal for Migrant Workers in Global Economy. 92nd Session*. http://www.ilo.org/public/english/standards/relm/ilc/ilc92/pdf/rep-vi.pdf.
International Labour Organization. Gender Promotion Programme. 2003. *Preventing Discrimination, Exploitation and Abuse of Women Migrant Workers: An Information Guide. Booklet 1-4*. International Labour Organization Website. http://www.ilo.org/employment/Whatwedo/Instructionmaterials/WCMS_116358/lang–en/index.htm.

International Law Commission. 2006. http://legal.un.org/ilc/reports/2006/2006report.htm.
Kim, Seung Min. 2014. *Eric Cantor Loss Kills Immigration Reform. Politico.* Accessed September 2, 2014. http://www.politico.com/story/2014/06/2014-virginia-primary-eric-cantor-loss-immigration-reform-107697.html
Kim, Seung Min, and Jake Sherman. 2014. *House Leaders Sell Immigration Blueprint. Politico.* Accessed September 2, 2014. http://www.politico.com/story/2014/01/immigration-house-republicans-102884.html
Legomsky, Stephen H. 1996. *The New Techniques for Managing High-Volume Asylum Systems, Retreating from the Refugee Convention?* http://www.ntu.edu.au/faculties/lba/schools/Law/apl/Retreating/legomsky.htm.
ILO 97, Migration for Employment Convention. 1949. UNTS Vol. 120, No. 1616, July 1. Geneva. https://treaties.un.org/pages/showDetails.aspx?objid=0800000280153c43.
Office of the United Nations High Commissioner for Refugees. 1999. *Information and Accession Package: The 1954 Convention Relating to the Status of Stateless Persons and the 1961 Convention on the Reduction of Statelessness.* January. http://www.refworld.org/docid/3ae6b3350.html.
Protocol Relating to the Status of Refugees. 1967. UNTS Vol. 606, No. 8791, January 31. New York. https://treaties.un.org/pages/showDetails.aspx?objid=0800000280048bb8.
Rosenberg, Lory D. (2003). *International Association of Refugee Law Judges Conference: The Courts and Interception: The United States' Interdiction Experience and Its Impact on Refugees and Asylum Seekers*, 17 Geo. Immigr. L.J. 199, 208.
Sale v. Haitian Centers Council, Inc. 1993. 509 U.S. 155 https://web.law.columbia.edu/sites/default/files/microsites/human-rights-institute/files/Sale.pdf.
Taran, Patrick. 2003. "The Key Role of International Labour Standards in Defending Rights of Non-Nationals." Paper prepared for Expert Meeting on 'Classifying and Expanding the Rights of Non-Nationals', Organized by the Open Society Justice Initiative, New York.
UN Committee on the Rights of the Child. 2002. *Concluding Observations of the Committee on the Rights of the Child: Lebanon.* U.N. Doc. CRC/C/15/Add.169, par. 32, March 21. http://www.refworld.org/cgi-bin/texis/vtx/rwmain?page=search&docid=3df5887b4&skip=0&query=rights%20of%20the%20child&coi=LBN.
UN Human Rights Committee (HRC). 1986. *General Comment No. 15: The Position of Aliens under the Covenant.* April 11. http://www.refworld.org/docid/45139acfc.html.
UN Human Rights Committee (HRC). 2002. *Concluding Observations of the Human Rights Committee: Yemen.* August 12. http://www.refworld.org/cgi-bin/texis/vtx/rwmain?page=search&docid=3df36fcb4&skip=0&query=Concluding%20Observations%20of%20the%20Human%20Rights%20Committee&coi=YEM.
UN Sub-Commission on the Promotion and Protection of Human Rights. 2003. Report of the Special Rapporteur on the Rights of Migrants. U.N. Doc E/CN.4/2003/85.
UNESCO. N.d. *Glossary: Asylum Seeker and Refugee.* http://www.unesco.org/most/migration/glossary_asylum_seeker.htm.
UNHCR. 1992. *Handbook on Procedures and Criteria for Determining Refugee Status under the 1951 Convention and the 1967 Protocol Relating to the Status of Refugees*, para. 16–17. http://www.unhcr.org/3d58e13b4.html.
UNHCR. *Washington. USA for UNHCR.* http://www.unrefugees.org/what-is-a-refugee/.
UN Sub-Commission on the Promotion and Protection of Human Rights. 2003. Report of the Special Rapporteur on the Rights of Migrants. U.N. Doc E/CN.4/2003/85.
Universal Declaration of Human Rights. 1948. G.A. Res. 217A (III), U.N. Doc A/810 at 71. http://www.un.org/en/documents/udhr/.
Vienna Convention on Consular Relations, Apr. 24, 1963, 21 U.S.T. 77, 596 U.N.T.S. 261.
Zlotnik, Hania. 2003. "The Global Dimensions of Female Migration." *Migration Information Source.* http://www.migrationinformation.org/Feature/display.cfm?ID=109.

The business of noncitizenship

Tendayi Bloom

Global Justice Program, Yale University, New Haven, CT, USA

ABSTRACT
Private actors play an increasing role in mediating the relationship between States and noncitizens and even in creating or perpetuating exclusions associated with noncitizenship. This paper offers a way to analyse the forms of engagement of the for-profit private sector in migration control and asks what it means for how noncitizenship is constructed. It presents the private sector as acting like a buffer, altering whether and how individuals may engage with a State constructing what noncitizenship means within a State's territory, and removing so-constructed individuals from a relationship with that State. It shows how this may occur directly or indirectly, explicitly or implicitly. The paper addresses two main concerns: the impact on the State-noncitizen relationship and whether there are some areas of the relationship between the State and the noncitizen that should not be so-delegated. It argues that privatised migration control raises problems for standard justifications of migration control and noncitizenship construction.

1. Introduction

The involvement of for-profit private entities in the construction of noncitizenship (either voluntarily or not) has implications for relationships between noncitizens and States and for the legitimacy of the way those relationships are constructed. The private migration sector is playing an increasing role in migration control, in terms of both enacting and developing policy. Private actors may act as a buffer between a State and a noncitizen, constructing the ways in which the individual may come into contact with the State, or even whether they may do so. Once an individual is within a State, private actors are involved in constructing what their noncitizenship means on that territory. Private entities are then also involved in removing so-constructed noncitizens from the State in question. Privatisation processes throughout this system may occur directly or indirectly, explicitly or implicitly. This contributes to a commodification of the construction of noncitizenship, which in turn emphasises economic considerations, illegality, security and risk. While the legitimacy of migration control itself should not be taken as given (for useful discussion see e.g. Cole

2000; Schotel 2012; Tonkiss 2013), this paper focuses upon particular problems that arise in the case of privatisation, raising questions about what sort of entities should be involved.

This paper draws attention to noncitizenship construction in privatised migration control, though this must be seen within a wider framework of private engagement with migration, including also facilitation. Privatisation in migration control is different from in other sectors. The role of private actors in this sector in the construction of the constituency of noncitizens sets this apart from traditional privatisation discourses. Involving private entities provides new locations and modes of noncitizenship construction which may fall outside some traditional justifications. The way in which the private sector is thereby involved in both decision-making and the use of force is problematic for justifications of noncitizenship construction that assume the State as the principal actor in the construction.

To focus discussion, this paper understands noncitizenship primarily in terms of a relationship between a person and a particular State (official noncitizenship), and a State in terms of its institutional structure or government, rather than its populace. While migration is not the only mechanism for becoming a noncitizen, this paper discusses only migration-related noncitizenship. This paper's discussion is directed principally at States based on liberal democratic and neoliberal models, both broadly understood.

2. The migration business

There are two sides to the migration business: facilitation and control.[1] Migration facilitation encompasses those entities enabling people to migrate, including: recruiters and travel agents helping persons navigate often complex migration laws and regulations; and those recruiters and agents, often called smugglers, who help individuals bypass legal systems when other routes are unavailable; the illegal and most extreme end of which is trafficking (Chuang 2006; Kyle and Koslowski 2011; de Haas 2013; see also classic discussion in Salt and Stein 1997). Migration control is the other side of this, and includes both: explicit contracts with visa-processing companies, security companies and transporters; and sanctions placed on carriers, employers and service-providers within the State. As the migration control industry expands, this drives facilitation industry development, and *vice versa*.[2] There is little regulation of the migration control industry, though there is much discussion of regulating facilitation, largely under the banner of combatting trafficking (e.g. UNODC 2004, 2008).

Robert Harney's 1977 article 'The Commerce of Migration' is often given as the starting point for discussion of the migration industry (e.g. Hernández-León 2013; Nyberg Sorensen and Gammeltoft-Hansen 2013, 4), though Harney's focus is migration *facilitation*, including a State mostly as an actor among others. Harney observed a network of agents, carriers, persons using ethnic ties, remittance - and labour-brokers, all profiting from the migration of Italians to Canada (and then also to the US) from the early twentieth century until the 1970s (e.g. Harney 1977, 49). Since Harney, others have observed similar systems in other migration contexts[3] and John Salt expands the theory to present a bigger, globally interconnected, phenomenon. Traditionally, Salt explains, migration is seen as a direct relationship between a migrant or migrant household and 'a government acting as gatekeeper' (Salt 2001, 88), but he argues that it is better understood to be:

> ... a diverse international business, with a vast budget, providing hundreds of thousands of jobs world-wide, and managed by a set of individuals, agencies and institutions, each of which has an interest in developing a sector of the business (Salt 2001, 89).

Like Harney, Salt places governments within this structure as business actors so that the role of a State, which benefits from certain aspects of migration and acts accordingly, is also theorised along a business model (Salt 2001, 91). While this paper builds upon this characterisation of an inter-sectorial, inter-national and global interconnectivity, it maintains that this takes place within a system for which legitimacy depends on a State being a special sort of actor, with a special role in noncitizenship construction.

Figure 1 maps the involvement of private entities throughout the migration process,[4] involving for-profit private actor involvement in both decision-making and the use of force in many areas usually seen as the preserve of the receiving State.[5] While the three crossing-points into a State are introduced briefly here, they and their role in noncitizenship construction will form the basis for more developed discussion in the main body of this paper.

The migration process begins on the left of the figure with visa processing companies, a sector supporting States to gather, process and store noncitizen data in a variety of ways, from data collection to 'entitlement credentialing' (e.g. see Bloom 2013). Companies such as Gerry's, Vfs Global, WorldBridge Services and CSC may have offices in countries where the visa applications are made and from there are involved, to different extents, in processing applications for visas to a range of countries. Still external to a State's borders, carrier companies may then be involved in two capacities: sending ahead passenger data to receiving ports, airports and terminals[6]; and enforcing documentation requirements for entering the receiving State (e.g. Mitsilegas 2015, 24–28 in European context).

Borders themselves may be controlled by privately contracted border guards from multinational companies like G4S and Prosegur alongside or instead of State agents. These guards may be contracted by private or public (or mixed public-private) port or airport companies, or by States at other border posts, and may fulfil a range of roles, from general security to document-checking and restraint of suspicious passengers.Privately supplied and/or privately manned surveillance and other technology supports control, whether through the collection of biometric data, or the surveillance of border zones. The final stage of the privatised migration control infrastructure is also involved in physical border crossing. This is the forcible removal from the State community through detention (Flynn and Cannon

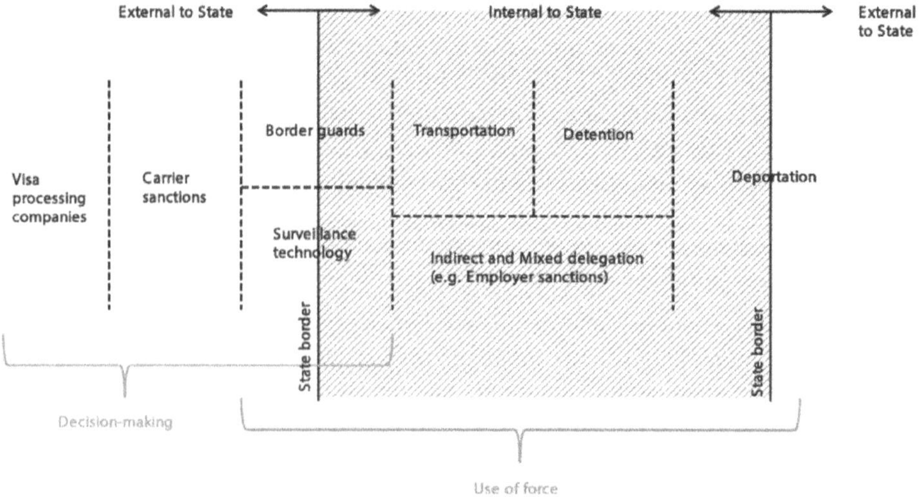

Figure 1. The structure of the business of migration control.
Note: First published at Bloom 2014, 152.

2009; Flynn 2012, 64–5)[7]; and from the State territory through deportation (recently characterised by Matthew Gibney as a form of forced migration; Gibney 2013). This may be at the direct request of a State or the role may be indirectly allocated.

Second, within the physical territory and at the border to the community of the State, there is another array of non-State actors, (often involuntarily) engaged in migration control, refining the construction of territorial noncitizenship. Some entities may be threatened with sanction if they do not participate in noncitizenship construction. This most commonly includes employers and landlords, but may also involve educators and health care professionals (Pham, 2008). In some jurisdictions, it may even include taxi drivers and religious leaders (e.g. see Clor 2014). These individuals are coerced against entering into relationships with certain members of society because of their immigration status, or to be suspicious of those who may lack the status requirements. This may construct noncitizenship beyond the exclusions of noncitizenship explicitly requested by the State, since private actors, to avoid sanction, may interpret policy to be more exclusionary than is explicit in State policy. It may indeed cultivate a wider suspicion within particular contexts of persons of specific ethnic groups, for example, locally most commonly associated with irregular migrant status (Pham 2008). As such, this may even extend the construction of a form of noncitizenship also to members of the citizenry, ostensibly not subject to immigration policy.

Third, and related, there is an overlapping crossing-point between delegation of decision-making and the use of force. This is found in all aspects of privatised migration control discussed here and is crucial to the problematisation of legitimacy.

Figure 2 analyses the mechanisms apparent in the delegation of migration control. It shows that this delegation may be explicit or implicit. Explicit delegation may occur through contracting a private security company to manage a detention centre, for example. Alternatively, the delegation may be implicit, when a State pressures a private sector actor to perform the role in question. The privatisation may also be direct or indirect. Transfer of responsibility for action may be directly from the State to a particular private entity or it may involve a further step of delegation such as when a private airline, to avoid sanction, hires a security company to detain persons before return (e.g. Gammeltoft-Hansen 2010, 68 gives example from Sheremetyevo 2 airport in Moscow, also discussed in Nicholson 1997). Figure 2 also includes the category of 'pseudo privatisation', to capture cases in which, rather than delegate in the first instance, a State may create a subsidiary entity, or collaborate with the private sector to create a semi-private entity. This five-way categorisation will be useful for examining effects on noncitizen-State relationships.

3. A peculiar sort of privatisation

Privatisation of migration control is peculiar. This can be seen in three main ways: (i) the private actors engaged in migration control are also involved in policy development; (ii) they are involved in creating the categories of humanity to be subjected to their activities; and (iii) the sector skews the composition of markets within a State. Privatisation is classically characterised as a moving of goods, services and assets from the public to the private sphere (e.g. from Starr 1988). Although there is no clear dividing line between public and private,[8] this paper assumes for-profit non-State entities to be private, the State to be public, and does not worry too much about other entities. Privatisation of migration control involves the transfer of functions through both contractual agreements and sanctions (see

Figure 2). There is some selling of assets (e.g. in the form of detention facilities), but this is only mentioned here in passing. Marketisation, as a key aspect of privatisation, involves publicly organised services being subjected to market forces. The role of the market in privatised migration control is of interest, though in opposing ways (calling for bids, and imposing sanctions).

Privatisation discourse entered the global mainstream in the 1970s, led by influential Member States of key organisations and influenced by the writings of figures like Milton Friedman (1962). Privatisation and de-regulation as a means to development became a key policy strategy of the International Monetary Fund and the World Bank, with these agencies promoting national privatisation schemes as conditions on loans, (e.g. Larner 2000, 7). For various reasons, then, countries in all global regions have engaged in some form of privatisation in recent decades (e.g. OECD 2003; Fink 2011, 111). There has been extensive study of the overall implications of privatisation policies in sectors like telecommunications, water, electricity, postal services, railways, airlines (e.g. OECD 2003, 9; Bakker 2010; Fink 2011, 113), as well as in security and military sectors (e.g. Donahue 1989; Avant 2005), but there is less analysis of the implications of migration control privatisation overall, though key exceptions are discussed in this paper.

Important for the current discussion has been the development of the private security sector. Despite a 'relatively depressed' post-cold war global arms market (Silverstein 2000), analysts suggest that private security and military services were booming. Elke Krahmann charts a historic use of private security services, which over three centuries had seen a 'progressive elimination due to the emergence of the State monopoly on the legitimate use of force' (Krahmann 2010, 2). The end of the cold war in the 1990s brought substantial cuts in States' military spending and analysts present the consequent sense of insecurity and the ready supply of unemployed personnel as key to the blossoming of the private military and security sectors (e.g. Vines 2000, 169; Krahmann 2010). Privatisation of migration control emerged within this context, using similar discourses (Menz 2013, 112). The relationship between the security industry and governments has long been subject to criticism, with private security firms both offering policy advice and bidding for the contracts developed on this advice (e.g. Leander 2007, 56). Several writers examine the migration industry through the same lens, arguing that private security companies involved in migration control have been part of the creation of the security discourse surrounding global migration, one in which the resources of the private sector are needed in order to meet emerging threats which are identified and characterised by the industry itself (Rodier 2012; Hidalgo 2014). Related, has been the development of the private prison industry and its sister sector, that of private immigration detention, in which there is economic incentive in 'winning and maintaining contracts and keeping their facilities full' (Bacon 2005, 2).

The notion of an 'immigration industrial complex' is introduced by theorists like Deepa Fernandez and Tanya Golash-Boza, though in different contexts. They draw on Eisenhower's notion of the military industrial complex (Eisenhower 1961). Golash-Boza writes that these 'three complexes [military, prison, migration] share three major features: (a) a rhetoric of fear; (b) the confluence of powerful interests; and (c) a discourse of other-ization'. (Golash-Boza 2009, 306).[9] All three elements can be seen in the privatised migration control sector described here. In migration control, however, the construction of the noncitizen as an object of fear is, if possible, more acute. A connection can be observed with facilitation discourse, according to which individual noncitizens may be seen at different times as non-threatening and vulnerable, as economically desirable, and as frightening threats to stability and security. This role of the private sector in constructing the policy landscape in this area is, then, peculiar, but not unique. However, the construction of noncitizenship is peculiar in its variety. Although the focus in migration control is on illegalisation and securitisation, in migration facilitation, it is on the possible contributions of skills and labour of migrants or on a vulnerability that reinforces the benevolent image of the receiving State.

Milton Friedman explains that a crucial driving principle behind the neoliberal free market project is that it should act as a mechanism for ensuring control and accountability of governments, providing 'a check on the powers of the governmental sector and an effective protection of freedom of speech, of religion, and of thought' (Friedman 1962, 3). He further explains that 'no exchange will take place unless both parties do benefit from it', so that co-operation 'is thereby achieved without coercion' (Friedman 1962, 13). Whatever problems there may be with this position, the types of marketisation shown in Figures 1 and 2 deviate from this neoliberal model, creating coercion without choice for the citizenry, let alone for noncitizens. The concern about implications of privatised migration control for citizen choice and the coercion of citizens is a worry also raised, for example, by Gallya Lahav.

This is seen most easily in QII (Figure 2), in which the State acts as sole customer of a direct contract. There are several sectors in which similar types of marketisation are found, such as publicly contracted health care providers, who then serve users on a no-choice basis (e.g. see the examples of direct contracting in UK health care discussed in Pollock 2004). This form of privatisation does not include the market checks and balances on treatment and conditions that are claimed to function in those privatised hospitals or schools, for example, where there is user-selection (e.g. see Minow 2002).[10] Put another way, and in the case of prison privatisation, 'prisoners are conspicuously unable to take their business elsewhere, however dissatisfied they might be' (Donahue 1989, 170). The same goes for those most directly affected by the migration control industry. Indeed, in their extensive study and critique of privatised detention in the US, Doty and Wheatley argue that while a belief in the market has been key to the private prison industry's success and 'market solutions

	EXPLICIT	**IMPLICIT**
	Direct, Explicit State directly contracts private entity to carry out activity in question *QII*	**Direct, Implicit** Sanction placed upon private actors to prevent certain activities *QI*
	QIII **Indirect, Explicit** State directly contracts one entity who delegates further	*QIV* **Indirect, Implicit** To avoid sanction, private actor uses services of a further private actor
QV **Pseudo Privatisation** State creates private entity to which to delegate activities, or State collaborates with private entity in creation of a delegatee.		

Figure 2. Taxonomy of privatisation of migration control.[16]

are [...] perceived as shrinking the size of the reach of government [...] this is not the case with prison privatisation' (Doty and Wheatley 2013, 434). They argue that the private prison industry increases both the reach of government and social control. The same happens with migration control and, by extension, in the construction of noncitizenship.

Moreover, as can be seen in other quadrants of Figure 2, the involvement of the private sector can remove activity from scrutiny. For example, it leads to 'hidden coercion' (Bloom and Risse 2014), whereby the nature and even existence of State coercion is hidden through the mediated role of private actors. As introduced above in the case of service providers, sanctions in this sector can lead to constructions of noncitizenship whose restrictions and whose scope go beyond those explicitly imposed by the State, as private entities take care to avoid risk of sanction, allowing the development of measures that are more exclusionary than *prima facie* apparent in policy and, as such, to use Aristide Zolberg's phrase, policy intentions are rendered 'highly ambiguous' (Zolberg 1999, 74). Carrier sanctions, for example, punish carriers that transport persons without required documentation, but do not punish those that leave behind persons with genuine humanitarian claims (e.g. pointed out by Kritzman-Amir 2011, 203; Feller 1989; Nicholson 1997). This releases States from needing to declare policy aims that would be problematic in the context of political and international legal commitments. The concern here is that it also removes legitimacy that may come from the democratic scrutiny of State decisions or the democratic delegation of power and decision-making to a State.

Perhaps the most profound peculiarity of privatised migration control, however, is that it commodifies the construction of humanity into two supposedly mutually exclusive constituencies, also commodifying this construction. The constituencies created are: the citizens on whose behalf the private actors are engaged, and the noncitizens as potential enemy or adversary to be controlled.[11] This construction happens at all stages of the migration control process, but detention provides a useful illustrative example of the peculiarity in this role. It could be proposed that criminal detention,[12] including privatised criminal detention, gives rise to a period of suspended citizenship, so that the entities involved could theoretically be seen as constructing a temporary form of noncitizenship. But this is unhelpful here. Criminal detention is based on an assumption that the incarcerated person, A, has a right not to be incarcerated which can be overridden because, according to certain agreed processes, it has been shown that A is in one or more of the following categories: a danger to others; deserving of punishment; needing to be reformed. Some cases of criminal incarceration may be functionally permanent, but usually A is released to re-join the citizenry after serving the sentence period. There is a different logic for immigration-related detention. The noncitizen is assumed not to be a member of society, lacking a right to be free within the State in question (note that even permanent residents may be subject to immigration-related detention or deportation e.g. LDSG 2009). The possibility of detention, then (and so it's enactment) is part of the construction of a central vulnerability of noncitizenship in the States under consideration. Involving the private sector here gives rise to three peculiarities: it risks 'diminishing basic services in order to increase profits' (Flynn 2012, 64); it changes the nature of the removal of noncitizen freedom, altering its justifiability; and it alters scrutiny. Consider these in reverse order. Scrutiny is reduced for two reasons: in criminal detention, citizens know that they could be in A's position; and information is so more freely available about conditions for inmates. The justification for the detention of noncitizens is based upon protection of State sovereignty. As such it is only derivatively for the benefit of that State's citizenry. The constructed illegalities involved in criminal and immigration-related detention are of different sorts, and the effects on legitimacy of the privatisation of detention are, therefore, different.

The final form of peculiarity in privatised migration control to be considered here is the special way in which it skews the market in a State. That is, as presented above, it skews the very *composition* of the labour and other markets through the construction of noncitizens as (i) welcome or unwelcome territorially, and then (ii) able or unable to access the internal State frameworks. This deviates from traditional neoliberal privatisation discourse. While Milton Friedman writes that the free market will protect the 'foreign-born' from xenophobia because it masks the producer and emphasises economic motivations (Friedman 1962, 21), the measures discussed here reintroduce distinctions, either stopping persons from participating in the market at all or constraining their participation. Friedman himself has identified such measures as problematic. In a lecture given in 1978, he said (Friedman 1978, min11–12):

> ... Mexican immigration over the border is a good thing. It's a good thing for the illegal immigrants. It's a good thing for the United States. It's a good thing for the citizens of the country. But it's only good so long as it's illegal.

It might appear from this that, for Friedman, people crossing the physical border is a good thing, so long as their entry into internal frameworks is restricted. This is not so. He wants immigrants to enter the work force freely. Friedman is against access for immigrants to the welfare state (hence the desire to keep them 'illegal'); which is problematic, but it is not the same thing (Moore 2013; see also argument between Rose and Milton Friedman in Varadarajan 2006). He is in favour of immigrants entering the State freely, and having full access to the social community of the State, where that community, for the neoliberal, does not include providing welfare services. This shows that the peculiar privatisation of migration control is problematic also within a neoliberal framework.

Privatisation measures in migration control are of a particular sort. Indeed, their peculiarity is found precisely in their role in the construction of noncitizenship and it is this special role that makes this difficult to analyse using standard understandings of privatisation and its impact upon States' human rights commitments.

4. Implications of commodifying noncitizenship construction

The involvement of the private sector transforms the construction of noncitizenship into commodity, illegallisation and risk-identification, driving the way noncitizenship is understood and the relationship of noncitizens with States. Moreover, new distances are created within that relationship, as this construction takes place in new spaces, sometimes far beyond State borders, or in aspects of daily life not usually subject to State control. Janine Brodie has noted that the welfare states that arose out of the Second World War were based on a 'notion of social citizenship', in which there were certain basic rights of the citizen, including protection from market forces (Brodie 1996, 60). She argues that the development of neoliberal State models changed this. The change is more marked with regard to noncitizenship construction. In conjunction with the migration facilitation industry, the migration control industry makes noncitizens and noncitizenship construction a commodity.

The commodification of noncitizen construction involves constructing the relationship of noncitizenship with States in terms of maximising the value of the goods involved – where the goods are represented either by the working presence of noncitizens, or by their enforced absence. Noncitizens come to be seen principally as part of an economic infrastructure, to be used for bargaining, as means to achieving certain ends. As a result, their humanity, and the attendant rights and needs, come second if at all. This commodification drives the private sector to find new forms of construction that maximise value. In particular, this has driven an escalation in a focus on illegality, security and risk in the construction of the relationships between noncitizens and States, in turn reinforcing the need for the private sector and increasing the value of private sector noncitizenship construction. It is the construction of a person's noncitizenship as a unit of risk, for example, that ensures that there is value to be gained from control.

One form of this is what has been referred to as an 'illegality industry' (Andersson 2014), whereby the construction of migrant illegality is crucial for some major international business sectors (Andersson 2012). Ruben Andersson argues that the industry described in this paper 'produces what it is meant to eliminate, curtail, or transform – more migrant illegality' (Andersson 2014, 6), as noncitizen illegality is constructed by private actors to support business interests. In turn, the relationship of illegalised noncitizens with a State comes second, driven by their constructed illegality. This is not to ignore the vast web of State-constructed illegality (e.g. see de Genova 2013), but to look at how commodification of noncitizenship construction may give rise to new constructions of illegality. This analysis also holds for security more widely. Until now, this paper has focused on the construction of the noncitizenship of individual noncitizens, albeit in large numbers. However, the use of for-profit non-State actors in migration control in fact reconfigures the State relationship with noncitizens as a whole by relocating emphasis, but also State monopoly on expertise and so decision-making in this area (see also crucial analysis in Betts 2013). This includes the configuration of noncitizenship itself as a security concern, the expertise about how to deal with which is increasingly held in the private sector.

The involvement of the private sector, then, contributes to what Engin Isin has called 'neuropolitics', a political decision-making based on anxiety, and the construction of noncitizens as a source of anxiety rather than sympathy. Isin presents this notion as arising out of his observation that there is an 'anxiety about the Other that has been articulating itself through various discourses on the border' (Isin 2009, 29). Indeed, the strategic locations held by Finmeccanica and other such companies in Brussels, for example, and the fact that others like Steria hold large amounts of sensitive data puts industry heavyweights in a position where they could influence policy. Moreover, the movement of high-ranking political personages into private sector boardrooms and of private sector leaders into political positions helps to reinforce the perception of shared interests. Crucially, this also creates a dependency of States on the private sector. This starts with the visa companies that increasingly hold the data on migrant admissions, visa applications and asylum claims, as well as the expertise regarding how to administer and organise such data. It includes also the security companies that enjoy an increasing monopoly on strategic and technical expertise in the area of migration and border management. In this way, the private sector could move towards becoming the primary repository of expertise and knowledge which once lay with States, making them crucial players in policy development as well as enactment.

Moving activities from a State into the private sector makes this emphasis on economic calculations more pronounced, potentially obscuring intended outcomes of policy. As argued in the section above, this is the case with regard to both explicit privatisation, and implicit forms. It is widely understood that private entities may be driven by profit, interested in quality of service-delivery insofar as it reinforces market-share, thought here are exceptions to this, as seen in the case of UK-based airline, XL Airways, which is reported to have refused to fly deportees, explaining that it had 'sympathy for all dispossessed people in the world (quoted in Verkaik 2007) and NGOs that also fulfil many contracts for non-State involvement in migration control. However, the focus here is on those private entities mostly driven by profit motives. Such motives, within existing structures, do not promote humanitarian considerations. Indeed, some, like Enrique Ballesteros, OHCHR Special Rapporteur on the Use of Mercenaries, go further. In the case of mercenaries, he has observed a *competitive advantage* for those able to act outside international law (quoted in Vines 2000, 172). This translates easily into the migration control sector, where several writers have suggested that the private actors are engaged by States *in order* to circumvent diplomatic limitations and international commitments which restrict the actions open to States acting as States (e.g. Gammeltoft-Hansen 2013, 36).

This is clearest in the case of 'externalisation of border control', or 'remote control' (e.g. Zolberg 1999, 75, 6, 2005; Gammeltoft-Hansen 2010). States are usually unable to carry out border control activities in other countries unless they have made special diplomatic arrangements. Involving the private sector actors in the ways shown to the left of Figure 1 above circumvents this, enabling non-State actors to construct the *territorial* meaning of noncitizenship before an individual even encounters the relevant State directly. As well as obstructing persons migrating in emergency conditions (Gammeltoft-Hansen 2013), this locates the private actor as the first layer of border control and, as such, as a (if not *the*) crucial player in noncitizenship construction. While some describe this as a moving of the border, it is also a crucial reconfiguring of the border-scape and, as such, the construction of noncitizenship.

In these new forms of noncitizenship construction, then, human elements become secondary to economic considerations, and as the noncitizenship construction is commodified, other aspects are magnified. The involvement of security and detention sectors may promote an emphasis on the construction of noncitizens as illegal and as threats to security. The use of sanctions may drive other companies and individuals to make decisions that are based principally on economic considerations.

5. Noncitizenship, force, decision-making and the limits of privatisation

The measures discussed here have been made more controversial by loss of life and reported inhuman treatment within privatised detention and deportation systems (e.g. cases against G4S on flights leaving the UK),[13] and claims that this is exacerbated by privatisation. However, similar things have happened in State-run facilities and at the hands of State agents (e.g. at the time of writing, new cases are being raised against the Guardia Civil on flights leaving Spain).[14] Indeed, privatisation does not necessarily produce worse conditions. In analyses of privatised detention facilities, for example, there are mixed views on whether or not individual cases of privatisation have been beneficial,[15] and perhaps systems could be developed to direct private interests in ways that would favour human rights. The concern raised here relates to the altered and hidden interests in the noncitizen construction and what privatisation itself means for more fundamental questions of the legitimacy of migration control itself, where control is justified on the basis of the specialness of the State entity and so its activity. Non-State actors come to take decision-making and enforcement roles relating to the construction of noncitizenship. Further, the privatised measures here, both explicit and implicit, engage commodification, illegality, risk and securitisation into noncitizenship construction, thereby also injecting these elements into the noncitizen-State relationship. This can be seen most clearly by considering how it affects each of the stages and forms of privatised migration control presented in Figures 1 and 2 at the beginning of this paper.

Writers from a range of theoretical frameworks support the idea that a State has a sovereign right to construct noncitizens, and to select among those noncitizens who wish to enter its borders. This need to make informed decisions could perhaps legitimise the State's collection of personal information from those who would immigrate, including data about salary, health, perhaps even finger prints and retina scans (though I am not sure it does). However, when the collection, storage, even analysis of such data is directly and explicitly contracted out to private companies, this changes the nature of what takes place. As has been shown in this paper, this cannot be seen simply as a private entity acting on the instruction of the State and its officials to support the State's construction of noncitizenship. Private entities here gain new sorts of power over noncitizens. Decisions on whether to accept visas (which may have been processed by private entities) and other documents may then be taken by the staff of private transport companies (possibly with the advice of public officials). This potentially builds two layers of private sector decision-making into the construction of an individual's ability to enter into a physical relationship with a State. When a person's claim to enter into such a relationship is controversial or rejected by the carrier, he or she may be detained. This detention may be further delegated. As a result, detention that may ostensibly be justified on the basis of State sovereignty considerations is carried out by one private entity at the instruction of another, arguably distanced from the direct command of the State. Irrespective of wider concerns with detention and its use in immigration governance, as this apparently brings it beyond traditional legitimising frameworks, theoretical work is needed if this detention is to be justifiable along these lines.

As has been shown, a State's relationship with noncitizens is further constructed through private entities within its physical territory. This mode of largely implicit delegation has the effect of changing both the constituency and the nature of noncitizenship. On the one hand, it means that some citizens may be constructed as noncitizens by private entities erring on the side of caution in their noncitizenship construction in order to avoid sanction. It also means that noncitizenship construction and enactment enters into new non-State spheres of engagement, within the social, spiritual and personal lives of individual so-constructed noncitizens as well as of citizens. That a State should control the activities of noncitizens within its borders is also controversial, as can be seen in the work of Bosniak and Carens, for example. However, when such control is relocated to private actors in the ways described in this paper, the situation becomes even more problematic.

This privatisation continues, as has been shown here, to follow the noncitizen out of the State. This includes the directly contracted entities and public private partnerships that set up and run detention centres and are involved in the transport of noncitizens. Private actors are also contracted to take persons out of a State's territory through deportation procedures, with private security firms providing onboard security, either contracted by the transport company or by the State. As was noted at the beginning of this concluding section, recent tragedies at the hands of both private and State actors in this last phase of the migration control process demonstrate that public migration control is not necessarily better in terms of humanitarian conditions. The worry raised here is that privatisation in this sector causes problems for legitimacy.

6. Conclusion

This paper has argued that there is a 'business of noncitizenship' in which private entities play key roles in the construction of noncitizenship and so of the relationships between non-citizens and States. It has raised concerns with privatisation of migration control activities in ways which relocate key powers away from States and so conflict with the assumption of States as the proper domain of competence in the construction of noncitizenship. It suggests that such privatisation weakens justification for the migration control activities themselves and gives rise to peculiar governance challenges. Aspects of noncitizenship are constructed by for-profit non-State actors outside the scrutiny and limiting mechanisms of the market (problematic for neoliberal frameworks), compromising the protection of the rights of noncitizens (problematic for liberal frameworks), the citizenries (problematic for democratic liberal frameworks) or the international community. It not only involves non-State actors using force and making decisions on behalf of States, but challenges the State's monopoly on official noncitizenship construction.

Notes

1. This view is widely defended, for example, Thomas Gammeltoft-Hasen and Ninna Nyberg Sorensen describe the 'Migration Industry' as complex, involving 'both facilitation and the control of migration' (Nyberg Sorensen and Gammeltoft-Hansen 2013, 4). Gammeltoft-Hansen's 2013 monograph, meanwhile, is the first to demonstrate the impact of this privatised system *as a whole* upon the international asylum system.
2. This has been presented before, perhaps most famously by Khalid Koser (e.g. Khoser 2005).
3. For example, Mexico, US (Hernandez-León 2013, 27); Bangladesh, Japan/US (Mahmud 2012); Peru, Italy (Berg and Tamagno 2013); and others.
4. For a classic analysis of this structure, see the writings of Gallya Lahav, e.g. at 2006.
5. Mitsilegas disagrees, arguing that new forms of control are created (2015).
6. Full list of countries with this requirement can be found on airline websites, e.g. Air Canada: http://www.aircanada.com/en/travelinfo/APIS/apis.html accessed 20/01/2015.
7. For detailed analysis of growing privatisation of immigration detention, see (Flynn and Cannon 2009); and (Flynn 2012, 64–5) for updated discussion.
8. For example, Starr 1988; Minow 2002, 29–35; Avant [on security] 2005, 23; Donahue 1989, 8 – government agencies are made up of private individuals.
9. Silverstein adds also financial contribution to political parties or policy initiatives (Silverstein 2000, 189).
10. For example, https://euobserver.com/justice/123711 [accessed 08/01/2015].
11. In this way, it is different from the dual constituencies commonly identified in other forms of privatisation: the receiving poor and the providing others (e.g. see Starr 1988).
12. Michael Flynn defines immigration-related detention as 'the deprivation of liberty of non-citizens because of their status', (Flynn 2012, 42–43). He emphasises that this must include 'both criminal incarceration and administrative detention', since 'many countries – from Malaysia to Lebanon to Italy to the US – charge irregular migrants with criminal violations

stemming from their status' (Flynn 2012, 43–44). In this paper, the term 'criminal detention' is used to refer to detention that is not immigration-related, though allowing that some immigration-related detention may also take place on the basis of criminal proceedings (this follows the convention adopted by Flynn). There are two key considerations: the mode of construction of the detainee; and the theoretical nature of the detention.

13. Extensive examples from the UK perspective can be found, for example, in the many writings of Clare Sambrook, http://claresambrook.com accessed 21/01/2015.
14. http://politica.elpais.com/politica/2015/04/17/actualidad/1429295054_780842.html
15. For example, Logan charts prisons improved by privatisation (Logan 1996; though with emphasis on employee experience rather than conditions for inmates), while the Swedish government reportedly decided to remove their immigration detention system from private operators because of what the government considered to be unethical malpractice.
16. This is adapted from a version first presented and defended in (Bloom 2013, 5), but with an additional fifth category.

Acknowledgements

I would like to thank the anonymous reviewers and Katherine Tonkiss for their careful reading, insight and comments which have certainly improved this piece, though errors that remain are mine. I began work on this paper whilst in post as research fellow at the United Nations University Institute on Globalisation, Culture and Mobility (UNU-GCM).

Disclosure statement

No potential conflict of interest was reported by the author.

References

Andersson, Ruben. 2012. "A Game of Risk: Boat Migration and the Business of Bordering Europe." *Anthropology Today* 28 (6): 7–11.

Andersson, Ruben. 2014. *Illegality Inc: Clandestine Migration and the Business of Bordering Europe*. Oakland: University of California Press.

Avant, Deborah. 2005. *The Market for Force*. Cambridge: Cambridge University Press.

Bacon, Christine. 2005. *The Evolution of Immigration Detention in the UK: The Involvement of Private Prison Companies*, Refugee Studies Centre Working Pâper No. 27. University of Oxford.

Bakker, Karen. 2010. *Privatizing Water*. Ithaca: Cornell University Press.

Berg, Ulla, and Carla Tamagno. 2013. "Migration Brokers and Document Fixers." In *The Migration Industry and the Commercialization of International Migration*, edited by Thomas Gammeltoft-Hansen and Ninna Nyberg Sorensen, 190–214. London: Routledge.

Betts, Alexander. 2013. "The Migration Industry in Global Migration Governance." In *The Migration Industry and the Commercialization of International Migration*, edited by Gamletoft-Hansen and Nyberg Sorensen, 45–63. London: Routledge.

Bloom, Tendayi. 2013. '*Statelessness and the Delegation of Migration Functions to Private Actors*', UNU-GCM Policy Report 02/04. Barcelona: UNU-GCM.

Bloom, Tendayi, and Verena Risse. 2014. "Examining Hidden Coercion at State Borders." *Ethics and Global Politics* 7 (2): 65–82.

Brodie, Janine. 1996. "Restructuring and the New Citizenship." In *Rethinking Restructuring: Gender and Change in Canada*, edited by I Bakker, 126–140. Toronto: University of Toronto Press.

Chuang, Janie. 2006. "Beyond a Snapshot: Preventing Human Trafficking in the Global Economy." *Indiana Journal of Global Legal Studies* 13 (1): 137–163.

Clor, Zaid. 2014. '*Targeting Undocumented Migrants*', UNU-GCM Working Paper. Accessed January 21 2015. i.unu.edu/media/gcm.unu.edu/publication/1087/ZAIDREPORT.pdf

Cole, Phillip. 2000. *Philosophies of Exclusion*. Edinburgh: Edinburgh University Press.
De Genova, Nicolas. 2013. "Spectacles of Migrant 'Illegality': The Scene of Exclusion, the Obscene of Inclusion." *Ethnic and Racial Studies* 36 (7): 1180–1198.
de Haas, Hein. 2013. '*Smuggling is a Reaction to Border Controls, Not the Cause of Migration', blog post Saturday 5th October 2013*. Accessed January 22 2015. http://heindehaas.blogspot.com.es/2013/10/smuggling-is-reaction-to-border.html
Donahue, John. 1989. *The Privatisation Decision*. New York: Basic Books.
Doty, Roxanne Lynn, and Elizabeth Shannon Wheatley. 2013. "Private Detention and the Immigration Industrial Complex." *International Political Sociology* 7: 426–443.
Drakeford, Mark. 2000. *Privatisation and Social Policy*. Harlow: Longman.
Eisenhower, Dwight. 1961. *January 17, 1961, President Eisenhower's Farewell Address to the Nation*. Accessed December 24 2014. https://www.youtube.com/watch?v=8y06NSBBRtY
Feller, Erika. 1989. "Carrier Sanctions and International Law." *International Journal of Refugee Law* 1: 48–66.
Fink, Simon. 2011. "A Contagious Concept." *Governance* 24 (1): 111–139.
Flynn, Michael. 2012. "Who Must Be Detained?" *Refugee Survey Quarterly* 31 (3): 40–68.
Flynn, Michael, and Cecilia Cannon. 2009. *The Privatisation of Immigration Detention*. A Global Detention Project Working Paper, Geneva.
Friedman, Milton. 1962. *Capitalism and Freedom*. Chicago, IL: University of Chicago Press.
Friedman, Milton. 1978. *'What is America?', lecture given at the University of Chicago*. Accessed January 22 2015. www.youtube.com/watch?v=fwDhx1XXO (uploaded by Basic Economics)
Gammeltoft-Hansen, Thomas. 2013. *Access to Asylum*. Cambridge: Cambridge University Press.
Gammeltoft-Hansen, Thomas. 2010. "Growing Barriers: International Refugee Law." In *Forgotten Genocides: Oblivion, Denial, and Memory*, edited by Rene Lemarchand, 55–81. Philadelphia: University of Pennsylvania Press.
Gibney, Matthew. 2013. "Is Deportation a Form of Forced Migration?" *Refugee Survey Quarterly* 32 (2): 116–129.
Golash-Boza, Tanya. 2009. "The Immigration Industrial Complex." *Sociology Compass* 3: 1–15.
Harney, Robert. 1977. "The Commerce of Migration." *Canadian Ethnic Studies/Etudes Ethniques Du Canada* 9: 42–53.
Hernández-León, Rubén. 2013. "Conceptualizing the Migration Industry." In *The Migration Industry and the Commercialization of International Migration*, edited by Thomas Gammeltoft-Hansen and Ninna Nyberg Sorensen, 24–44. London: Routledge.
Hidalgo, Susan. 2014. *El Último Holocausto Europeo*, Akal.
Isin, Engin. 2009. "The Neurotic Citizen." In *Securitizations of Citizenship*, edited by Peter Nyers, 15–33. Abingdon: Routledge.
Khoser, Kalid. 2005. *Irregular Migration, State Security and Human Security*. A Paper Prepared for the Policy Analysis and Research Programme of the Global Commission on International Migration. Accessed January 08 2015. www.iom.int/iahia/webdav/site/mviahiasite/shared/shared/mainsite/policy_and_research/gcim/tp/TP5.pdf
Krahmann, Elke. 2010. *States, Citizens and the Privatisation of Security*. Cambridge: Cambridge University Press.
Kritzman-Amir, Tally. 2011. "Privatisation and Delegation of State Authority in Asylum Systems." *Law and Ethics of Human Rights* 5 (1): 193–215.
Kyle, Davd, and Rey Koslowski. 2011. "Introduction." In *Global Human Smuggling*, edited by David Kyle and Rey Koslowski, 1–30. Baltimore: Johns Hopkins Press.
Lahav, Gallya. 2006. "The Rise of NonState Actors in Migration Regulation in the United States and Europe." In *The Migration Reader*, edited by Anthony Messina and Gallya Lahav, 290–314. Boulder, CO: Lynne Rienner.
LDSG. 2009. *Detained Lives*. London: London Detainee Support Group.
Leander, Anna. 2007. "Regulating the Role of Private Military Companies in Shaping Security and Politics." In *From Mercenaries to Market: The Rise and Regulation of Private Military Companies*, edited by Simon Chesterman and Chia Lehnardt, 49–64. Oxford: Oxford University Press.
Logan, Charles. 1996. "Public vs. Private Prison Management." *Criminal Justice Review* 21 (1): 62–85.

Mahmud, Hasan. 2012. "Enemy or Ally." *Migration and Development* 2 (1): 1–15.
Menz, Georg. 2013. "The Neoliberalized State and the Growth of the Migration Industry." In *The Migration Industry and the Commercialization of International Migration*, edited by Thomas Gammeltoft-Hansen and Ninna Nyberg Sorensen, 128–151. London: Routledge.
Minow, Martha. 2002. *Partners, Not Rivals*. Boston, MA: Beacon Press.
Mitsilegas, Valsamis. 2015. *The Criminalisation of Migration in Europe*. Heidelberg: Springer.
Nicholson, Frances. 1997. "Implementation of the Immigration (Carrier's Liability) Act 1987." *International and Comparative Legal Quarterly* 46: 586–634.
Nyberg Sorensen Ninna, and Thomas Gammeltoft-Hansen. 2013. "Introduction." In *The Migration Industry and the Commercialization of International Migration*, edited by Thomas Gammeltoft-Hansen and Ninna Nyberg Sorensen, 1–23. London: Routledge.
OECD. 2003. *Privatising State-owned Enterprises*. Paris: OECD.
Pham, Huyen. 2008. "The Private Enforcement of Immigration Laws." *The Georgetown Law Journal* 96: 777–826.
Pollock, Allyson. 2004. *NHS Plc: The Privatisation of Our Health Care*. London: Verso.
Rodier, Claire. 2012. *Xénophobi Business: A Quoi Servent Les Contrôles Migratoires?*. Paris: La Découverte.
Salt, John. 2001. "The Business of International Migration." In *International Migration into the 21st Century*, edited by MAB Siddique, 86–108. Cheltenham: Edward Elgar.
Salt, John, and Jeremy Stein. 1997. "Migration as a Business: The Case of Trafficking." *International Migration* 35 (4): 467–494.
Schotel, Bas. 2012. *On the right of Exclusion*. London: Routledge.
Silverstein, Ken. 2000. *Private Warriors*. New York: Verso.
Starr, Paul. 1988. "The Meaning of Privatisation." *Yale Law and Policy Review* 6: 6–41.
Tonkiss, Katherine. 2013. "Constitutional Patriotism, Migration and the Post-national Dilemma." *Citizenship Studies* 17 (3–4): 491–504.
UNODC. 2008. *Toolkit to Combat Trafficking in Persons*. New York: United Nations.
UNODC. 2004. *United Nations Convention against Transnational Organised Crime and the Protocols Thereto*. New York: United Nations.
Varadarajan, Tunku. 2006. "The Romance of Economics." *The Wall Street Journal* July 22. Accessed January 08 2015. www.wsj.com/articles/SB115352827130914276
Verkaik, R. 2007. "Major Airline Refuses to Help with Forcible Removal of Immigrants." *The Independent* October 8. Accessed May 4 2015. http://www.independent.co.uk/news/uk/crime/major-airline-refuses-to-help-with-forcible-removal-of-immigrants-394451.html
Vines, Alex. 2000. "Mercenaries, Human Rights and Legality." In *Mercenaries*, edited by Abdel-Fatau Musah and J. Kayode Fayemi, 169–197. London: Pluto Press.
Zolberg, Aristide. 2005. "The Archaeology of 'Remote Control'." In *Migration Control in the North Atlantic World*, edited by Andreas Fahrmeir, Olivier Faron, and Patrick Weil, 195–222. New York: Berghahn Books.
Zolberg, Aristide. 1999. "Matters of State: Theorizing Immigration Policy." In *The Handbook of International Migration*, edited by Charles Hirschman, Philip Kasinitz, and Josh DeWind, 71–93. New York: Russell Sage.

Rooted displacement: the paradox of belonging among stateless people

Kristy A. Belton

Human Rights Center, University of Dayton, Dayton, OH, USA

ABSTRACT

Stateless people are noncitizens everywhere. Yet, unlike many noncitizens, they are not border crossers. Despite the majority's physical rootedness in the countries of their birth, the stateless are nonetheless forcibly displaced. Their peculiar form of noncitizenship displaces them *in situ* as they lack the right to choose to belong to the specific communities within which they were born and raised. Using The Bahamas and the Dominican Republic as case studies, this article illustrates how the stateless are either forcibly cast into liminality or made to take on the nationality of a country with which they do not identify when the State can no longer tolerate their noncitizen status.

Introduction

The interview is conducted in a hushed tone. Gillard Louis does not want the other college students to overhear our conversation. We are discussing a highly sensitive subject that has affected him directly. 'To be stateless,' he says, is 'to not have a nationality that is publicly known or I can say that falls under a country's group of identity.'[1] Marie St. Cecile, a prominent figure in the Haitian-Bahamian community, concurs: 'To be stateless means you have no identity … It feels like you're nonexistent … You have no identity … in the community that you live.'[2]

While statelessness is generally treated as an issue of whether a person formally belongs to a State or not through the legal bond of citizenship (UN 1954), these interviewees' quotes reveal the important role that identity plays in citizenship construction and the uncertainty that surrounds belonging when one is a noncitizen everywhere. Unlike asylum seekers, refugees, migrants, and other types of noncitizens who are noncitizens in their States of residence, but who are generally recognized as citizens under the operation of some State's laws, the majority of stateless people are 'noncitizen insiders' (Belton 2011). They have not migrated from elsewhere and remain, for the most part, in the countries where they were born.

Although physically emplaced, I illustrate via the comparative case study of The Bahamas and the Dominican Republic that the stateless' sense of identity is ambiguous at best or nonexistent at worst. Unlike many other types of noncitizens who come from elsewhere, they are unable to answer, or are prevented from answering, the question of 'Where do I belong?' (Cuba and Hummons 1993, 112) via practices of citizenship denial or deprivation in the countries of their birth. As Natacha Jn-Simon, another college student explains, 'to be stateless means that [to] you … and to others, it's confusing as to which country you belong to.'[3] Noncitizenship, then, is much more than legal exclusion from the State for the stateless. As I argue in this article, it is a form of forced displacement that immobilizes them *in situ*.

In order to make the case that stateless people face a peculiar and injurious form of displacement, even as they remain physically rooted in the countries of their birth, the article is divided into three sections. The first part situates the argument in the extant literature on citizenship, noncitizenship, and forced displacement, underscoring the lack of attention that has been paid to the stateless noncitizen and critiquing the emphasis that has been placed on examining displacement under crisis or conflict conditions. The second and third portions use data gathered from interviews, supported by other primary and secondary sources, to explain how the noncitizenship generated by statelessness is a form of forced displacement that can be produced by liberal democracies. Specifically, these sections illustrate how the stateless are either forcibly cast into liminality or made to take on the nationality of a country with which they do not identify (that of their parents or grandparents) when the polity can no longer tolerate their ambiguous status. In both cases, the stateless are forcibly displaced while remaining 'in place.' The article concludes that the greatest 'calamity' (Arendt [1948] 2004, 377) to befall the stateless is their inability to choose to belong to the communities of their birth.

Statelessness as forced displacement

Writing in the immediate aftermath of World War II, Hannah Arendt, herself a stateless person, described how millions of people were essentially rendered nonhuman through denationalization procedures and forced migratory movement. Such people 'lived outside the pale of the law' ([1948] 2004, 353) and were homeless, unprotected beings that no State was willing to adopt. Human rights had ceased to exist for them because 'it turned out that the moment human beings lacked their own government and had to fall back upon their minimum rights, no authority was left to protect them and no institution was willing to guarantee them' (370).

Although the loss of human rights was disturbing, Arendt argued that it was not the loss of this or that specific right that mattered as much as the loss of 'a right to have rights.' That is, the 'right to the human condition itself, which depends upon *belonging to some human community*' (631; italics added). Unlike Arendt, who lamented that the stateless were referred to as '"displaced persons" … for the express purpose of liquidating statelessness once and for all by ignoring its existence' (Arendt [1948] 2004), I contend that the forced displacement framework is necessary to demonstrate that the stateless face similar challenges to those whom we typically associate with forced displacement (such as refugees and the environmentally displaced) and, as such, deserve the attention of policy-makers and scholars alike in their work with/on the forcibly displaced.

Displacement is not a typical lens through which to analyze statelessness or the condition of being a noncitizen everywhere. Instead, other noncitizens, such as refugees, travelers, and different types of migrants, have been the subjects of 'an explosion of work which considers the role of place in the production of outsiders' or people 'who are said to be "out-of-place"' (Cresswell 2004, 103). A recent theoretical and empirically informed work that is an exception in this regard is Redclift's *Statelessness and Citizenship: Camps and the Creation of Political Space* (2013). Through her study of the camp-based displacement of the Biharis of Bangladesh, Redclift exposes the messiness of contemporary membership and how individuals are able to negotiate, and maneuver between, the boundaries of citizenship inclusion and exclusion. '[C]itizenship and "statelessness" are not stable identities of law and fact,' she finds, 'but a shifting assortments [*sic*] of exceptions, rejections, inclusions and denials' (2013, 170).

Prior to Redclift's assertion that 'displacement cannot be reduced to mobility' (2013, 4), Lubkemann (2008) presented such an argument in 'Involuntary Immobility: On a Theoretical Invisibility in Forced Migration Studies.' In this insightful work, which does not focus on stateless populations but on those who have been rendered immobile as a result of government and insurgent practices during wartime, Lubkemann argues for the need to critically examine the assumed relationship between displacement and mobility that permeates forced migration and refugee studies. Examining the case of the 1977–1992 Mozambican civil war, Lubkemann describes how those who were unable to flee the conflict suffered 'a form of displacement in place' (2008, 457) as the war prevented them from using various forms of 'mobility-based' coping strategies (464). Based on his findings, Lubkemann consequently argues for a redefinition of displacement as 'immobilization' generated by the involuntary 'disruption of key life projects' (468 and 471, footnote 8).

Like Lubkemann, I examine how forced displacement can occur without migration and how this form of 'displacement in place' generates various forms of immobilization, especially in the areas of identity formation and the ability to pursue 'key life projects.' Akin to Redclift, I use the lens of displacement, albeit from a different perspective than her, to analyze the under-examined phenomenon of stateless noncitizens. In contradistinction to these authors, however, I do not focus on those who find themselves in situations of protracted camp displacement due to 'war-related' migration (Redclift 2013, 8) or on those who are rendered immobile due to wartime conflict (Lubkemann 2008). Just as Lubkemann argues 'for the usefulness of analytically de-coupling displacement from migration' (455), we must not assume that forced displacement is only generated under crisis conditions and/or by illiberal States. Thus, while the focus within forced migration studies has been upon those who are made to move, whether internally or externally, as a result of ethnic conflict, insurgency, persecution, foreign invasion, and other types of crises (Wood 1994, 612; Troeller 2003, 50),[4] I examine how forced displacement, as defined by Lubkemann, is generated by liberal democracies in nonconflict or noncrisis situations when it comes to the stateless.

Liberal democracies allegedly allow for a person to enjoy rights, freedoms, and protections – allowing for the fulfillment of 'key life projects' – without formally belonging to the State. The argument is that such polities respect the principle of personhood, as opposed to formal citizenship, as a basis for granting rights. In her seminal work on the rights of guest workers, for example, Soysal finds that '[r]ights that used to belong solely to nationals are now extended to foreign populations, thereby undermining the very basis of national citizenship' (1994, 137) and Jacobson similarly finds that 'the distinction between "citizen" and "alien"' has eroded (Jacobson 1996, 8–9 and 39). In a more recent work, Bosniak argues that 'the status of aliens in liberal democratic societies is, in many respects, hardly distinguishable from that of citizens' (2006, 34) as 'a great many of the rights commonly associated with equal citizenship and economic citizenship are not confined to status citizens at all but are available to territorially present persons' in 'most other liberal democratic states' (ibid., 117).[5]

Much of this scholarship is limited by its focus on developed world, liberal democracies, and their provision of rights and protections to noncitizens, however. Very few works have examined the relationship between noncitizenship and access to rights and protections in developing world, liberal democracies. Moreover, none to date has used a forced displacement perspective to investigate how stateless people suffer *in situ* from the disruption of 'key life projects' and how this form of displacement is just as immobilizing as other types of forced displacement that garner the attention of policy-makers and academics alike.

To illustrate how the stateless are rooted yet displaced, and what noncitizenship means in reality for those who are born into liberal democracies that deny or deprive them of citizenship,[6] I conducted 55 semi-structured interviews in the Caribbean from 2009 to 2013. I chose the Caribbean because 'no other region' in the developing world 'has had, for so long, so many liberal democratic polities' (Domínguez 1993, 2)[7] and I focused specifically on The Bahamas and the Dominican Republic because they are the primary destination sites of Haitian migrants in the region (Lanzoni 2013; Marcelino 2013). They have also recently pursued questionable practices that have largely affected persons of Haitian descent on their territories.

In The Bahamas, I conducted 16 anonymous, elite-level interviews in 2009[8] and 21 elite and nonelite interviews in 2012.[9] In the summer of 2012 and the spring of 2013, I conducted fieldwork in the Dominican Republic where I interviewed 11 individuals in the capital, Santo Domingo, and five in the *batey*[10] of El Caño in the province of Monte Plata. Study participants included former or current government officials[11] from The Bahamas, the Dominican Republic, and Haiti, civil servants, United Nations (UN) program officers, community leaders and activists, educators, lawyers, businesspersons, health care professionals, a police and a defense force officer, an amateur film documentarian, and persons at risk of being rendered, or who had been, stateless.[12]

In addition to interviews,[13] I engaged in participant observation in a number of settings[14] and analyzed various primary and secondary sources to understand how individuals should be covered under a given nationality law in theory and how they are covered in practice. I thus examined the nationality, migration laws, and Constitutions of The Bahamas, the Dominican Republic, and Haiti, as well as legal assessments by experts on the latter country. I assessed the status of these countries' treaty ratifications regarding statelessness and the human right to a nationality, pertinent judicial cases, newspaper accounts, and the reports of various NGOs and the UN on the subjects of racial discrimination, statelessness, and nationality. The evidence gathered through my fieldwork and primary and secondary source analyses reveals that The Bahamas and the Dominican Republic are both engaging in practices that paradoxically forcibly displace and immobilize persons of Haitian descent born on their territories.

The liminality position

Liminality refers to the condition of being between statuses (Riggan 2011), 'be these fixed cultural classifications or more formalised legal statuses' (Hynes 2011, 2). While migrants of diverse kinds – such as rejected asylum seekers, the undocumented and refugees – have been the subject of a turn to liminality in migration and citizenship studies,[15] statelessness as a form of liminality has not received as much attention. Even when it does appear (for example, Redclift 2012), it is not in the form of an analysis of how the stateless meet the criteria of being liminals or how they are thrust into this ambiguous and paralyzing space without consent.

Liminality is supposed to be a temporary condition wherein a person becomes separated from his or her former identity and, through a rite of passage, takes on another identity. It is often portrayed as a freeing and creative time (Thomassen 2014, 10). Sometimes the transition from one identity to the next does not go as expected, however, and people become stranded in the liminal stage (Higgot and Nossal 1997, 170). They remain in limbo, as 'entities that are neither here nor there; they are betwixt and between the positions assigned and arranged by law, custom, convention, and ceremonials' (Turner ([1969] 1995), cited in Rumelili 2003, 220).

The stateless have undergone the first stage of the initiation rite, separation. They are separated from formal citizenship in the countries of their birth through practices of citizenship denial or deprivation; yet, they unable to acquire an effective nationality from another State. As such, they remain 'betwixt and between,' in a space of invisibility, impurity, rightlessness, and reflection. That they may wish to take on – or retain – the identity of the political community on whose territory they were born has little or no bearing on their ability to actually transition to this status and identity. The rite of passage is generally thus not an option and they must bear the consequences of being legally and/or socially rejected by both their 'home-State' communities (where they feel they belong due to birth and residence) and their purported State of nationality (in this case, Haiti).

This liminal status often translates into invisibility in diverse spheres. As Beech, interpreting Turner (1984), explains, 'the liminar is socially if not physically invisible. Their ambiguity means that they are outside definition' (2011, 287). Although the previously stateless or at-risk participants interviewed for this study do not describe themselves as invisible, those who were not stateless, but citizens of the Dominican Republic, Haiti or some other third country, do use the term to describe them. A Dominican UN Development Program officer, for example, explains how without a national ID card (cédula), people are 'invisible … They are not subjects of the law. They don't exist as citizens.'[16] While admitting that 'Yes, as human beings [they exist] because they are present,' the officer emphasizes that they 'do not exist in the civil sense of the word.'

Those who are stateless are rendered invisible in other ways as well. Whether due to perceived racial, ethnic or class differences, individuals of Haitian descent are either considered 'an undifferentiated mass' (Craton and Saunders 1998, 455) or labeled 'illegal' persons (Marshall 1979, 54; Fielding et al. 2008, 44). As one interviewee of Haitian descent observes, '[t]hat's where the problem comes, they just say illegal for everyone … because to most people, every Haitian born in The Bahamas is an illegal.'[17] Similar public sentiment courses through Dominican society, which also considers persons of Haitian descent to be an undifferentiated mass and/or illegals.[18] The leitmotif is that 'you are not one of us' and individuality consequently becomes hidden from view.

Even when not rendered invisible, individuals of Haitian descent are often described in derogatory terms or associated with unclean or impure practices.[19] This is a common phenomenon 'when people … are seen as "out-of-place"' or not belonging (Cresswell 2004, 103). During Arendt's time the stateless were described as 'the scum of the earth' (Arendt [1948] 2004, 341), 'outlaw(s)' (360, 363) and 'barbarians' (384). In the Caribbean context, they are often associated with unclean animals such as pigs, hogs, and dogs. For instance, Dominican anthropologist Tahira Vargas comments on how Dominicans often say that 'all Haitians are dogs'[20] and one of the two local politicians I interviewed in Abaco, Bahamas, consistently compares the people living in Haitian settlements on that island to hogs. When describing the living conditions of those of Haitian descent, the person says that 'only hogs can live like that.'[21] When discussing crime in the settlements and how 'locals' (that is, those accepted as 'Bahamians') attempt to get a 'Haitian Bahamian' informant from within the communities to identify any illegal activity, the interviewee says that 'the Bahamian-Haitian will say yes, but he never does [act as an informant] because *they don't squeal on their own breed*.'

Associations with impurity are also present when the Bahamian-born persons of Haitian descent are associated with criminal activity due to their 'betwixt and between' status. As one Abaconian official asserts, 'The Haitian Bahamians is the ones that's breaking in and stealing. They're the worst. The Haitian-Haitians aren't half as bad as the Haitian Bahamians.'[22] The interviewee attributes the alleged criminal nature of Bahamian-born persons of Haitian descent to the fact that '[t]hey don't know where they belong … They're not accepted by the Haitians and they're not accepted by the Bahamians.' The other Abaconian official affirms that '[a]ny time you find these fellas getting out of hand and they're doing the serious, serious cruel acts, check it close–some kind of Haitian blood mix.'[23] That they are neither Bahamian nor Haitian – 'neither fish nor fowl'[24] – but some 'impure' mixture of the two, results in their criminal inclinations in these interviewees' eyes.

During the 'impurity' stage of liminality, death is also an ever-present possibility as the liminal 'may be ritually buried/lie motionless/stained black/covered in blood' (Beech 2011, 287). The 'link to death' reveals itself primarily in the act of civicide in both cases. The practice of 'kill[ing] the juridical personality' of an individual (Arendt [1948] 2004, 577) through citizenship denial and deprivation is both a legal and 'sociological but no less real' means of 'kill[ing] in human community' (Odinkalu 2009, n. pag.). As the Inter-American Court of Human Rights (IACHR) asserts,

> The right to the recognition of juridical personality implies the capacity to be the holder of rights (capacity and exercise) and obligations; the violation of this recognition presumes an absolute disavowal of the possibility of being a holder of such rights and obligations. (2005, 66)

A stateless individual, the Court continues, 'ex definitione, does not have recognized juridical personality, because he has not established a juridical and political connection with any State' (ibid., 66–67). Lacking this connection, stateless people are unable to lawfully acquire property, obtain loans, credit, enter into contracts or sue, among other acts. Key life projects are disrupted as a result.

Although I elsewhere expand upon the rightlessness generated by this liminal condition (Belton 2013, 2014, forthcoming), it is important to point out here that citizenship is both an intrinsic and an instrumental human right. Its nonfulfillment leaves almost every other right in the Universal Declaration of Human Rights and international human rights treaties susceptible to violation. As individuals who occupy a liminal space, the stateless encounter difficulties in accessing many of the rights, freedoms, and protections that citizens take for granted. Specifically, I found that those who are stateless, or at risk of statelessness, in The Bahamas and the Dominican Republic face obstacles in the areas of education, employment, freedom of movement, family unity, access to health care, and justice (Belton 2014). Moreover, unlike other types of noncitizens who possess a juridical personality, the stateless lack a 'country of origin' to which they can be returned. Indefinite detention is thus a real possibility. Unlike immigrant noncitizens, the stateless are not necessarily considered 'lawful' residents by the States within which they reside either, exacerbating their precarious status and further immobilizing them *in situ*.

The immobilization they feel as a result of their forced displacement is revealed in comments such as: 'growing up there are many opportunities that came my way, but because I didn't have a passport, it kind of like *hindered me*' (Louis); 'There's a lot of talented kids out there who *could have been achieving so much more*' (Dumercy); 'They want opportunities, but it gets to the point where *they are stagnated* from these opportunities' (Mark Desmangles)[25]; 'They *cannot advance* … they are *faced with this roadblock*' (former Attorney General Alfred Sears).[26] Interviewees in Civolani Hischnjakow's study (2011) also remark on how their limbo-like status prevents them from taking the Dominican national exam, continuing their post-secondary studies, taking part in overseas athletic opportunities or obtaining secure employment, all of which greatly affects their future prospects and displaces them 'in place.'

Lack of citizenship from the countries of their birth not only immobilizes the stateless in terms of life opportunities and rights enjoyment, but it also leaves them without a psychological home, even though they remain physically rooted in the countries of their birth. As persons stuck in a state of liminality, stateless interviewees, or those who had been at risk of statelessness, readily reflect upon what their 'betwixt and between' status means for them in terms of their place identity (where they belong).

It was commonplace for Dominican interviewees who were or who had been at risk of statelessness to evince a sense of Dominican identity. The individuals interviewed in El Caño felt Dominican despite facing problems in obtaining their cédula or in registering their children as Dominican.[27] The participants in Civolani Hischnjakow's study also '[a]ll felt very Dominican despite the discrimination they had received' (2011, 45), but readily admit that they become 'confused about what their nationality is and where they belong' (24). They add that their noncitizen status affects them to the point where 'your personality changes. If you're not from here or there, where are you from?' (ibid.). One declares that '[w]e don't know where we belong' (25), while a second explains that without recognition as a Dominican citizen, it is as if 'I were a stranger, but in my own country or in my own nation … it's like I am physically here, but when it comes to the laws it's as if I don't exist' (26).

In contrast, Bahamian-born interviewees of Haitian descent were under no illusion that they were Bahamian, but they did not necessarily consider themselves Haitian either. They describe how they did not have Haitian nationality or identity documents growing up. '[F]rankly, I didn't even want one,' Dumercy admits. 'I'm like why should I have to get a Haitian passport when I was born here?' Others comment on the strangeness of renouncing a nationality (Haitian) that they never felt they had as part of the Bahamian citizenship application process at 18. 'That was always something that I questioned,' says Louis. 'Why? Because I am denouncing a nationality that genetically I have. However, according to [the] State, I am not a Haitian.' When I ask why he thought he was not considered a Haitian by Haiti, he responds, 'I did not have a Haitian passport. I was not born in Haiti.' Bernard Petit-Homme concurs, 'I felt like I wasn't really a Haitian citizen because I never saw the place and I didn't really feel a direct connection to Haiti other than through my parents and speaking some of the language and some of my associations.'

Due to their lack of identification with Haiti, Bahamian-born study participants typically refer to themselves as 'Haitian Bahamian.' Dumercy, for example, explains how growing up there were two soccer teams in her neighborhood. One 'was a "real" Haitian team,' while the other was made up of 'Haitian Bahamians.' 'I'd side with the Haitian Bahamians as a spectator compared to the real Haitians,' she says, 'because I'm Haitian Bahamian.' Despite her self-identification as 'Haitian Bahamian,' Dumercy reveals that she feels 'conflicted' over where she belongs. She feels rejected by both the Haitian and Bahamian communities. 'I don't feel like, you know, if they had to pick between me and them, they'd pick me. They would always pick themselves.' She continues, 'The Bahamas don't want to claim you and Haiti don't either … So we are on our own basically. We're in limbo.'

Harry Dolce, a Bahamian police officer of Haitian descent, agrees, 'You have one group of people saying, "You are this" and the other person saying that you are not. It's like you are stuck in between … You're saying I am Haitian, but if I go to Haiti they say that I am not Haitian. I am Bahamian.'[28] Even Haitian President Michel Martelly admits these Bahamian-born persons are in a liminal state. In a revelatory comment made during his 2012 Bahamas country visit, President Martelly stated that 'until they're 18 [persons born in The Bahamas of Haitian descent] *don't belong to anywhere*' (Rolle 2012; italics added). Dumercy concurs, 'They don't make us feel like we belong here [in The Bahamas]. *You shouldn't be stateless in the place [where] you were born and where you feel like you're not included or not wanted.*' When these individuals are removed from their enforced liminality, however, it is only to be forcibly emplaced within the classification of Haitian national by the country of their birth.

The imposed nationality position

Until quite recently, individuals born of Haitian descent in The Bahamas and the Dominican Republic were allowed to languish in their limbo-like status. Physically present, they were in practice neither nationals of the country of their birth nor of their parents' country of birth. Over the past few years, however, both The Bahamas and the Dominican Republic have engaged in practices that force these individuals to seek proof of their purported 'Haitian' nationality, whether such persons consider themselves Haitians or not and whether such persons should be recognized as, or have the option by law to register as, citizens.

In the case of The Bahamas, neither its Constitution nor any of its Acts dealing with nationality[29] specifically targets Haitian migrants or their descendants when it comes Bahamian citizenship acquisition. A child born in The Bahamas may only become a citizen if one of his or her parents is a Bahamian citizen (Government of The Bahamas 1973a, Article 6). Those persons born in the country who do not have a Bahamian citizen parent are permitted to apply for Bahamian citizenship via registration within 12 months of turning 18 (Article 7), but there is no guarantee that the person will obtain Bahamian citizenship. As a former Free National Movement official makes clear, 'it's not an automatic entitlement.'[30] Statelessness may therefore result if the child does not possess another nationality in practice.

Beside protection gaps in Bahamian law,[31] children born of noncitizens in the country are at risk of statelessness due to bureaucratic inefficiencies, obscure citizenship decision-making rules and practices, and the politicized nature of citizenship bestowal.[32] Recent changes in Bahamian immigration policy have only exacerbated the situation. As of 1st November 2014, the Department of Immigration (DoI) put into effect a new policy, which '*forces them* [noncitizens born on Bahamian soil] to apply for a passport from their parents' country of origin' (Robles 2015; italics added).

As part of this new policy, Certificates of Identity, which used to be issued to children born of noncitizen parents in The Bahamas, 'enabling the holder to remain in The Bahamas, and re-enter The Bahamas during the processing of the application for registration as a citizen,'[33] are no longer being issued (Mitchell 2014). Moreover, whereas it used to be that '[t]he last Certificate of Identity will be issued on the eighteenth birthday and is valid for five years,' carrying the Bahamian-born noncitizen child through to the age of 23, Dumercy explains that the Bahamian Government is refusing to renew these certificates for those who have not gone to the Haitian Embassy to acquire Haitian identity documents. '[W]hat they're making the kids do,' she says, is 'go and apply to the Haitian Embassy in Nassau … in order to get a valid ID.'

Requiring noncitizen children to obtain proof of another nationality is no easy feat for the offspring of many Haitian migrants. The Haitian Embassy in Nassau cannot provide Haitian citizenship to those who are unable to provide proof of their parent's Haitian nationality or who cannot produce two witnesses to attest to the citizenship of the child's parents. Ambassador Antonio Rodrigue describes how many parents 'cannot get a birth certificate [from Haiti]' and that this is 'the big, big, big problem' when it comes to obtaining Haitian citizenship for their Bahamian-born children. 'If you come to the consular section and ask me for a passport,' he says, 'if you cannot prove [to] me beyond any doubt that you [are] Haitian, I'm not going to give you the passport,[34] Thus despite the DoI's best efforts at forcing these Bahamian-born persons to acquire Haitian nationality documents by refusing to issue further Certificates of Identity, circumstances on the ground in Haiti,[35] combined with some parents' inability to return to Haiti for proof of their own citizenship, leaves many susceptible to statelessness.

Nationality imposition on those deemed 'noncitizen' is also apparent in the Dominican case. The Dominican Republic has engaged in various exclusionary membership practices toward individuals of Haitian descent for several years and faced international condemnation for doing so. From the denial of birth certificates to children born of Haitian descent, the illegitimate sale of their identity documents to others, the issuance of various resolutions that place people in membership limbo, the insertion of Dominicans of Haitian descent into a 'foreigners' book,' and a reinterpretation of the 'in-transit' clause of the Dominican Constitution, all such acts have adversely impacted persons of Haitian descent born on Dominican territory.[36]

It was not until the Dominican Constitutional Court issued Sentence TC/0168/13 (Government of the Dominican Republic 2013a) in 2013, however, that the denationalization of tens, if not hundreds, of thousands of Dominicans of Haitian descent found judicial sanction. In this Sentence, the Court heard the case of Juliana Deguis Pierre who claimed that when she had tried to obtain her cédula at her local civil registry office, they took away her birth certificate and told her that she could not have a cédula because she was not Dominican. The Court stated that Deguis' Haitian parents were 'in transit' (nonresident) at the time of her birth and she did not, therefore, satisfy the requirements for Dominican *jus soli* citizenship acquisition (ibid., 29–30).[37]

Deguis, however, was born in the Dominican Republic in 1984, well before the creation of Ley 285-04[38] and the 2010 Constitutional amendment retroactively made her parents 'illegals.' Deguis' parents used their fichas (a work permit generally issued by the owners of sugarcane estates to temporary foreign sugarcane workers) to register her birth. Despite the fact that fichas were used to register the births of Haitian workers' Dominican-born children in past decades, the President of the Junta Central Electoral (JCE),[39] Roberto Rosario, states that children born to foreigners who registered them with fichas or 'other documents not permitted or authorized by law' are 'irregularly' registered as Dominicans (Government of the Dominican Republic 2013b, 7; author's translation). The Constitutional Court agreed with this position and found that Deguis' parents lacked the requisite ID to be able to declare her birth as a Dominican (Government of the Dominican Republic 2013a, 36). The Court thus ruled that civil registry officers were not acting unconstitutionally when they refused to issue citizenship and identity documents to persons whose parents' residency status was unclear or illegal when they were born in the country.

The Court's decision, and its order that the JCE create special birth registration books that extend the reach of contemporary law as far back as 1929 (to determine whether or not a Dominican was 'irregularly' registered based on the documentation used by their parents or grandparents) directly contravenes international doctrine. Both the Convention on the Rights of the Child,[40] which the Dominican Republic ratified in 1991, and the IACHR's 2005 judgment against the Dominican Republic, state that the migratory status of one's parents has no bearing upon a child's migratory status. Moreover, not only was Deguis denied Dominican citizenship, but the Court also opined that she had the right to Haitian nationality and had not, therefore, been rendered stateless (Government of the Dominican Republic 2013a, 75). Importantly, in her dissenting opinion to Sentence TC/0168/13, Justice Katia Jiménez Martínez argued that the verdict issued in the Deguis case was one 'not only [of] denationalization, but [of] *being forced to be Haitian*' (Government of the Dominican Republic 2013a, 140; italics added).

The Dominican Government had found a means by which to forcibly displace those who once held – or by law in operation at the time should have held – Dominican citizenship into having to acquire another nationality or else become liminal subjects. Thus, while some find that migrants and their host State-born children 'are defined in essentialist terms as representatives of their heritage countries' and 'are symbolically returned to their native lands' in the process (Hanauer 2011, 203), the practices of both the Bahamian and Dominican Governments reveal that the displacement of the Bahamian- and Dominican-born offspring of Haitian migrants is much more than symbolic. They are effectively 'returned' to a 'native land' they have never seen (Haiti) even though they remain physically rooted in the countries of their birth.

Conclusion

This article demonstrates that noncitizenship, in its extreme form of statelessness, is a form of forced displacement that can be generated under noncrisis or nonconflict situations. The stateless are either forced to be liminal subjects – detached from any national home – or are made to take on a nationality with which they do not identify when the State of their birth can no longer tolerate their ambiguous status. Although they are not literally defined by forced movement, their particular form of displacement has repercussions that can be just as severe as those faced by forced migrants. Lacking a recognized juridical existence, being socially excluded, confronting diverse human rights violations and being denied or deprived of a 'national' home are all significant barriers to the stateless' ability to fulfill 'key life projects' and be self-determining agents. The main difference is that the stateless are forcibly displaced *in situ*.

Unlike other types of noncitizens, the stateless do not come from elsewhere. They do not know any other 'place' than the one into which they were born. Yet, they are prevented from belonging by practices of citizenship denial and deprivation in the countries of their birth. Their lack of a national home affects their 'expectations for the future' (Weil (1955) cited in Relph (1976), 38) and psychosocially displaces them, even as they remain physically rooted in the countries of their birth. They consequently lack 'a secure point from which to look out on the world, a firm grasp of [their] position in the order of things' (Relph 1976, 38).

This affects their sense of identity and belonging in very concrete ways, demonstrating how the realm of statelessness is more than one where the law ceases to operate or where rights are difficult to achieve. It is one, as Arendt recognized, in which one's place in the world becomes ambiguous, or even outright negated. At the most fundamental level then, the article demonstrates that the great 'calamity' that befalls these noncitizens is not that they lack the 'right to belong to *some kind* of organized community' (Arendt [1948] 2004, 377; italics added), but that they lack the right to choose to belong to the *specific* communities within which they were born and raised.

Notes

1. Personal interview, Nassau, November 5, 2012. All quotations attributed to Louis throughout the rest of the article are from this interview.
2. Personal interview, Nassau, November 1, 2012.
3. Personal interview, Nassau, November 1, 2012.
4. See also Forced Migration Review's issue on 'Crisis' (2014) and Forced Migration Online's digital resources, especially their three-pronged understanding of forced displacement (2015). A plethora of scholarship also exists on the forced movement of the internally displaced and refugees as a result of crises or conflicts.
5. See also Brubaker (1989, 146 and 155).
6. Although this article is a comparative case study, the arguments made here are not unique to the cases at hand. Other liberal democracies (in noncrisis situations), such as Canada and the United Kingdom, generate stateless populations that face similar experiences of displacement *in situ*.
7. Freedom House, which scores States according to their practices in the areas of civil liberties and political rights, classifies all the countries in the Caribbean – with the exception of Cuba and Haiti – as 'free' (2013). The Bahamas earns the highest freedom scores possible (1 out of 7) in both civil liberties and political rights, while the Dominican Republic scores slightly lower, earning a score of 2 (out of 7) in each category.
8. Interviews were carried out under IRB Protocol I109-130. Interviews lasted an average of 51 min. No pseudonyms are used for the interviews conducted under this protocol, which took place under the condition of anonymity. Fourteen of these interviews were held in Nassau and two were conducted via telephone.
9. Interviews were carried out under IRB Protocol I111–261, which allowed me to interview 'Special Populations.' Interviews lasted an average of 57 min. Only one pseudonym is used from this study – 'Marie St. Cecile' – because, as a formerly stateless person, she did not want her real name to be used.
10. A *batey* is the traditional name for a settlement where sugarcane workers resided during the heyday of the sugarcane industry in the Dominican Republic, from the 1930s to the 1980s. Today, these settlements are primarily shanty towns where many Dominicans of Haitian descent live.
11. An official from the Ministry of Foreign Affairs provided the Ministry's position via email.

12. I performed purposeful and snowball sampling for both case studies (see Belton 2014 for an elaboration of my methodology).
13. Additional interviews were conducted in New York City with two other program officers of OSJI – Sebastian Kohn and Indira Goris – on February 7, 2012 and February 22, 2012, respectively.
14. Also note, as a Bahamian, I have spent many hours in The Bahamas informally chatting with 'citizens' and 'noncitizens' at supermarkets, retail stores, religious venues, and their homes about Bahamian membership practices, statelessness, Haitian migrants, and discrimination.
15. See, for instance, Marcelino and Farahi (2011), Menjívar (2006), Hynes (2011), Menjívar and Bibler Coutin (2014), Riggan (2011) and Torres and Wicks-Asbun (2014).
16. Personal interview, Santo Domingo, July 13, 2012.
17. Personal interview, Nassau, July 29, 2009.
18. See Wooding and Moseley-Williams (2004, 33–34), Martínez in IACHR (2005) and Aber and Small (2013, 81).
19. Kristeva's work (1980) focuses on the impurity that results from abjection in the spheres of literature, psychology, and religion.
20. Vargas was one of the presenters at the 'Simposio sobre Derecho a la Nacionalidad' in Santo Domingo where I also presented.
21. Personal interview, Marsh Harbour (MH), Abaco, November 12, 2012.
22. Personal interview, MH, Abaco, November 12, 2012.
23. Personal interview, MH, Abaco, November 14, 2012.
24. Personal interview, Nassau, August 4, 2009.
25. Personal interview, Nassau, October 30, 2012.
26. Personal interview, Nassau, 8 November 2012.
27. Interviews took place in El Caño on February 7, 2013.
28. Personal interview, Nassau, October 29, 2012.
29. For example, Chapter 190/Bahamas Nationality Act (Government of The Bahamas 1973b) and Chapter 191/Immigration Act (Government of The Bahamas 1967).
30. Personal interview, Nassau, July 27, 2009. The Free National Movement is one of the two major political parties in The Bahamas.
31. Such 'gaps' affect all children born of noncitizens, as well as children born overseas to Bahamian women married to foreigners.
32. Details of each of these processes are found in chapter 3 of 'Precarious Belonging: Stateless People in a "Postnational" World' (Belton 2014).
33. Email correspondence, Ministry of Foreign Affairs, April 15, 2013.
34. Personal interview, Nassau, July 28, 2009.
35. For example, most civil registries are located in urban settings that are often difficult to access by the largely rural population. Additionally, many civil registries were destroyed during the 2010 earthquake.
36. See chapter four of Belton (2014) for an elaboration of these practices.
37. All quotes from Sentence TC/0168/13 are my own translations.
38. Whereas a person was considered 'in transit' if s/he were in the Dominican Republic 10 days or less (Government of the Dominican Republic 2013a, 118), Ley 285-04 (Government of the Dominican Republic 2004) reinterpreted the 'in-transit' clause to equate it with not being legally present in the country (Government of the Dominican Republic 2013a, 62–3).
39. The JCE is the Central Electoral Board. It is the body mandated with setting elections and issuing Dominican identity documents.
40. Article 2 of the CRC states that 'States Parties shall take all appropriate measures to ensure that the child is protected against all forms of discrimination or punishment on the basis of the status, activities, expressed opinions, or beliefs of the child's parents, legal guardians, or family members' (UN 1989).

Disclosure statement

No potential conflict of interest was reported by the author.

References

Aber, Shaina, and Mary Small. 2013. "Citizen or Subordinate: Permutations of Belonging in the United States and the Dominican Republic." *Journal on Migration and Human Security* 1 (3): 76–96.

Arendt, Hannah. (1948) 2004. *The Origins of Totalitarianism*. New York: Schocken Books.

Beech, Nic. 2011. "Liminality and the Practices of Identity Reconstruction." *Human Relations* 64 (2): 285–302.

Belton, Kristy A. 2011. "The Neglected Non-Citizen: Statelessness and Liberal Political Theory." *Journal of Global Ethics* 7 (1): 57–69.

Belton, Kristy A. 2013. "Statelessness and Economic and Social Rights." In *The State of Economic and Social Rights: A Global Overview*, edited by Lanse Minkler, 221–248. Cambridge: Cambridge University Press.

Belton, Kristy A. 2014. "Precarious Belonging: Stateless People in a 'Postnational' World." *Doctoral Dissertations*. Paper 465. University of Connectict. Accessed March 17, 2015. http://digitalcommons.uconn.edu/dissertations/465

Belton, Kristy A. 2015. "The Legal Status of Statelessness: An Overview." In *The Human Right to Citizenship: A Slippery Concept*, edited by Rhoda Howard-Hassmann and Margaret Walton-Roberts. Philadelphia, PA: University of Pennsylvania Press. 31–42.

Bosniak, Linda. 2006. *The Citizen and the Alien: Dilemmas of Contemporary Membership*. Princeton, NJ: Princeton University Press.

Brubaker, William Rogers. 1989. "Membership without Citizenship: The Economic and Social Rights of Noncitizens." In *Immigration and the Politics of Citizenship in Europe and North America*, edited by William Rogers Brubaker, 145–162. Lanham, MD: University Press of America.

Civolani Hischnjakow, Katerina. 2011. *Vidas suspendidas: Efectos de la Resolución 012-07 en la población dominicana de ascendencia haitiana [Suspended Lives: The effects of Resolution 012-07 on the Dominican population of Haitian descent]*. Santo Domingo: Centro Bonó.

Craton, Michael, and Gail Saunders. 1998. *Islanders in the Stream: A History of the Bahamian People*. 2 vols. Athens: The University of Georgia Press.

Cresswell, Tim. 2004. *Place: A Short Introduction*. Malden, MA: Blackwell.

Cuba, Lee, and David M. Hummons. 1993. "A Place to Call Home: Identification with Dwelling Community and Region." *The Sociological Quarterly* 34 (1): 111–131.

Domínguez, Jorge I. 1993. "The Caribbean Question: Why Has Liberal Democracy (Surprisingly) Flourished?" In *Democracy in the Caribbean: Political, Economic, and Social Perspectives*, edited by Jorge I. Domínguez, Robert A. Pastor and R. DeLisle Worrell, 1–25. Baltimore, MD: The Johns Hopkins University Press.

Fielding, William, Virginia Ballance, Carol Scriven, Thaddeus McDonald, and Pandora Johnson. 2008. "The Stigma of Being 'Haitian' in the Bahamas." *The College of the Bahamas Research Journal* 14: 38–50.

Forced Migration Online. 2015. "What is Forced Migration?" Accessed June 5, 2015. http://www.forcedmigration.org/about/whatisfm/

Forced Migration Review. 2014. "Crisis." Accessed June 5, 2015. http://www.fmreview.org/crisis/contents

Freedom House. 2013. "Freedom in the World 2013: Democratic Breakthroughs in the Balance." Accessed May 27. http://www.freedomhouse.org/sites/default/files/FIW%202013%20Booklet%20-%20for%20Web_1.pdf

Government of The Bahamas. 1967. "Immigration Act." Accessed March 17, 2015. http://laws.bahamas.gov.bs/cms3/images/LEGISLATION/PRINCIPAL/1967/1967-0025/ImmigrationAct_1.pdf

Government of The Bahamas. 1973a. "The Constitution of the Commonwealth of the Bahamas." Accessed March 17, 2015. http://www.lexbahamas.com/bahconcontents.htm

Government of The Bahamas. 1973b. "Bahamas Nationality." Accessed March 17, 2015. http://laws.bahamas.gov.bs/cms36/images/LEGISLATION/PRINCIPAL/1973/1973-0018/BahamasNationalityAct_1.pdf

Government of the Dominican Republic. 2004. "Ley General de Migración No. 285-04." Accessed March 17, 2015. http://www.mip.gob.do/Portals/0/docs/Marco_Legal_Transparencia/2013Actualizacion/Ley%20No.285-04%20Migración.pdf

Government of the Dominican Republic. 2013a. "Sentencia TC/0168/13 [Sentence TC/0168/13]." Accessed March 17, 2015. http://tribunalconstitucional.gob.do/sites/default/files/documentos/Sentencia%20TC%200168-13%20-%20C.pdf
Government of the Dominican Republic. 2013b. "Junta Central Electoral. 'Entrevista: Roberto Rosario' [Central Electoral Board. 'Interview: Roberto Rosario']." *El Demócrata*. No. 32. Accessed March 17, 2015. http://issuu.com/publicacionesjce/docs/el_democrata_32.
Hanauer, David Ian. 2011. "Non-Place Identity: Britain's Response to Migration in the Age of Supermodernity." In *Identity, Belonging and Migration*, edited by Gerard Delanty, Paul Jones and Ruth Wodak, 198–217. Liverpool: Liverpool University Press.
Higgot, Richard A, and Kim Richard Nossal. 1997. "The International Politics of Liminality: Relocating Australia in the Asia Pacific." *Australian Journal of Political Science* 32 (2): 169–186.
Hynes, Patricia. 2011. *The Dispersal and Social Exclusion of Asylum Seekers: Between Liminality and Belonging*. Bristol: Policy Press.
IACHR (Inter-American Court of Human Rights) 2005. *Case of Yean and Bosico V. the Dominican Republic*. Accessed March 17, 2015. http://www.corteidh.or.cr/docs/casos/articulos/seriec_130_%20ing.pdf
Jacobson, David. 1996. *Rights across Borders: Immigration and the Decline of Citizenship*. Baltimore, MD: The Johns Hopkins University Press.
Kristeva, Julia. 1980. *Powers of Horror: An Essay on Abjection*. Translated by Leon S. Roudiez. New York: Columbia University Press.
Lanzoni, Ilaria. 2013. "Haitian Migrants, Desperate for Survival, Find Death on High Seas." *International Organization for Migration*. Accessed March 17, 2015. https://www.iom.int/cms/en/sites/iom/home/news-and-views/press-briefing-notes/pbn-2013/pbn-listing/haitian-migrants-desperate-for-s.html
Lubkemann, Stephen C. 2008. "Involuntary Immobility: On a Theoretical Invisibility in Forced Migration Studies." *Journal of Refugee Studies* 21 (4): 454–475.
Marcelino, Pedro F, ed. 2013. "Si Proches et Si Lointaines: Les diasporas haitiennes aux Caribe [So Close and Yet so Far: The Haitian Diaspora in the Caribbean]." Accessed May 28, 2015. http://www.acpmigration-obs.org/sites/default/files/Haiti%20Diasporas%20Research%20Rep.pdf
Marcelino, Pedro F, and Hermon Farahi. 2011. "Transitional African Spaces in Comparative Analysis: Inclusion, Exclusion and Informality in Morocco and Cape Verde." *Third World Quarterly* 32 (5): 883–904.
Marshall, Dawn. 1979. *'The Haitian Problem': Illegal Migration to the Bahamas*. Mona: Institute of Social and Economic Research, University of the West Indies.
Menjívar, Cecilia. 2006. "Liminal Legality: Salvadoran and Guatemalan Immigrants' Lives in the United States." *American Journal of Sociology* 111 (4): 999–1037.
Menjívar, Cecilia, and Susan Bibler Coutin. 2014. "Challenges of Recognition, Participation, and Representation for the Legally Liminal: A Comment." In *Migration, Gender and Social Justice: Perspectives on Human Insecurity*, edited by Thanh-Dam Truong, Des Gasper, Jeff Handmaker and Sylvia L. Bergh, 325–330. Berlin: Springer.
Mitchell, Fred. 2014. "Minister Mitchell on Bahamas Immigration Regulatory Changes." *The Bahamas Weekly*, October 25. Accessed March 10, 2015. http://www.thebahamasweekly.com/publish/bis-news-updates/Fred_Mitchell_on_Bahamas_Immigration_Regulatory_Changes37798.shtml
Odinkalu, Chidi Anselm. 2009. "Nigeria: The Right to a Passport." *This Day*. Accessed March 17, 2015. http://allafrica.com/stories/200910200930.html
Redclift, Victoria. 2012. "Ilimitable Liminality or the Return to Structure? Locating Displacement in Bangladesh." In *Robert Kennedy, Margaret Greenfields and Jonathan Rollins*, edited by Diasporic Identities and Spaces Between, 33–66. Oxford: Inter-Disciplinary Press.
Redclift, Victoria. 2013. *Statelessness and Citizenship: Camps and the Creation of Political Space*. London: Routledge.
Relph, Edward. 1976. *Place and Placelessness*. London: Pion Limited.
Riggan, Jennifer. 2011. "In between Nations: Ethiopian-Born Eritreans, Liminality, and War." *PoLAR: Political and Legal Anthropology Review* 34 (1): 131–154.

Robles, Frances. 2015. "Immigration Rules in Bahamas Sweep up Haitians." *New York times*, January 30. Accessed February 1, 2015. http://nyti.ms/1vijdjA
Rolle, Krystel. 2012. "Ingraham: Haitian Leader 'Mistaken'." February 13. Accessed March 17, 2015. http://www.thenassauguardian.com/index.php?option=com_content&view=article&id=24004&Itemid=27
Rumelili, Bahar. 2003. "Liminality and Perpetuation of Conflicts: Turkish-Greek Relations in the Context of Community-Building by the EU." *European Journal of International Relations* 9 (2): 213–248.
Soysal, Yasemin Nuhoglu. 1994. *Limits of Citizenship: Migrants and Postnational Membership in Europe*. Chicago: University of Chicago.
Thomassen, BjØrn. 2014. *Liminality and the Modern: Living through the in-between*. Surrey: Ashgate.
Torres, Rebecca Maria, and Melissa Wicks-Asbun. 2014. "Undocumented Students' Narratives of Liminal Citizenship: High Aspirations, Exclusion, and 'in-Between' Identities." *The Professional Geographer* 66 (2): 195–204.
Troeller, Gary. 2003. "Refugees and Human Displacement in Contemporary International Relations: Reconciling State and Individual Sovereignty." In *Refugees and Forced Displacement: International Security, Human Vulnerability, and the State*, edited by Edward Newman and Joanne van Selm, 50–65. Tokyo: United Nations University Press.
Turner, Victor W. (1969) 1995. *The Ritual Process: Structure and Anti-Structure*. New York: Aldine De Gruyter.
Turner, Victor W. 1984. "Liminality and Performance Genres." In *Rite, Drama, Festival, Spectacle: Rehearsals toward a Theory of Performance*, edited by John J MacAloon, 19–41. Philadelphia, PA: Institute for the Study of Human Issues.
United Nations. 1954. "Convention Relating to the Status of Stateless Persons." Accessed May 28, 2015. http://www.unhcr.org/3bbb25729.html
United Nations. 1989. "Convention on the Rights of the Child." Accessed March 17, 2015. http://www.ohchr.org/en/professionalinterest/pages/crc.aspx
Wood, William B. 1994. "Forced Migration: Local Conflicts and International Dilemmas." *Annals of the Association of American Geographers* 84 (4): 607–634.
Wooding, Bridget, and Richard Moseley-Williams. 2004. *Needed but Unwanted: Haitian Immigrants and Their Descendants in the Dominican Republic*. London: Catholic Institute for International Relations.

Citizenship and inclusion: rethinking the analytical category of noncitizenship

Paulina Tambakaki

Department of Politics and International Relations, Centre for the Study of Democracy, University of Westminster, London, UK

ABSTRACT

The paper problematises the category of noncitizenship. It traces its trajectory in accounts of inclusive citizenship and argues that it is difficult to theorise it as a distinct theoretical category outside of citizenship. To support this argument, the paper distinguishes between a pluralist, political and democratic variant of accounts of inclusive citizenship and it shows how they all end up reducing noncitizenship to a journey to citizenship. To overcome this limit, the paper develops the idea of subversive politicisation and suggests that injustices and inequalities can be challenged without falling back on the vocabulary of citizenship.

Introduction

In the 'Decline of the Nation State and the End of the Rights of Man', a short chapter in *The Origins of Totalitarianism*, Hannah Arendt famously (and ambiguously) defined citizenship as the 'right to have rights' (Arendt 1968, 296). Writing in the aftermath of the Holocaust and in the wake of the emergence of statelessness as a mass phenomenon, it was clear to Arendt that 'the loss of citizenship deprived people not only of protection, but also of all clearly established, officially recognised identity' (1968, 287). Does Arendt's emphasis on the primacy of citizenship still resonate today? The answer one gives to this question bears strongly on discussions of noncitizenship. Seeking to contribute to such discussions, this special issue on *Theorising Noncitizenship* exploits the ambivalence of the prefix *non* and enquires into the primacy of citizenship. In so doing, it carves out a space for noncitizenship as a distinct analytical category and invites contributors to reflect on its nature. The paper responds to this invitation. It problematises the distinctiveness of noncitizenship as an analytical category and explores its relationship with citizenship.

For the purposes of this paper, noncitizenship is taken to denote the condition of being where access to basic political rights is precarious and insecure. Noncitizenship is not the same as bare humanity, by which I mean a state of existence stripped of all rights and dependent on international human rights law (see Agamben 1998). Although the conditions of existence that define the life of the noncitizen can be likened to conditions of bare humanity, the way I use the concept here steers away from such comparisons. This is because the underlying objective of the paper is to draw out and explore the political dimension of noncitizenship – the extent to which noncitizenship, as an umbrella term, successfully captures *and* challenges the exclusions, inequalities, injustices and naturalisations that accompany citizenship politics. Does noncitizenship transgress the relationship with citizenship, in line with the intentions of the special issue, or does it end up reproducing the relationship with citizenship that it seeks to overcome?

To address this question, the paper traces the trajectory of the concept of noncitizenship in accounts of inclusive citizenship and shows its floating nature. In particular, the paper distinguishes between a pluralist, political and democratic variant of accounts of inclusive citizenship and highlights the shifts and turnings in the meaning of noncitizenship within such accounts. The paper argues that although all variants seek to interrogate and blur the binary citizen/noncitizen, they end up reinstating it. On the assumption that citizenship is the most valuable practice, the benchmark for evaluating – acknowledging and noticing – the demands raised by a variety of groups, the three variants, cancel out noncitizenship as an analytical category. Noncitizenship becomes reduced to a journey to citizenship and, as such, it loses meaning and force. What are the implications of this loss? Although the paper suggests that it is possible to challenge exclusions, inequalities and injustices without references to noncitizenship, it does not altogether dismiss noncitizenship as a concept. Instead, the paper develops a comparison with the concept of politicisation and suggests that the first step in consolidating the analytical force of noncitizenship lies in the attenuation of the relationship with citizenship.

This argument develops in two sections. The first section starts with the examination of the concept of noncitizenship within accounts of inclusive citizenship, giving an idea of their limitations. The second section explores these limitations further through the comparison with the concept of politicisation.

Citizenship, inclusion and noncitizenship

The category of noncitizenship confronts the theorists with a challenge. While it is apparent who the noncitizen is – anyone who does not have access to the formal rights of citizenship – the prefix *non*, that simultaneously affirms and negates citizenship, bears the marks of a challenge. How do we determine the usage of the term? That is, how do we interpret and theorise it, as an affirmation or as a negation of citizenship, or both? Seeking to offer an answer to these questions, the section explores the category of noncitizenship through the lens of accounts of inclusive citizenship. By accounts of inclusive citizenship, I mean the growing body of work that highlights and challenges the exclusions that accompany citizenship politics, with the aim of extending – redescribing and opening up – the practices that are considered to be citizenic (Andersen and Siim 2004; Gaventa and Tandon 2010; Kabeer 2005; Lister 2007; Marin 2010, Soysal 1994). While accounts of inclusive citizenship come in many forms, in this section, I distinguish and focus on the three variants that I term pluralist, political and democratic. The terms 'pluralist' and 'democratic' issue from a retrospective reading of work on citizenship. They selectively capture the common threads running through this body of work and bring attention to the shifts and turnings in the meaning of noncitizenship. By contrast, the term 'political' stems from the intention to politicise the experience of noncitizenship – that is characteristic of the type of work that the section focuses on.

There are three reasons why the frame of inclusive citizenship offers a fertile ground for theorising noncitizenship. First, accounts of inclusive citizenship problematise the relation between citizen and noncitizen, and in so doing, accentuate the ambivalence at the heart of the category of noncitizenship. Second, they expose the difficulty facing theorisations of noncitizenship as a distinct analytical category, namely, the reproduction of the relationship with citizenship. Third, they foreground inclusion as an inescapable dimension of theories of noncitizenship. Seeking to isolate this dimension and, thus, show the conceptual overlap between theories of noncitizenship and accounts of inclusive citizenship, the section subsumes the former under the latter and it discusses work on noncitizenship as the political variant of accounts of inclusive citizenship. Before this, however, the section explores the pluralist variant.

The pluralist variant develops on the terrain of identity politics, particularly in work that seeks to address the challenges currently confronting multicultural and multinational democracies – such as ensuring democratic equality while respecting difference (see Kymlicka 1996, 2001; Lister 2007). It takes issue with the formalistic and universal dimensions of citizenship and highlights issues of entry, recognition and rights (Isin and Wood 1999; Kymlicka 1996, 2001; Pakulski 1997; Parekh 2000; Philips 2003; Stevenson 2003; Young 1995, 2000). Concerned with the ways in which liberal democracies exclude, assimilate and discriminate against difference, theorists in the pluralist canon seek to renegotiate the terms and modes of membership. The term 'pluralist' derives from this renegotiation, for the primary aim here is to challenge the uniformity of citizenship by opening up and accentuating modes of membership that differ from and often challenge its dominant mould. Indeed, citizenship denotes membership on this account. It is associated with the typical Marshallian rights – civil, political and social – and it has liberal and legalistic overtones that carry over to the requisites for inclusive citizenship (see Marshall 1950). These consist of less stringent criteria for entry into citizenship – ranging from residence to universal personhood (Soysal 1994); formal recognition of particularity, the different ways one is and acts as a citizen (Young 1995); and the expansion of formal legal rights to include (often by differentiating) excluded groups (Kymlicka 1996, 2001; Parekh 2000). Formal rights and rules ease the passage to citizenship. More importantly, they initiate a shift in the very norms and practices of citizenship.

To see this shift more clearly – that the second and third variants of inclusive citizenship rely on – it is important to notice the three key contributions of the pluralist account to narratives of inclusive citizenship. The first consists in its sophisticated account of exclusion. By distinguishing between outer and 'inner exclusion'[1] (Taylor 1999, 276) work on identity politics brings attention to the continuous interplay between citizen and noncitizen, to the back and forth movement between experiencing political life as a citizen and as a noncitizen. If the rights-holder experiences exclusion (because of her identity, lifestyle, culture or religion), then the analytical category of noncitizenship does not just emerge when there is limited (or no) access to rights, but also when there is access to citizenship. Second and closely related, the pluralist variant notably expands the realm of noncitizenship. The noncitizen is the outsider, the different, the denizen, the third-country national, the illegal immigrant, the refugee, the woman – that is, anyone mistrusted, marginalised or stigmatised by dominant norms. While this expansion subverts the divide between inside–outside which citizenship perpetuates, it does not do away with the divide itself. Citizenship remains the most important form of membership and the noncitizen, as I will explain later in the section, is only seen to strive for inclusion (even when this is conceived in differential terms).

Third, the attention to law – that is to the range of measures necessary to alleviate exclusionary politics ranging from multicultural policies to positive discrimination and human rights law – fosters democratic practice. This means that inclusive citizenship is not simply seen as a moral good that liberal societies aspire to, but as a distinctly democratic good that can in fact be put into practice. Therefore, the focus on the legal and liberal dimensions of political membership, pressed by the pluralist variant, opens the way for attending to practice and, in so doing, it casts light on the everyday, political and democratic parameters of this practice. Of course, it might be more accurate to use the past tense here and take the pluralist variant as the predecessor to what I here designate as the democratic and political variants – especially if we consider that work on identity politics was at its height in the 1980s and 1990s. However, I think it is more useful to avoid a linear narrative and emphasise their interlacing. This interlacing becomes more evident when we direct attention to the work of specific theorists. Seyla Benhabib's work serves as a good example here (Benhabib 2005, 2007, 2009).

Benhabib is deeply dissatisfied with liberal accounts of citizenship as a status. However, she neither rejects rights-based approaches to citizenship nor does she reconceptualise citizenship with the aim of making it more inclusive – at least not explicitly. Instead, she strongly defends the idea of 'citizenship of place', citing the disaggregation of citizenship rights in international legislation (Benhabib 2005, 2007; see also Gordon-Zolov 2010, 275) and she argues that the jurisgenerative capacity of international human rights law has the potential to 'develop new vocabularies for public claim making, by encouraging new forms of subjectivity to engage with the public sphere, and by interjecting existing relations of power with anticipations of justice to come' (Benhabib 2009, 696). Therefore, the point here is that Benhabib turns to (international) law to ascertain the rights and, crucially, subjectivities of noncitizens. She distinguishes between rights, subjectivity and membership to the nation state and, in so doing, she prefigures the distinction that the political variant draws between citizenship as membership status and noncitizenship as emergent condition. At the same time, Benhabib's focus on democratic iterations (2009), that is on deliberative exchanges that contest, expand and transform existing practices of citizenship, interlaces with the emphasis that the democratic variant places on practice. Indeed, it can be argued that the reason that Benhabib's work perfectly illustrates the interlacing between the three variants of inclusive citizenship is because it combines the focus on the practice of noncitizenship (that perforates the political and democratic variants) with an account of noncitizenship as an often permanent, outside yet inside, legal and political status (pluralist and political variants). This account of noncitizenship lies at the centre of the political variant of inclusive citizenship that I now move on to examine.

In particular, the political variant encompasses ethnographic and sociological work on noncitizenship. In contrast with the other two variants that expand on the realm of noncitizenship, the political variant narrows it down to the field of migration. This means that the noncitizen denotes a particular form of exclusion that challenges the inside–outside boundaries of the political community. She is, for example, the long-term migrant who has temporary and often precarious access to citizenship rights or little to no access to such rights by virtue of her irregularity (De Genova and Peutz 2010; Hepworth 2014a, 2014b;

Squire 2010). The noncitizen, so articulated, foregrounds a more nuanced relationship with citizenship than the one that we notice in the pluralist variant. For example, on some accounts, the noncitizen is expelled from the order of citizenship (see Hepworth's account of abject citizenship 2014b); on other accounts, she oscillates between security and insecurity (see the account of precariousness developed by Goldring, Berinstein and Bernhard 2009); and yet on other accounts, the noncitizen challenges the juridical world of citizenship (Nyers 2003). Despite such understandable variations, however, this critical literature on noncitizenship agrees that far from being the mere victim of state-policies, the noncitizen exposes, disrupts and exceeds such policies. The type of negotiations that noncitizen actions elicit, such as unauthorised cross-border mobility, question the meaning of legal citizenship and also, crucially, *enact* citizenship (Hepworth 2014a). That is, they express a form of embodied and emergent citizenship that directly undermines the legal status of (non) citizenship (Hepworth 2014a, 2014b; Mezzadra and Neilson 2012).

This emphasis on citizenship enactment constitutes the most important contribution of this variant to accounts of inclusive citizenship. First, it shows that political agency, far from being confined to citizens, attaches also to noncitizens. Noncitizens contest and challenge the inside–outside distinction that the state system perpetuates and, by so doing, they politicise, claim and embody a type of citizenship that exists alongside standard accounts. Second, the emphasis is placed upon political agency, showing that far from seeking to open up or modify the legal order of citizenship, theorists of noncitizenship interrogate and, notably, defy the distinction between legality and illegality pressed by vocabularies of citizenship. Understood as a permanent condition, noncitizenship exceeds and subverts the limits set on politicisation by legal rules. This primacy given to politics over law has a noteworthy implication for accounts of inclusive citizenship. Although inclusion into citizenship looses the legal overtones that it carries in the pluralist variant, it finesses a socio-political process that at once augments and reinstates the citizenic logic of politics. While noncitizens politicise against the legal rules of citizenship, their politicisations, anchored as they are in the language of citizenship, precipitate nothing less but the expansion of its politics – or, at least, the expansion of what is considered as citizen politics. Therefore, the third, related, contribution to accounts of inclusive citizenship is the move away from the pluralist variant's focus on membership to highlight the limits of (non)citizenship as a legal status. By identifying ways of being a citizen outside of and beyond the legal parameters of citizenship, it paves the way for the democratic variant that probes deeper into the conditions of this emergent, disruptive and political noncitizenship.

In particular, the first thing to notice about the democratic variant is that it breaks further away from accounts of citizenship as legal status (political variant) and membership (pluralist variant). Instead, it focuses on the participatory dimension of citizenship and draws attention to political practices that challenge and transgress conventional ways of contributing to citizen politics – such as, for example, voting (Cornwall and Coelho 2006; Desforges, Jones and Woods 2005; Kopf 2010; Mohanty and Tandon 2006; Pateman 2012). In line, therefore, with the political variant, the democratic one accentuates the focus on political practice – on the many sites and scenes of citizenship (Isin 2008). However, in contrast with the political variant, it does neither limit this practice to migrants nor to politicisation. Instead, the democratic variant opens up noncitizen practice to other actors (such as the poor as we will shortly see) and it ties politicisation with democratisation – that is, with other ways of experiencing and practicing democracy. Thus, the first distinctive contribution of this variant to narratives of inclusive citizenship issues from its expanded account of practice.

Two theoretical ideas underpin this account: citizenship practice as an everyday, lived, experience and citizenship practice as participation/deliberation in dynamics of governing. Ruth Lister explains that lived experiences of citizenship consist of renegotiations of rights and responsibilities in the everyday and not just in moments conventionally considered to be democratic – such as protests or elections (Lister 2007). Lived citizenship, as renegotiation, emerges in the workplace, the private realm and/or the domain of the intimate (see Cohen 2009). Of course, the citizen qualities of such everyday renegotiations of rights, duties and obligations might be critically questioned. However, to confine thinking to such criticisms would be to miss the emphasis on the lived and experienced. This emphasis, as Lister highlights, draws attention to the system, to those enabling/disabling conditions (material and cultural) that carry implications for the everyday life of (non)citizens (Lister 2007). The participatory form that citizenship action takes in the democratic variant further accentuates this focus on the systemic conditions that often hinder citizen involvement and input to ways of governing. By drawing attention to persistent inequalities of wealth, position, societal status, skills and abilities, and the way these undermine democratic life, the deliberative perspective[2] has developed a large body of empirical work that tackles conditions of unequal participation (see De Souza Santos 2006; Pateman 2012). Citizen juries, panels, participatory budgeting, all constitute attempts to secure participation from marginalised groups of citizens unable to have a say about the way they are governed – and this is especially the case when we look at deliberative/participatory initiatives in the Global South (see Kopf 2010; Thompson and Tapscott 2010).

Therefore, the important point here is that with this variant, we have a stronger emphasis on the conditions for exercising citizenship – rather than the measures for securing inclusive citizenship (that we find in the pluralist variant). With this emphasis, an additional dimension of noncitizenship comes to the fore. Noncitizens are not only those excluded, marginalised, stigmatised or demonised by the formal and uniform politics of citizenship, but also the poor, the unskilled, the exploited or the unequal (a more refined category than the excluded). Noncitizens, in other words, are the non-actors – those who lack the resources to act and, thus, miss out on the benefits of citizenship in their everyday life where meaningful access to citizenship matters the most.

This brings us to the second, perhaps more crucial, contribution of the democratic variant to narratives of inclusive citizenship: the citizenisation of noncitizens. By citizenisation,[3] I mean processes of citizen formation – that is processes of citizen-becoming or citizen-constitution as these arise in particular (though various) locales, as a result of specific enabling conditions (or their lack thereof).[4] The primacy given to practice by the democratic variant encases this promise of citizenisation and, in so doing, it gives the idea of inclusionary citizenship its most radical 'twist': everyone can *become* a citizen, even though not anyone *is* a citizen (see Tully 2008b, 99). By engaging in practices that converse with the institutional politics of the given citizenship order, contesting or going against these, political subjects become citizens. This insight into processes of citizenisation evades the divide between the citizen and the noncitizen, democracy (citizenship) and politics (noncitizenship) that is still folded into the political variant with its limited focus on the migrant. So long as someone acts with the aim of drawing attention to injustice, inequality, subordination or marginalisation, one acts as, and thus is, a citizen. Whether the actor has access to rights is irrelevant.

Instead, what is relevant is that the citizen emerges out of *this* struggle for democracy. That is why she is now seen as a democratic actor, and not merely as a political subject because she seeks such distinctly democratic idea(l)s as equality, justice, recognition and inclusion. At the same time, the very focus on citizen-becoming, rather than citizen-being, inverts the meaning of inclusive citizenship (Isin 2008). It is not the inclusion of the 'other' that makes citizenship inclusive, but the reverse; it is the expansive account of democracy that invites the inclusion of the noncitizen into the world of citizenship. It is noteworthy, then, that both citizenship and inclusion, albeit their reconception, remain firmly at the centre of the democratic variant, much like in the pluralist and political ones.

This is where, I now argue, the limits of all three variants lie. By retaining the focus on citizenship and inclusion, the pluralist, political and democratic variants end up reproducing, if not consolidating, the binary between citizenship and noncitizenship. Of course, the underlying argument here is not that we need to turn away from the order of citizenship, dismissing its politics, that are, after all, the last stronghold of state sovereignty and, as such, the subject in need of continuous interrogation; nor does the argument intend to gloss over or undermine demands and struggles for inclusion. Rather, the point here is that it is one thing to recognise the reality of citizenship and its exclusionary implications for those who are not part of it, and quite another to see citizenship as the highest, most valuable practice, the benchmark for evaluating – acknowledging and noticing – the demands raised by a variety of groups. The second assumption, which is exactly what I find limiting here, perforates all three variants. In so doing, it reproduces, through the back door, the very binary between inside and outside that the pluralist, political and democratic variants problematise. Indeed, whether we view the noncitizen as the subject who seeks to be recognised and included in the liberal order of citizenship through changes in law and access to rights (pluralist variant); or as the migrant who enacts citizenship (political variant); or even as the non-actor who citizenizes through spontaneous and/or deliberative practice (democratic variant), it is difficult to escape the conclusion that the noncitizen is the inevitable victim of the state system that occasionally subjectifies to seek inclusion in that system, the highest order of citizenship.

To explicate the point further, the problem with this conclusion is not victimhood per se – that as we have seen the political variant does a good job challenging – but the primacy given to *citizen*-isation, that potentially undermines claims and demands for a better life in the here and now. By pointing to the larger scripts of citizenship that implicate institutions, state actors and societal attitudes, citizenship-construed demands displace the particular by the general – on the assumption that references to the general *of* citizenship give weight to particular claims *to* citizenship. However, do we need the lens of citizenship to respond to and address injustice, exclusion and discrimination? I will return to this question in the next section. Here, suffice to notice that by taking citizenship as the benchmark for all political practice, the pluralist, political and democratic variants reinstate the binary citizen/noncitizen that they seek to disturb and unsettle.

The second limit of the pluralist, political and democratic variants is closely related to the first one. It concerns the interrelation between citizenship and noncitizenship that runs through the three variants of inclusive citizenship. By tying noncitizenship with citizenship, that is by tying the being of noncitizens with that of the citizens, all three variants cancel out noncitizenship as an analytical category. Noncitizenship becomes reduced to a journey to citizenship and, as such, as a journey, it loses meaning and force. At the same time, a retrospective reading arises that assimilates struggles for new kinds of politics into the canonical narrative of modern citizenship. James Tully is particularly attuned to this danger when he points out that even when the rights of noncitizens are institutionalised and their conditions bettered, this betterment 'is redescribed retrospectively as a stage in the development of modern citizenship and incorporated within its framework' (Tully 2014, 18–19). The danger, therefore, that Tully's point alerts us to is that the very category of non-*citizenship* might inadvertently undermine struggles for another politics, by limiting these to struggles for and against citizenship. However, as the next section shows, it is possible to take such struggles seriously without falling back on the vocabulary of noncitizenship. To this end, the next section explores the idea of politicisation and contrasts its analytical force with that of the category of noncitizenship.

Rethinking noncitizenship

The previous section developed two arguments. The first argument was that the analytical category of noncitizenship is closely entangled not just with citizenship by way of antithesis, but with accounts of inclusive citizenship in particular. By tracing the shifts and turnings in the concept of noncitizenship *within* such accounts, the previous section highlighted the floating nature of the concept that the pluralist, political and democratic variants exploit to the full. Three particular moments in the account of these variants are noteworthy. The first is that noncitizenship significantly expands and blurs with citizenship – once exclusion, marginalisation and stigmatisation are seen to be experienced by anyone whose identity does not conform to dominant norms. The second noteworthy moment in discussions of inclusion is that noncitizenship becomes synonymous with non-action – in the absence of enabling resources (material and cultural). Finally, processes of citizenisation – or citizen enactment in the vocabulary of the political variant – displace the analytical and legal categories of noncitizenship. Although access to rights still formally distinguishes citizens from noncitizens, political agency and practice that are common to both categories ensure that noncitizens become citizens when they politicise and engage in practices that challenge the exclusionary politics of citizenship. Does this indicate that noncitizenship is a superfluous category? The second argument of the previous section was that the very persistence of the binary between citizen/noncitizen undermines the analytical force of the category of noncitizenship.

Of course, it might be objected that there are examples of noncitizenship that point to the opposite direction – particularly when noncitizenship is taken to denote partial access to the rights of citizenship in the state (or region) one resides but is not a full citizen of – as a result of multi-level governance (for a critical account of multi-level citizenship see Bauböck and Guiraudon 2009). Denizenship, for example, as exemplified in the case of European citizens who 'carry their citizenship abroad and exercise it from outside', has often been construed as a transgressive category that undermines, rather than reinforces, the citizen/noncitizen binary (Bauböck and Guiraudon 2009, 440). However, it is also a more limited category in that it simply taps into and expands rights-based accounts of citizenship, leaving the exclusivity of the status of citizenship either untouched – as is the case with the pluralist variant – or only partly questioned (when the focus is on the national dimension of citizenship). Nevertheless, cases of multi-level citizenship raise the question: Is it possible to leave the citizen/noncitizen binary aside and see some strengths in noncitizenship as an analytical category?

On the one hand, it can be argued that noncitizenship is a necessary category because it captures the excess of politics. So long as there are citizens, there will be noncitizens, that is a surplus or excess of politics – a political difference – that either does not conform to the given citizenship order and/or challenges the dominant norms of this order (see Honig 1993). At the same time, it can be argued that noncitizenship is not just a necessary category, but also a useful one. It alerts us to the exclusions, inequalities, marginalisations and naturalisations that accompany citizenship politics. Therefore, by continuously interrogating who the noncitizens are, we keep an eye on democratic exclusions and, in so doing, we ward off – or at least we attempt to ward off – closures and exclusions. On the other hand, however, it can also be argued that we do not need the category of noncitizenship to notice and attend to democratic closures and exclusions. After all, instances of injustice and inequality can be recognised without resorting to the vocabulary of noncitizenship, as any newspaper reader will immediately confirm. More than that, terms such as 'inequality', 'destitution' and 'injustice' are more powerful than 'noncitizenship' to capture attention and stirring action.

Of course, it can be argued that noncitizenship foregrounds questions of democracy. By enquiring into democratic exclusions – the ways in which liberal democracies fail to admit, integrate and support 'difference' or 'otherness' – the concept of noncitizenship forces us to continuously assess and evaluate the ways in which democratic idea(l)s translate into democratic practice. But, still, do we need the category of noncitizenship to evaluate the quality of democratic life? As the previous section argued, there is something disturbing in the idea – in vogue today – that all politics be read as citizenship politics to gain democratic ground. The assumption that informs this idea, that citizenship is the most valuable practice, the door to a better politics, tends not just to underplay the particularity of the given demand and struggle, but also to undermine the very plurality of politics. To be sure, it is vital that struggles against exclusion, inequality and injustice gain democratic ground (and are translated into measures that reflect these gains). However, it is questionable whether they need the lens of noncitizenship to do so. Politicisation can do the same work. The remaining of this section explains why. It starts by identifying the overlap between politicisation and noncitizenship and it moves on to discuss the two components of the politicising process that make it a better alternative to noncitizenship.

By politicisation, I mean a process of political subjectification where subjects excluded from the institutional world direct attention to their situation and, through public action, bring visibility to the inequalities and injustices permeating this world (see Rancière 1999). Politicisation, therefore, like the category of noncitizenship, confronts relations of power and inequality, presupposes agency and involves practice. In particular, subjects who politicise seek to challenge the established order. They bring into view the power dynamics behind this order – its closures, injustices and inequalities and, in so doing, they openly unsettle these. Although it can be credibly objected here that the noncitizens (the poor, excluded and marginalised) are not always in a position to politicise and confront the power order – and this alone reveals the force of noncitizenship as an analytical category – it can be argued that noncitizenship, much like the concept of politicisation in this sense, promises something more than a comprehensive exposé of the inequalities perforating a given power order. It promises citizenisation. Citizenisation involves political subjectification – as is the case with politicisation. At the same time, politicisation, like citizenisation or noncitizenship for that matter, gains momentum through references to a variety of scripts, from 'justice' and 'equality' to even 'citizenship' – and this means that either sections of society politicise to give visibility to the position/demands of those who cannot, or the excluded and marginalised subjectify and politicise. Therefore, the point here is that there is significant overlap between the concepts of politicisation and noncitizenship when it comes to matters of subjectification and counter-power. There is also overlap with respect to practice. Politicisation *is* practice, for subjects politicise against or for something – for example, by setting up a sit-in, a protest, an occupation, etc. In fact, political protests (against the state) can be seen as exemplary moments of politicisation, where the binary citizen/noncitizen becomes redundant.

In particular, what makes protests exemplary moments of politicisation (at least in the way I use the term here) is their public nature – the publicity, connection, openness and generality that they encase. Protests publicise exclusion X; they make it visible. They are public events and this means that they both reach out to the public and draw in (the support of) the public – broadly understood. At the same time, public protests are sites of assembling. They gather the people together and, in this gathering, it makes little difference who is the citizen and who is not, or who initiated the protest and who did not. What matters is that protests remain open and, as a result of this openness, demands flesh out, intermesh and expand. More than that, the openness of the protests compounded by the indeterminacy of the subject 'people' as a democratic actor has the additional effect of drawing sharper attention to the political demand or claim eliciting the protest. This is where, in the end, the greatest difference between the concepts of politicisation and noncitizenship lies: in their *telos*. Whereas the *telos* of politicisation, say in the case of public protests to stay with the same example, is to have the particular (series of) demands or claims met in the here and now – thus, it has a rather limited, provisional, target that does not always or necessarily coincide with an expansion of rights; the telos of the category of noncitizenship is often, inadvertently, citizenship – and, this implicitly enfolds the aspiration to expand on existing rights.

By defending, therefore, politicisation, I move a step further from the critical literature that sees the politicisations of noncitizens as intrinsic to the enactment of citizenship (Hepworth 2014a, 2014b; Isin 2008). More than that, as William Walters warns,

> we should not overlook those moments when political interventions refuse to make strong claims in the name of citizenship … because subjects explicitly reject the rights, responsibilities and commitments that are associated with the citizen, or out of preference for other identities. (2008, 185, 193)

Attending to such moments of struggle, that Walters refers to as 'acts of demonstration', opens the way for noticing new possibilities that arise in the course of such struggles (2008, 194). To be sure, what Walters calls 'acts of demonstration' is what I here refer to as politicisation, for acts of demonstration 'occur when an injustice is revealed, a relationship of power is contested, or a particular wrong is protested, but when the identity of the subjects, at the heart of the protest is left relatively open' (Walters 2008, 194). But there is a difference. Whereas Walters suggests that 'acts of demonstration' supplement political acts of noncitizenship, I suggest that politicisations blur with acts of noncitizenship.

There are two reasons behind this suggestion. The first reason is that politicisations that do not tie the identity of the political subject with that of the citizen promote a stronger conception of agency. This is particularly important for those subjects who are noncitizens for their entire life, such as, for example, Palestinian refugees in Lebanon and/or the occupied territories who do not struggle for either Lebanese or Israeli citizenship (Allegra 2009; Salih 2013). However, they do struggle to improve and renegotiate the conditions of their life in the here and now. This is a continuous and ordinary struggle, neither exceptional nor just disruptive as the literature on noncitizenship would have it (Hepworth 2014a, 2014b). In this ongoing struggle, agency dissociates from identity (Salih 2013). That is, political agency exceeds the identity of (non)citizenship and it is important that work on citizenship studies acknowledges and recognises the indeterminacy of this agency. At the same time, politicisations that do not tie the identity of the subject with that of the citizen are potentially more effective in drawing attention to the exclusions and injustices of citizenship. Construed as political acts, they open up possibilities that resist the normalisations, naturalisations and framings that accompany references to citizenship. Thus, the following question arises: If politicisation is a potentially more effective – target specific – process of interrogating exclusions, then is it possible to give it some form beyond the setting of the public protest? In other words, is it possible to identify some of the components that contribute to its weight as a process?

James Tully gives us a good idea of one of these components. In his discussion of civic freedom, he offers sufficient cues to enable us to envision politicisation outside the setting of the public protest (2008a, 2008b). In particular, practices of civic freedom consist, according to Tully, of the freedom to question, renegotiate and, as a result, renew the terms of the political game. For example, if there is, say, inequality and exploitation in the work place, the moment that groups of unequal/exploited workers question (from their different positions and for their different reasons), these relations of inequality, practices of civic freedom come into play. Indeed, practices of civic freedom, according to Tully, arise *together* with practices of governance – understood in an expansive sense as relations of control (see Tully 2008a, 24–25). In a typical Foucauldian way, therefore, what Tully tells us here is that wherever there is power, closure and exclusion, there is resistance. There is the possibility to interrogate power and domination, confront and change it. Now, what I find useful in the idea of 'practices of civic freedom' is, first, that they arise wherever there is domination, control and exclusion – thus, the concept attends to the omnipresence of power, exclusion and inequality. Second, practices of civic freedom appear to have the same effect as noncitizenship, that is they challenge exclusions without, however, pinning down the political subject behind them. Third, and perhaps more importantly, practices of civic freedom are neither necessarily nor exclusively aimed at introducing a change in the order of citizenship (by expanding, for example, its rights). They are just that: practices *of* freedom *against* relations of control, domination or subordination. Thus, practices of civic freedom can be seen as the politicised moment par excellence. What is missing from this moment is the focus on demands/claims that I previously tied with the idea of politicisation.

To attend to this moment, and thus explore the second component of politicisation, we need to move a step further from Tully and return to the idea of claims-making that I have already discussed in passing. The aim here is to make the connection between claims-making and politicisation explicit. Saward (2006) talks about claims. Claims are, for Saward, performative, creative and representative. They can be taken up by all kinds of actors and they produce subjects, objects and audiences. For Saward, therefore, it is the claim *itself* that has productive effects (produces representation), not the subject who formulates the claim. Or, as he puts it: 'what exists are *claims* and their receptions' (Saward 2006, 306). Indeed, by highlighting the constituting and everyday dimension of claims-making, Saward opens interesting lines of enquiry into its role in interrogating exclusive politics. To see these, we need to briefly look at the nature of claims-making. In particular, claims-making puts emphasis on the claim itself – since it is the specificity of the claim that constitutes political projects. At the same time, the claim does more than facilitate the expression of a grievance or issue. Claims-making seeks to reformulate and, indeed, re-negotiate the given unequal power distribution – this is why it is also relevant to long-term noncitizens. Claims open the way to re-negotiation because they are, first, necessarily narrower, target specific and more limited than citizenisations are. Second, claims *to* someone or something establish a relation of interdependence between the side that produces the given claim (the noncitizens) and the side that responds to the claim (the state). Third, and perhaps more importantly, claims *already* envelop alternatives to the existing order since this is precisely what defines and distinguishes them *as* claims, the requests or demands they encase.

Indeed, the very possibility of transforming the world of citizenship politics, by challenging and exposing the exclusions and injustices that define it in the here and now, is one dimension that for the time being escapes attempts to theoretically refine the category of noncitizenship. One reason for this is perhaps innate to the category of noncitizenship. Non*citizenship* captures the journey to citizenship, the quest to be included in citizenship. It is a telic process and its telos, as I have been arguing throughout the paper, constitutes its key limit. Politicisation, by contrast, evades this limit because it draws attention to process, subjectification, agency and claims-making. Although the binary citizen/noncitizen can inform the politicising process, it does not define it. This makes politicisation a potentially richer category than noncitizenship for theorising contentious politics over and against set frames of citizenship. Of course, the emphasis that I here place on politicisation does not imply that we altogether give up on the category of noncitizenship, for noncitizenship does not necessarily preclude politicisation. As the section showed, there is considerable overlap between the two concepts. However, what my emphasis on politicisation does imply is that we need to start by problematising the binary citizen/noncitizen that taps into attempts to theorise noncitizenship. Although this is a difficult task, the undecidability of the prefix *non* invites attempts, such as this one, to travel the road away from citizenship.

Conclusion

The paper explored the implications of the case for noncitizenship as a distinct analytical category. By tracing the nature of the concept in trajectories of inclusive citizenship, it argued that its key limit issues precisely from its entanglement with citizenship and citizenisation. To support this argument, the paper distinguished between a pluralist, political and democratic variant in accounts of inclusive citizenship and it showed how they end up reinstating the very binary citizen/noncitizen that they intend to interrogate. Seeking to overcome this limitation, the paper discussed the idea of politicisation and contrasted its empowering potential with that of noncitizenship. Do we need, in the end, the category of noncitizenship to acknowledge and challenge relations of exclusion, power, inequality, injustice and discrimination? The paper answered this question by suggesting that to consolidate the analytical force of the category of noncitizenship, we need to start with the difficult task of attenuating its relationship with citizenship.

Notes

1. In contrast with outer exclusion that captures the reluctance to either admit outsiders into citizenship or trust them as co-citizens, 'inner exclusion' designates the subordination of other ways of being a citizen into the dominant mould of citizenship. This dimension of exclusionary politics has been heavily criticised by the literature on gender politics (Taylor 1999; see also Lister 2003; Young 1995, 2000).
2. Here, it is important to note that I use the terms deliberation and participation interchangeably. For the opposite view, see Mutz 2006.
3. I borrow the term 'citizenisation' from the work of James Tully (2008a, 2008b).
4. Isin (2008) gives the most sophisticated account of such processes of citizenisation when he distinguishes between acts of citizenship (that involve disruption, rupture and a break with an order) and citizenship action (that envelops routine, habit and order).

Disclosure statement

No potential conflict of interest was reported by the author.

References

Agamben, G. 1998. *Homo Sacer: Sovereign Power and Bare Life*. Stanford, CA: Stanford University Press.
Allegra, M. 2009. "Citizenship in Palestine: A Fractured Geography." *Citizenship Studies* 13 (6): 553–573.
Andersen, J., and B. Siim, eds. 2004. *The Politics of Inclusion and Empowerment: Gender, Class and Citizenship*. Basingstoke: Palgrave Macmillan.
Arendt, H. 1968. "The Decline of the Nation State and the End of the Rights of Man". Chap. 9 in *The Origins of Totalitarianism*. New York: Harcourt.
Bauböck, R., and V. Guiraudon. 2009. "Introduction: Realignments of Citizenship: Reassessing Rights in the Age of Plural Memberships and Multi-level Governance." *Citizenship Studies* 13 (5): 439–450.
Benhabib, S. 2005. "Disaggregation of Citizenship Rights." *Parallax* 11 (1): 10–18.
Benhabib, S. 2007. "Twilight of Sovereignty or the Emergence of Cosmopolitan Norms? Rethinking Citizenship in Volatile times." *Citizenship Studies* 11 (1): 19–36.
Benhabib, S. 2009. "Claiming Rights across Borders: International Human Rights and Democratic Sovereignty." *American Political Science Review* 103 (4): 691–704.
Cohen, E. 2009. *Semi-Citizenship in Democratic Politics*. Cambridge: Cambridge University Press.
Cornwall, A., and V. S. Coelho. 2006. *Spaces for Change? The Politics of Citizen Participation in New Democratic Arenas*. London: Zed Books.
De Genova, N., and N. Peutz, eds. 2010. *The Deportation Regime: Sovereignty, Space and the Freedom of Movement*. Durham: Duke University Press.
De Souza Santos, B. 2006. *Democratizing Democracy: Reinventing Social Emancipation*. London: Verso.
Desforges, L., R. Jones, and M. Woods. 2005. "New Geographies of Citizenship." *Citizenship Studies* 9 (5): 439–451.
Gaventa, J., and J. Tandon. 2010. *Globalising Citizens: New Dynamics of Inclusion and Exclusion*. London: Zed.
Goldring, L., C. Berinstein, and J. K. Bernhard. 2009. "Institutionalizing Precarious Migratory Status in Canada." *Citizenship Studies* 13 (3): 239–265.
Hepworth, K. 2014a. "Encounters with the Clandestino/a and the Nomad: The Emplaced and Embodied Constitution of Non-citizenship." *Citizenship Studies* 18 (1): 1–14.
Hepworth, K. 2014b. "Topologies of Citizenship." In *Routledge Handbook of Global Citizenship Studies*, edited by Engin F. Isin and Peter Nyers, 110–118. Abingdon: Routledge.
Honig, B. 1993. *Political Theory and the Displacement of Politics*. Ithaca: Cornell University Press.

Isin, E. 2008. "Theorising Acts of Citizenship." In *Acts of Citizenship*, edited by Engin F. Isin and Greg Nielsen, 15–43. London: Zed Books.
Isin, E. F., and P. K. Wood. 1999. *Citizenship and Identity*. London: Sage.
Kabeer, N., ed. 2005. *Inclusive Citizenship*. London: Sage.
Kopf, B. 2010. "The Geography of Participation". *Third World Quarterly* 31(5): 709–720.
Kymlicka, W. 1996. *Multicultural Citizenship*. Oxford: Clarendon Press.
Kymlicka, W. 2001. *Politics in the Vernacular*. Oxford: Oxford University Press.
Lister, R. 2003. *Citizenship: Feminist Perspectives*. Basingstoke: Palgrave Macmillan.
Lister, R. 2007. "Inclusive Citizenship: Realizing the Potential." *Citizenship Studies* 11 (1): 49–61.
Marin, R. 2010. *Immigration as a Democratic Challenge: Citizenship and Inclusion in Germany and the United States*. Cambridge: Cambridge University Press.
Marshall, T. H. 1950. *Citizenship and Social Class*. Cambridge: Cambridge University Press.
Mezzadra, S., and B. Neilson. 2012. "Between Inclusion and Exclusion: On the Topology of Global Space and Borders." *Theory, Culture and Society* 29 (4–5): 58–75.
Mohanty, R., and R. Tandon, eds. 2006. *Participatory Citizenship: Identity, Exclusion, Inclusion*. London: Sage.
Mutz, D. 2006. *Hearing the Other Side*. Cambridge: Cambridge University Press.
Nyers, P. 2003. "Abject Cosmopolitanism: The Politics of Protection in the Anti-deportation Movement." *Third World Quarterly* 24 (6): 1069–1093.
Pakulski, J. 1997. "Cultural Citizenship." *Citizenship Studies* 1 (1): 73–86.
Parekh, B. 2000. *Rethinking Multiculturalism: Cultural Diversity and Political Theory*. Basingstoke: Macmillan Press.
Pateman, C. 2012. "Participatory Democracy Revisited." *Perspectives on Politics* 10 (1): 7–19.
Phillips, A. 2003. "Recognition and the Struggle for Political Voice." In *Recognition Struggles and Social Movements*, edited by Barbara Hobson, 263–273. Cambridge: Cambridge University Press.
Rancière, J. 1999. *Disagreement: Politics and Philosophy*. Translated by J. Rose. Minneapolis: University of Minnesota Press.
Salih, R. 2013. "From Bare Lives to Political Agents: Palestinian Refugees as Avant-Garde." *Refugee Survey Quarterly* 32 (2): 66–91.
Saward, Michael. 2006. "The Representative Claim." *Contemporary Political Theory* 5: 297–318.
Soysal, Y. N. 1994. *Limits of Citizenship: Migrants and Postnational Membership in Europe*. Chicago, IL: University of Chicago Press.
Squire, V., ed. 2010. *The Contested Politics of Mobility: Borderzones and Irregularity*. Abingdon: Routledge.
Stevenson, N. 2003. *Cultural Citizenship*. Buckingham: Open University Press.
Taylor, C. 1999. "Democratic Exclusion (and Its Remedies?)." In *Citizenship, Diversity and Pluralism: Canadian and Comparative Perspectives*, edited by Alan C. Cairns, John C. Courtney, P. MacKinnon, H. J. Michelmann and D. E. Smith, 265–286. Montreal: McGill-Queen's University Press.
Gordon-Zolov, T. 2010. "A Conversation with Seyla Benhabib and Judith Resnik." *WSQ: Women's Studies Quarterly* 38 (1–2): 271–286.
Thompson, L., and C. Tapscott, eds. 2010. *Citizenship and Social Movements: Perspectives from the Global South*. London: Zed.
Tully, J. 2008a. *Public Philosophy in a New Key. Volume I, Democracy and Civic Freedom*. Cambridge: Cambridge University Press.
Tully, J. 2008b. *Public Philosophy in a New Key. Volume II, Imperialism and Civic Freedom*. Cambridge: Cambridge University Press.
Tully, J. 2014. *On Global Citizenship: James Tully in Dialogue*. London: Bloomsbury.
Walters, W. 2008. "Acts of Demonstration: Mapping the Territory of (Non-) Citizenship." In *Acts of Citizenship*, edited by Engin F. Isin and Greg M. Nielsen, 182–206. London: Zed Books.
Young, I. M. 1995. "Polity and Group Difference: A Critique of the Ideal of Universal Citizenship." In *Theorizing Citizenship*, edited by Ronald Beiner, 175–208. Albany: State University of New York Press.
Young, I. M. 2000. *Inclusion and Democracy*. Oxford: Oxford University Press.

Contractualization, depoliticization and the limits of solidarity: noncitizens in contemporary Australia

Shanthi Robertson

Institute for Culture and Society, Western Sydney University, Sydney, Australia

ABSTRACT

This paper seeks to analyze a particular form of noncitizenship – arising from legal long-term temporary migration – that is increasingly significant to the contemporary Australian context and to understand some of its consequences. It argues that traditional pathways of permanent settlement and full citizenship are being disrupted by new temporary migration schemes that create 'middling' noncitizen subjects who experience 'patchwork' rights and statuses across complex and diverse migration pathways. Through a close analysis of policy narratives and discourses, as well as of the existing literature on the social conditions and emerging solidarities of these noncitizens, the paper shows the various ways that noncitizenship is depoliticized and citizenship contractualized in Australia. These entwined processes of depoliticization and contractualization have intimate effects on the lives of noncitizens, and also limit and constrain the emerging solidarities that seek to challenge their exclusion. The analysis has a number of implications for the ongoing study of contemporary transformations in citizenship in other 'immigrant democracies' globally.

Introduction

In 2011, an Australian federal court ruled that the owners of a popular Melbourne dumpling restaurant must pay $AU200,000 in unpaid wages and superannuation to Chinese immigrant chef Chang Chang. Sponsored by the restaurant to work in Australia under the 457 temporary skilled worker programme,[1] Chang had worked 13-hour days for an illegally low wage. Aware he was being exploited, he waited three years until he was able to secure permanent residency before taking legal action against his employer. In 2009, accounting graduate and Indian national Nitin Garg was fatally stabbed in a Melbourne park while walking to his job at a fast-food restaurant, in one of a chain of attacks on Indian student-workers in Melbourne and Sydney across 2009 and 2010. The stories of these two men, both noncitizen workers seeking out permanency, speak to a wider picture of how immigration in Australia is changing, and how forms of noncitizenship are central to these changes.

Since the 1990s there has been an expanding population of legal noncitizen residents, like Chang and Garg, living and working in Australia, largely through the expansion and diversification of temporary visa schemes. While there is emerging work in Australia on temporary migrants, particularly their impact on the labour market (see e.g. Hugo 2006; Khoo, McDonald, and Hugo 2005) there is little broad analysis of what increases to temporary migration mean politically or theoretically, and particularly what they mean for noncitizenship as well as transformations to the relationship between noncitizenship and citizenship.

This paper thus seeks to engage with policy discourses and existing literature to theorize temporary migrants as an emerging form of noncitizen in the contemporary Australian context. It uses the specific case of Australia to contribute to what Shachar (2014, 114) establishes as a 'crucial task' of contemporary migration and citizenship scholarship: 'to identify the political, institutional and ideological conditions that define, reify or unsettle the boundary between inclusion and exclusion.' It adds generally to the emerging body of literature that analyses the new permutations of noncitizenship in the traditional 'immigrant democracies'. In engaging with the ways that temporary migration processes contractualize citizenship and depoliticize noncitizenship, this paper also goes beyond the more common analyses of temporary migration in immigrant democracies that tend to focus primarily on labour experiences and migrant rights (see e.g. Dauvergne and Marsden 2014; Goldring and Landolt 2011; Lenard and Straehle 2012). While not based on any specific empirical data-set, the paper engages with a range of existing empirical work (including my own) on temporary migrants, as well as an analysis of policy developments, advocacy interventions and media reports in order to theoretically position this particular form of noncitizenship within the wider citizenship literature. This is an important first step in furthering a research agenda around temporary migrants and their noncitizenship in the Australian context, given that existing literature on the rapid increases in temporary migration rarely touch on noncitizenship or on political identities more generally.

First, I provide a brief outline of the immigration policies that shape the specific noncitizen subjectivities that are the main concern of this paper, and argue how this policy context transforms citizenship and noncitizenship, particularly in relation to contract and consumption, and to the intimacies of state power in noncitizen lives. I then establish three key ways in which noncitizen identities are depoliticized by particular discourses surrounding temporary migrants. Finally, I look at some of the emerging forms of resistance and solidarity among noncitizens in Australia and question whether they have the power to be truly transformative of trends towards depoliticization and contractualization.

Staggered pathways, 'middling' noncitizens and 'patchwork' belongings

Noncitizenship in the post-colonial Australian context concerns a far broader spectrum of experiences than those of voluntary migrants, who are the main focus of this paper. Recent policies around asylum seekers, particularly those arriving by boat, have seen a warping of the relationship between asylum, territory and citizenship on several fronts. Indigenous Australians are also of great significance to any debate on the limits and edges of citizenship in Australia, with the majority of Aboriginal and Torres Strait Islander people denied citizenship and its attendant rights until the 1960s. Ongoing questions about their distinctive rights and the recognition of indigenous social orders continue to challenge the post-colonial state's taken-for-granted principles of Western citizenship (Peterson and Sanders 1998).

This paper looks, therefore, only at a specific form of noncitizenship in Australia, manifested specifically through the management of voluntary forms of migration. The definitions and analytic boundaries discussed in this paper reflect only this particular subsection of noncitizenship, although as the scope of the papers in this Special Issue attests, noncitizenship has varied manifestations globally. What this paper provides is a detailed case study of how, as Landolt and Goldring (2015) note in this issue, state policies and discursive practices construct variegated memberships. This case reflects more broadly some of the current contestations around citizenship and noncitizenship globally, indicating some of the new challenges to inclusion and exclusion in multicultural democracies in an era of increased global mobility.

Immigration policy in Australia has historically tended to emphasize permanent settlement (Khoo 2002). Post-war migration was built predominantly through chains of permanent settlement, with the majority of migrants granted permanent residency (PR) upon selection or arrival. Permanent residency offered a full complement of social rights, and progression to full citizenship through naturalization was positioned as the desirable and desired norm (Jordens 1997; Ongley and Pearson 1995). Over the last fifteen years, however, there has been a rapid increase in the number of noncitizens living and working in Australia for relatively extended periods of time, reflecting a global shift in international migration patterns from permanent settlement and to temporary mobility (Allon, Anderson, and Bushell 2008, 74). For the purposes of this paper, I discuss a subset of noncitizens, defined as those who have the right to work and reside in Australia for 12 months or more, and who do not have Australian permanent residency or citizenship.[2] As shorthand, unless otherwise stated, when I refer to 'noncitizens' throughout this paper, the reference is to this subgroup in particular. At the end of 2013, there were nearly 1.4 million of these noncitizen residents living in Australia, the vast majority with work rights (DIBP 2013). This includes migrants on a range of different visas, which fall into several categories – employer-sponsored temporary migrants (457 visas), international students, graduate workers (485 visas), tourist-workers (those on the working holiday scheme) and New Zealand citizens. It also includes the spouses and dependents of primary holders of these visas as well as those who are working illegally, either by overstaying or through working outside the specific conditions of their temporary visa.

Most noncitizen residents in Australia are legally temporary but often reside within the nation-state for extended periods of time on a succession of different temporary visas (Birrell and Healy 2012a). In addition, the resident population of temporary migrants has now become a key pool from which permanent migrants are selected. One third of all permanent migrant 'arrivals' between 2000 and 2011 were onshore applicants (ABS 2013), and of the total permanent residence visas granted in 2012–2013, 50% were issued to people already living in Australia on a temporary visa (DIAC 2013a). As Mares (2013a) points out, this represents a fundamental change in the way immigrant selection works in Australia, yet this change often goes unrecognized in both political and academic discourse. Australia differs from similar immigrant democracies like Canada and New Zealand in that there are no guaranteed pathways from a temporary visa to permanent residency. Churn between temporary statuses, is however, mostly unfettered. As a result of this, many migrants are able to create pathways between temporariness and permanence, but this often involves protracted and uncertain journeys of multiple 'status mobilities' (Schuster 2005, 758). For example, a migrant could spend 3 years on a student visa, 2 years on a 485 temporary graduate visa, and then 4 years on a 457 temporary skilled visa before finally obtaining sponsorship for a permanent visa. These types of pathways mean that noncitizens often spend extended periods living and working in Australia with a series of precarious statuses, often investing significant amounts of time and money into the journey towards PR, with no certainty that they will achieve it (Mares 2013a; Robertson and Runganaikaloo 2014). This 'insecurity of presence' (Rajkumar et al. 2012, 488) across multiple statuses keeps workers flexible and expendable, and means migrants contribute economically with their labour, spending and taxes for longer periods before they may be able to access any of the benefits of the welfare state.

This experience of noncitizenship in Australia is a more 'middling' one than is often explored in the migration studies and citizenship literature, which has tended to focus on the stateless and the undocumented (McGregor 2011; McNevin 2006, 2007; Mountz et al. 2002; Somers 2008) or on low-skilled contract workers (Parreñas 2010; Silvey 2004). Most noncitizens in Australia are legal residents and from the middle class of their home country (Colic-Peisker 2011), due to the minimum levels of education and the expense required to obtain most temporary visas. However, the breadth of this 'middling' experience is also wide. Noncitizens encompass elite knowledge workers, mid-level professionals, retail and hospitality workers, skilled tradespeople, taxi drivers, cleaners and sex workers.[3] The categories of skilled and unskilled, elite and disenfranchised are increasingly complex in the context of noncitizenship in Australia. Those on 'skilled' visas do not always occupy the upper echelons of the labour market (Janda 2015; Velayutham 2013; Xiang 2001) and many of those picking fruit or driving taxis have tertiary qualifications (Tan et al. 2009). Nitin Garg and Chang Chang are quite typical examples here – Garg was a graduate of a local university but was doing unskilled work in the fast-food industry, while Chang, as a chef, was on a skilled visa but was forced to work in virtual servitude.

The current situation in Australia is emblematic of the fact that contemporary mobilities are highly heterogeneous and produce a 'complex field of differentiated economic and social statuses, ethnicities, identities, rights and entitlements and (it is important to remember) ambitions' (Lewis and Neal 2005, 426). The rights and statuses of migrants, and the subsequent ways citizenship and noncitizenship function, have thus been increasingly fragmented and diversified in Australia. Different rights, resources and belongings are sutured together at different points in a migrants' journey – as migrants 'churn' across different visa categories they can lose and gain different sets of rights and subjectivities. My approach here sees noncitizenship in this specific context not as an absence or lacuna – reminiscent of Agamben's (1998) 'bare life' of the stateless person – but as an 'intersectionist' (Shachar 2014, 122) position within which 'patchworks' of rights and belonging are ever evolving. Although this intersectionist noncitizenship can provide mobility and flexibility, it remains at heart exclusionary in form. Although noncitizens in Australia have varying degrees of rights, power and embeddedness within the community or nation-state, these are always partial, contingent, conditional and revokable. It is important to note here that migrants' own agencies and desires shape the nature of risk and vulnerability as much visa status or formal rights – most significantly the desire to stay.

As Shachar (2014, 121) notes, states' desires to manage migration and create 'flexible' migration programmes are destabilizing the pathways from immigrant to citizen in many of the traditional immigrant democracies, including Australia. There is thus a proliferation of 'in-between categories' (Shachar 2014, 121) in the grey area between inclusion and exclusion that need to be more fully understood. With race-based criteria for entrance and belonging removed at the end of the White Australia Policy in the early 1970s and the subsequent introduction of 'points-based' systems of immigrant selection, Australian immigration and citizenship policy has constructed itself as politically 'neutral' and non-discriminatory. The removal of overtly discriminatory criteria like race and ethnicity from states' immigration and citizenship policies, however, often serves to mask ongoing and emerging forms of exclusion (Clifton 2010, 412) – in particular in this case the diversification of migrant statuses that each contain their own 'patchwork' of rights and entitlements, as well as the lack of direct and explicit pathways from temporariness to permanence that can leave migrants in precarious situations.

Contract, consumption and the intimacies of state power

Staggered journeys towards citizenship create a framework within which the relationship between the noncitizen migrant, state and society is understood through forms of contract and consumption. Particular kinds of labour market participation and investment in national economies now act, as in many of migrant-receiving states, as the main criterion for individuals' membership, and migrants are also seen to desire these memberships for primarily instrumental reasons (Nagel and Staeheli 2004; Ong 1999; Somers 2008). Temporary migration schemes in particular reinforce logics that noncitizens must 'earn' (van Houdt, Suvarierol, and Schinkel 2011) citizenship through economic contributions. This in turn engenders precarity for noncitizen migrants as citizenship becomes 'increasingly precarious and conditional on requirements that are often difficult to meet or maintain' (Goldring, Berinstein, and Bernhard 2009, 245). This instrumentalist perspective colours discourse around temporary migrants in Australia, with uncertain migration trajectories often framed through a consumption-based metaphor of 'try before you buy' migration (Hawthorne 2013; Mares 2013a).

Although an instrumental turn is only one form of recent transformations in citizenship, it is the most relevant to the subjects of this paper. There has also been in Australia, as there has internationally, a contrasting political discourse around 'integration conditions' and 'civic citizenship' (see e.g. Goodman 2010; Joppke 2007), and calls to 're-nationalize' (Levey 2014) citizenship. In Australia, this has largely taken the form of a conservative discourse around commitment to 'Australian values' as a condition of citizenship. In practice, however, civic citizenship is only marginally part of the lived migration process in Australia. It is reflected mostly in the citizenship test, introduced in 2007, which in comparison to eligibility for permanent residency, remains a marginal hurdle for most migrants – unlimited re-sits are permitted, failing does not affect permanent resident status, and pass rates on the first or second attempt are around 99% for skilled migrants and 79% for humanitarian migrants (McNamara and Ryan 2011).

Analyses of neoliberalized citizenship that refer to the way in which citizenship has become 'contractualized' (Somers 2008) are highly relevant to the noncitizen subjects I am discussing here. 'Contract', however, implies an agreement that is binding, and also implies an exchange of agreed upon value and agreed terms. Yet the journey from noncitizen to citizen in Australia is in fact a nonlinear process of often unequal transaction in which criteria can shift instantaneously and migrant investments of time, money, consumption and labour are given dynamic values by the regime in different contexts and at different times. I thus refer to these processes as 'uneven contractual exchanges'. Criteria to obtain permanent residence (and thus become eligible for citizenship) can be revoked or reframed at any time, which often disrupts migrants' investments of time and labour and makes their migration goals inherently tenuous (Robertson and Runganaikaloo 2014, 214).

A noncitizen who may be eligible to eventually gain citizenship when she arrives in Australia can find that changes to points systems, the national lists of priority skills, or other requirements mean that she becomes ineligible even if she has been living and working in Australia for some time. Falling into ineligibility can happen to individual noncitizens (see e.g. the story of nurse Claire Hewitt who was denied a permanent visa after being injured in a workplace accident (Mares 2013b)) or to particular groups en masse, sometimes even after their applications for permanent residency have been lodged. This was the case for a large group of mostly student-migrants in 2010, with overnight policy changes rendering many previously eligible onshore PR applicants either ineligible or placed at the end of a continually growing processing queue. Verma (2013) describes the over 120,000 would-be citizens affected by the changes as 'a cohort who had paid thousands for an education never obtained, who had worked the most violent and precarious jobs imaginable in the Australian economy.' Yet, any hope of a return on their long-term investment in fulfilling the 'citizenship contract' were instantaneously revoked by the immigration regime in the face of processing backlogs and public backlash against student to migrant policies. Despite such risks of precarity, student-migrants are often still understood through consumption-based metaphors of privileged mobility, described for example by Hawthorne (2010, 30) as 'highly discerning education and migration consumers – researching global options to select the optimal study, migration and lifestyle "package"'.

Within uneven contractual exchanges, the criteria for ongoing membership are sometimes determined by the state, sometimes by the employer, and sometimes highly contingent on the amount of material resources that a noncitizen has. The dominance of consumption within processes of uneven contractual exchange shores up inequalities and uncertainties. This is exemplified by the burgeoning transnational migration industry of lawyers, agents, loan sharks and labour recruiters. Usually paid for by migrants themselves but occasionally by employers, these capitalist operations outsource the management of migrant labour away from state apparatuses, and often operate in the grey areas between legality and illegality. These processes of exchange place noncitizens at a level of distance from the state and the likelihood of successfully gaining citizenship also becomes, often to a large extent, dependent on one's consumer capital. For example, those who can afford to undertake further study (such as further tertiary study or preparation courses for the mandatory English language tests), to pay agents and lawyers to develop their application, or to pay corrupt recruiters or agents to falsify documents, are at a distinct advantage in gaining new visas.

The work of Lee and Pratt (2012) is particularly instructive here, as it highlights 'the violence that can attend the promises and practices of inclusion through citizenship' (890). Their work on Filipino undocumented migrants in the US, as well as work by Culic (2010) on the disciplining of skilled migrants through their visa application processes, clearly shows how the 'promise' of citizenship becomes a process of moulding subjects to fit state criteria. Migrants in this context must 'prove their "worthiness" of the ultimate prize of membership' (Shachar 2014, 118). While Culic (2010) looks at skilled migrants before they enter the nation-state and Lee and Pratt (2012) look at the undocumented in the Australian context, this 'worthiness' is both constructed and contested while subjects are legally resident in the territory of host state and often have been for some time. The processes of citizenships of uneven contractual exchange thus often put migrants in vulnerable positions in the workforce, willing to put up with exploitative conditions for the promise of employer sponsorship for new visas. This is apparent in both my own work on student-workers and tourist-workers (Robertson 2014, 11–12) as well as in reviews of the 457 scheme from the Australian Industrial Relations Commission, which showed that the power of the employer to give or withhold support for permanent residency makes noncitizens vulnerable to poor living conditions, illegal wage deductions and other forms of exploitation (Mares 2013a).

The precarity of noncitizens surrounds not just their labour, however, but in fact bleeds in to the most intimate spheres of their lives. State power infiltrates the 'intimate' (and by this, I mean the personal and domestic lives of noncitizens) largely due to the inherent uncertainty of the 'promise of citizenship' and the biopolitical approach of the immigration regime in deciding who meets the criteria for permanent belonging. In my previous work on the protracted journey from international student to citizen in Australia (Robertson 2013; Robertson and Runganaikaloo 2014) I found that romantic relationships with partners with PR or citizen status may be accelerated so that spouse visas can be obtained. Having children may be delayed until residency or citizenship is confirmed, because of the higher costs of healthcare and education for noncitizens in comparison to citizens, as well as concerns about starting or growing a family in a situation of immigration precarity. Noncitizens on bridging visas (often while in the process of 'churning' from one visa to another) were unable to care for ailing parents overseas or attend family funerals because of restrictions on their right to travel. For many, passions, interests and established career trajectories were put aside for career pathways that would garner immigration points (Robertson and Runganaikaloo 2014, 217). The general uncertainty of the 'promise of citizenship' had a strong psychological impact on noncitizens: their sense of security, their relationships, their sense of self, and their relationship to the nation-state (Robertson 2013). The biopolitical nature of migrant selection can also have a highly significant impact on long-term family investments in migration goals – this is exemplified in the recent stories of 457 skilled health workers denied permanent residency because of children with disabilities or their own disabilities (Dobbin 2008; Mares 2013b), as well as the fact that 'ageing out' of eligibility (younger migrants achieve more 'points') is always a risk in staggered migration pathways.

Although these intimate forms of state power are incomparable with the 'bare life' that Agamben (1998) prescribes to the stateless noncitizen, they are nonetheless a type of what Žižek (2008) calls 'systemic violence' – in which the structures that dominate economic and political life perpetuate 'hidden' oppression on large groups of people. The 'promise of citizenship' makes noncitizens complicit in their own governance and their own exclusion, and subject to rigorous biopolitical criteria for membership. This resonates with Bailey et al.'s (2002, 139) analysis of the ways in which temporary status allows immigration regimes to hold 'disciplining power over bodies, families, and social fields'.

Beyond the impact on the lives of individual migrants, however, these processes reframe the way citizenship and noncitizenship are understood, particularly in the context of settler migration in immigrant democracies. The transition from noncitizen to citizen in an immigrant democracy has traditionally been symbolic of national social, cultural and political belonging (initially assimilationist in Australia but increasingly integrationist and multicultural from the 1970s). The contractualization of citizenship and the increase in temporary migration means that the boundary between noncitizen and citizen becomes less about belonging and civic participation, and more about the fulfilment of particular economic criteria. Resident noncitizens are no longer either short-term visitors or settler citizens-in-waiting, but occupy a complex and ambiguous space as often long-term residents who may have a varied range of subjective senses of belonging to Australia, and similarly varied and contingent access to crossing the boundary from noncitizen to citizen.

The depoliticization of noncitizenship

As outlined above, immigration systems and criteria can mean that the state plays a highly amplified role in the lives of noncitizens in comparison to citizens – that is, it can have a more tangible presence in everyday decisions and experiences, often constraining both work and social conditions in specific ways. There have also been an increasing number of visible breaches of the rights of noncitizens in Australia, including 'subjective' (Žižek 2008) acts of racist violence as well as the systemic violence of workplace exploitation. Yet noncitizens in Australia remain a considerably depoliticized group, particularly in comparison to other noncitizen groups globally, such as undocumented workers and asylum seekers (see this volume). In this section, I identify three key elements of depoliticization that work through the discursive framings of noncitizen subjects in Australia: the subsumption of noncitizen lived experiences and labour under sojourner-consumer and elite identities; the hierarchy and fragmentation of various noncitizen statuses and the weak links to existing political collectivities.

Policy frameworks and political discourse render the presence of noncitizens, and in particular their contributions and vulnerabilities as labour, largely invisible. Dauvergne and Marsden (2014, 226) note how the very category of 'temporary migrant' belies a kind of political 'neutrality'. Temporary migrants are most commonly presented as self-sufficient and transient subjects who therefore justifiably sit outside the rights and social protections afforded to citizens. This is achieved through government policy and discourse that subscribes sojourner-consumer identities to many noncitizens, particularly students, graduates and working holiday makers. The Knight Review, for example, the key document framing the temporary graduate worker policy, insists that the visas are for temporary residence only, that they function as 'an adjunct to study' and should not be seen as pathways to permanent migration (Knight 2011, 40). Official information targeted towards potential working holiday makers and the general public continues to position the visa as for 'cultural exchange' and to place the work component as secondary to the tourism component (DIAC 2013b), despite the fact that these workers can stay for two years, provide crucial labour to the agricultural sector, and often move on to further temporary and permanent visas.

These 'sojourner-consumer' discourses work to position many noncitizen groups within a specifically Western cultural imaginary of why and how young people choose to live and work aboard. These imaginaries centre on Western 'rite of passage' constructs, popular with Australian middle-class young people, such as the 'gap year' or the 'working holiday.' But such constructs imply temporary mobilities for purposes of self-actualization, professional development and leisure travel (Hirschorn and Hefferon 2013; Simpson 2005), rather than, as is the case for many noncitizens in Australia, labour migration or citizenship pathways. These discourses, which often do not fit with the realities of noncitizens' desires and practices, reinforce ideas of noncitizens as independent, self-reliant and transient, excising their identities as workers and as potential citizens. Even 457 workers, who are explicitly in Australia to work, are prescribed an identity of 'highly skilled'. This denotes an elite mobility characterized by self-resourcing and self-reliance, obscuring the fact that, as work by Xiang (2001) and Velayutham (2013) shows, and the story of Chang Chang exemplifies, 457 status does not necessarily denote either an elite status in the labour market or an immunity to vulnerability.

The hierarchies and heterogeneity within the broad category of noncitizenship in Australia also have a depoliticizing function. Unlike undocumented workers in the EU or US, who have mobilized under the political subjectivity of 'undocumented', different categories of noncitizens in Australia often have little common ground politically. Any movements to claim further rights tend to be fairly localized and narrowly focused on a particular noncitizen group. For example, in 2006 international students in the states of Victoria and New South Wales lobbied for the same public transport concessions as local students, and in 2011 New Zealand citizens living in Queensland campaigned to be eligible for government disaster relief after flooding and a cyclone. There has been, however, little collective politicization around a noncitizen or a temporary migrant identity. This is largely because of the highly 'patchworked' nature of rights and statuses I have described earlier and the subsequent diversity of experiences, vulnerabilities, concerns and claims among the noncitizen population. International students and graduate workers, for example, are unlikely to feel support for the ire of New Zealanders on the 'protected special category visa' at being left out of new bonuses in unemployment benefits, when students and graduate workers are not eligible for any benefits at all. Similarly, 457 workers in primarily skilled trades and professions in urban centres are unlikely to find collective ground or even opportunities to interact with working holiday makers doing agricultural work in remote areas, despite the fact that both groups are subject to labour exploitation on the basis of their visas. The fragmentation and hierarchies of rights mean that although there are over one million noncitizen workers in Australia, they are as yet unable to form a cohesive sense of political community as a basis to resist state practices and make claims for more rights for noncitizens or fairer access to citizenship.

The status of many noncitizens in Australia also sets them apart from existing ethnic communities made up primarily of 'settled' migrants. Tensions between permanent and temporary migrants of the same ethnicity, based on class, religious and cultural differences, but also on the perceived 'short-termism' of temporary migrants are emerging in the Australian migration literature (see e.g. Baldassar and Pyke 2014; Han and Han 2010; Singh and Cabraal 2010). Noncitizens in Australia can often live in a segregated subcultural space, mostly only interacting with others of their own visa status as well as nationality (Allon and Anderson 2010; Maksay 2007). The uncertain futures of noncitizens may also find them excluded from established diaspora communities, who are associated with long-term settlement (Cwerner 2001). This relative segregation from the established ethnic community of settler migrants thus makes it difficult for noncitizens to mobilize from an ethnic base, despite the strong presence of ethnic lobbies and advocacy groups throughout Australia, developed over the course of nearly 40 years of official multiculturalism. Ethnic lobbying in Australia tends to be based on a settler paradigm – lobbing for the recognition of full members of an established multicultural society to practice their culture without harm or derision, and for government-funded services to meet the specific needs of various ethnic groups. Because they lack full membership and are overall ineligible for most government support services, noncitizens often fall outside of this type of ethnic politics.

The limits and possibilities of solidarity

Despite the depoliticization discussed above, there are some incipient solidarities that work towards a recognition of noncitizens' unique position. Here, I understand the concept of 'solidarities' in Featherstone's (2012) sense as transformative political relations. These movements, usually still relatively small in scale, have been most successful when embedded, even in a fragmented and uneven way, within existing local labour solidarities or broader social movements, such as antiracism. As Rosenblum and Tivig (2014, 126–127) argue, for noncitizen subjects, the moral and symbolic significance of political participation is amplified through established, institutionalized channels.

The taxi driver strikes in Melbourne in 2008 after the stabbing of an Indian driver and the general protests in 2009 in the wake of continuing violent street attacks on Indian students, including the murder of Nitin Garg, are good examples. Although much of the strike action was undertaken by Indian noncitizen taxi drivers, a key component of the labour force, the strike action garnered broader support from the national Transport Workers Union as well as a great deal of media attention. This led to successfully lobbying for legislative change within the taxi industry, and brought public attention to noncitizens' contributions as labour (Robertson 2011, 9–10). The anti-violence protests rallied thousands of Indian student-migrants and supporters. These actions also gained significant traction politically because they tied in to the existing antiracist and multicultural politics of the Australian Left, and because they had potential to damage the reputation of Australia's multimillion-dollar international education industry. Although the initial protests were organized by the Indian student lobby, they eventually grew to include broad-based community support. The 'Vindaloo against Violence' campaign that emerged after the street protests was initiated by Anglo-Australian citizens and supported by the settled Indian community, particularly through engagement with the owners of Indian restaurants.

However, protests and contestations more particular to the noncitizen identity itself, and not embedded within local solidarity networks have gained far less traction. For example, the 'G4/G5' movement conducted online protests and attempted legal action against the Australian government when immigration policy change left thousands of would-be citizens with limited access to residency. This was one of the few movements that provided a direct challenge to the ways that migration governance itself had crafted inequalities for particular groups of noncitizens. Yet, sitting outside of labour politics or existing non-discrimination advocacy, this movement gained very little political purchase or mainstream publicity. Advocacy groups for noncitizen student-workers and tourist-workers have also emerged often based around particular nationalities. They work primarily to help noncitizen workers understand their workplace rights and entitlements and to have support in labour disputes. Groups like this do very significant outreach work and are beginning to build important links across noncitizen groups and with existing organizations such as unions. However, at present these organizations are grassroots, largely unfunded and run mostly by volunteer noncitizens, and thus lack resources or capacities to lobby for broader structural changes.

As I have written elsewhere (Robertson 2011, 14), even when noncitizen politics does gain visibility and support, the actual discursive politics of some of these movements are not always a direct resistance to the ideological underpinnings of citizenships of contract and consumption. The discourses of noncitizens in their 'acts of citizenship' (Isin 2009) often co-opt the rhetoric of consumption and exchange as grounds of their claims to rights. For example, noncitizen groups have often cited their economic contributions to Australia in education fees, labour and taxes as evidence that they are 'deserving' citizens, and even as a grounds to protest subjective violence. Unlike irregular migrant politics, noncitizen solidarities do not always make direct claims for legal citizenship (Walters 2008, 185). Their agendas are diverse, from ensuring workplace rights to combating racist violence to addressing claims of injustice in the immigration system. The 'process of becoming' here is not just about gaining legal membership – rather it is about developing a political subjectivity in relation to the nation-state in which they are resident, about 'acts of citizenship' (Isin 2009) that make claims to rights despite their ambiguous statuses.

Conclusions

I have argued in this paper that the proliferation of temporary migration schemes in contemporary Australia has led to increased numbers of noncitizens on 'staggered' and uncertain pathways from noncitizenship to citizenship, and that citizenships based on uneven contractual exchanges and consumption ideologies have come to dominate these pathways. I have analysed how these ideologies and practices of citizenship create a highly intimate intrusion of state power into migrants' daily lives, and how the 'promise of citizenship' subjects noncitizens to systemic violence and intensified regulation. Further, I have shown that noncitizen identities are depoliticized through their heterogeneity, fragmentation and invisibility. Acts of citizenship by noncitizens thus have limited traction unless they are embedded into local solidarity networks and their concerns. This conceptualization of noncitizenship in relationship to intimacies of state power and the 'promise of citizenship' seek to look beyond the presence or absence of legal rights in theorizing noncitizenship and emerging forms of migration. It focuses in contrast on the intensified governance of the noncitizen subject, whose hours and patterns of work and study can be regulated and monitored by the regime, and who must self-regulate aspects of their health, relationships and finances in order to meet unstable criteria for ongoing membership or citizenship. It also shows how long-term and often familial investments (both financial and personal) in a migration journey can be severely disrupted by the state's ever present power to exclude.

Noncitizens in Australia sit within the broad and diverse 'middle' spectrum between the elite flexible citizen, often seen as the beneficiary of emerging 'mutations' in sovereignty and citizenship (Ong 2006), and the low skilled and often exploited contract or undocumented workers who are often constructed subject to 'fragmented citizenship.' Analysis of this heterogeneous 'middle space' of Australian noncitizenship is instructive to citizenship studies more broadly, in that it shows how regimes shape and reshape the criteria that make a 'desirable' migrant, and that nominal 'skills' classification and visa categories can obscure a vast array of subjectivities, social practices and labour practices. Official status and migrant practice often exist in a contradictory tension, such as the skilled worker who does unskilled work, or the 'student' or 'tourist' who in fact operates as a labour migrant. These patchwork subjectivities can depoliticize noncitizen identities through their invisibility as labour, their lack of a collective agenda of claims, and their limited embeddedness in traditional ethnic politics. Yet new political identities and solidarities involving noncitizens are emerging, and very much exemplify Agamben's (2000) argument about the interstitial zones between inclusion and exclusion, as their political claims negotiate 'the social condition of being neither fully excluded nor fully recognized' (Walters 2008, 185).

Noncitizenship in this context is a position of exclusion in contrast to permanent residents and citizens (which is what makes the promise of citizenship so alluring), but it cannot be merely framed as a condition of the absence of rights or legal membership. It is rather a mutable space that can be orientated towards a future citizenship, as well as a highly fragmented space in which a 'patchwork' of rights, legitimacy and claims operate at different levels and morph across time as temporary migrants become mobile across different visa statuses. This analysis of citizenship and noncitizenship in Australia raises avenues for further analysis of other contexts globally: namely, how transnationally mobile, noncitizen labour is rendered invisible by various political discourses and processes in different political contexts; how the 'middling' experience of noncitizenship plays out under different immigration regimes and what incipient strategies of resistance are emerging to the contractualization of citizenship and the depoliticization of noncitizenship in different global contexts.

Notes

1. The 457 visa subclass was introduced in 1996. It is the main programme under which Australian or overseas employers can sponsor skilled migrants to work in Australia on a temporary basis, for a period of up to four years.
2. I do not include migrants with permanent residency (PR) under the noncitizens category in this paper, because permanent residents in Australia are effectively 'citizens-in-waiting' – they have full social rights and are virtually guaranteed access to full citizenship once they have been legally resident in Australia for the required time. I also exclude the small number of short-term workers who enter Australia under the Seasonal Workers Program (SWP), who have a vastly different experience from the majority of noncitizen workers in Australia – most notably they have little to no chance of extended temporary stays or permanent residency.
3. It is difficult to ascertain the proportion of temporary migrants across employment sectors or skilled/unskilled work. There are no existing sources of population level socio-economic or employment data on temporary migrants in Australia (Birrell and Healy 2012b; Hugo 2006), with the Department of Immigration and Border Protection only releasing regular data on 457 workers, and many noncitizens, particularly working holiday makers and students, working in the informal economy. Existing surveys do show that the significance of different employment sectors varies greatly across visa categories, with the vast majority of working holiday makers in low or unskilled work in accommodation and food services or agriculture, forestry and fishing (Tan et al. 2009), while over a half of 457 workers are engaged in professional work (DIBP 2014).

Disclosure statement

No potential conflict of interest was reported by the author.

References

Agamben, Giorgio. 1998. *Homo Sacer. Sovereign Power and Bare Life*. Stanford: Stanford University Press.
Agamben, Giorgio. 2000. *Means without End: Notes on Politics*. Minneapolis: University of Minnesota Press.

Allon, Fiona, and Kay Anderson. 2010. "Intimate Encounters: The Embodied Transnationalism of Backpackers and Independent Travellers." *Population, Space and Place* 16 (1): 11–22.
Allon, Fiona, Kay Anderson, and Robyn Bushell. 2008. "Mutant Mobilities: Backpacker Tourism in 'Global' Sydney." *Mobilities* 3 (1): 73–94.
ABS (Australian Bureau of Statistics) 2013. "3417.0 – Understanding Migrant Outcomes – Enhancing the Value of Census Data, Australia, 2011." Accessed July 17, 2014. http://www.abs.gov.au/ausstats/abs@.nsf/latestproducts/3417.0main%20features22011?opendocument&tabname=summary&prodno=3417.0&issue=2011&num=&view
Bailey, Adrian J., Richard A. Wright, Alison Mountz, and Ines M. Miyares. 2002. "(Re)Producing Salvadoran Transnational Geographies." *Annals of the Association of American Geographers* 92 (1): 125–144.
Baldassar, Loretta, and Joanne Pyke. 2014. "Intra-Diaspora Knowledge Transfer and 'New' Italian Migration." *International Migration* 52 (4): 128–143. doi:10.1111/Imig.12135.
Birrell, Bob, and Ernest Healy. 2012a. "Immigration Overshoot." In *CPUR Research Report*, 1–37. Melbourne: Centre for Population and Urban Research, Monash University.
Birrell, Bob, and Ernest Healy. 2012b. "Scarce Jobs: Migrants or Locals at the End of the Queue." In *CPUR Research Report*. Melbourne: Centre for Population and Urban Research, Monash University.https://theaustralianpopulationresearchinstitute.files.wordpress.com/2015/01/birrell-healy-scarce-jobs-aug-2013.pdf
Clifton, Jonathan. 2010. "Fragmented Citizenship: Canadian Immigration Policy and Low-skilled Portuguese Workers in Toronto." *Journal of Immigrant and Refugee Studies* 8 (4): 409–430.
Colic-Peisker, Val. 2011. "A New Era in Australian Multiculturalism? From Working-class "Ethnics" to a "Multicultural Middle-class"." *International Migration Review* 45 (3): 562–587.
Culic, Irina. 2010. "State of Imagination: Embodiments of Immigration Canada." *The Sociological Review* 58 (3): 343–360.
Cwerner, Saulo B. 2001. "The Times of Migration." *Journal of Ethnic and Migration Studies* 27 (1): 7–36.
Dauvergne, Catherine, and Sarah Marsden. 2014. "The Ideology of Temporary Labour Migration in the Post-global Era." *Citizenship Studies* 18 (2): 224–242.
DIBP (Department of Immigration and Border Protection) 2013. "Temporary Entrant and New Zealand Citizens in Australia, as at 31 December 2013". Accessed September 7, 2014. http://www.immi.gov.au/media/statistics/pdf/temp-entrants-newzealand-dec13.pdf
DIBP (Department of Immigration and Border Protection) 2014. "Subclass 457 Quarterly Report, Quarter Ending at 31 December 2014." Accessed April 8, 2015. http://www.immi.gov.au/media/statistics/pdf/457-quarterly-report-2014-12-31.pdf
DIAC (Department of Immigration and Citizenship) 2013a. "2012–13 Migration Program Report." Accessed August 22, 2014. https://www.immi.gov.au/media/statistics/pdf/report-on-migration-program-2012-13.pdf
DIAC (Department of Immigration and Citizenship) 2013b. "Visas, Immigration and Refugees: Working Holiday." Accessed May 6, 2013. http://www.immi.gov.au/visitors/working-holiday/
Dobbin, Marika. 2008. "Doctor Denied Visa as Son has Down Syndrome." *Sydney Morning Herald*, October 31. http://www.smh.com.au/news/national/doctor-denied-visa-as-son-has-down-syndrome/2008/10/31/1224956298223.html
Featherstone, David. 2012. *Solidarity*. London: Zed Books.
Goldring, Luin, and Patricia Landolt. 2011. "Caught in the Work-citizenship Matrix: The Lasting Effects of Precarious Legal Status on Work for Toronto Immigrants." *Globalizations* 8 (3): 325–341.
Goldring, Luin, Carolina Berinstein, and Judith K. Bernhard. 2009. "Institutionalizing Precarious Migratory Status in Canada." *Citizenship Studies* 13 (3): 239–265.
Goodman, Sara Wallace. 2010. "Integration Requirements for Integration's Sake? Identifying, Categorising and Comparing Civic Integration Policies." *Journal of Ethnic and Migration Studies* 36 (5): 753–772.
Han, Joy J., and Gil-Soo Han. 2010. "The Koreans in Sydney." *Sydney Journal* 2 (2): 25–35.
Hawthorne, Lesleyanne. 2010. "How Valuable is "Two-step Migration"? Labor Market Outcomes for International Student Migrants to Australia." *Asian and Pacific Migration Journal* 19 (1): 5–36.

Hawthorne, Lesleyanne. 2013. "Identification and Retention of the Globally Mobile 'Elite' Workforce." *International Metropolis Conference*, Tampere, Finland, September 9–13.
Hirschorn, Sara, and Kate Hefferon. 2013. "Leaving It All behind to Travel: Venturing Uncertainty as a Means to Personal Growth and Authenticity." *Journal of Humanistic Psychology* 53 (3): 283–306.
van Houdt, Friso, Semin Suvarierol, and Willem Schinkel. 2011. "Neoliberal Communitarian Citizenship: Current Trends towards 'Earned Citizenship' in the United Kingdom, France and the Netherlands." *International Sociology* 26 (3): 408–432.
Hugo, Graeme. 2006. "Temporary Migration and the Labour Market in Australia." *Australian Geographer* 37 (2): 211–231.
Isin, Engin F. 2009. "Citizenship in Flux: The Figure of the Activist Citizen." *Subjectivity* 29 (1): 367–388.
Janda, Michael. 2015. "Australia's 457 'King of Visas' is a Road to Serfdom for Many Migrants." *ABC News*, January 7. Accessed April 8, 2015. http://www.abc.net.au/news/2013-09-06/27king-of-visas27-a-road-to-serfdom-for-many/4941980
Joppke, Christian. 2007. "Beyond National Models: Civic Integration Policies for Immigrants in Western Europe." *West European Politics* 30 (1): 1–22.
Jordens, Ann-Mari. 1997. *Alien to Citizen: Settling Migrants in Australia, 1945–1975*. St. Leonards, Sydney: Allen and Unwin.
Khoo, Siew-Ean. 2002. "Immigration Issues in Australia." *Journal of Population Research* (Special Ed.): 67–68.
Khoo, Siew-Ean, Peter F. McDonald, and Graeme Hugo. 2005. *Temporary Skilled Migrants in Australia: Employment Circumstances and Migration Outcomes*. Canberra: DIMIA.
Knight, Michael. 2011. "Strategic Review of the Student Visa Program." Accessed May 7, 2013. http://www.immi.gov.au/students/_pdf/2011-knight-review.pdf
Landolt, Patricia, and Luin Goldring. 2015. "Assembling noncitizenship through the work of conditionality." *Citizenship Studies* 19 (8): 1–17. doi:10.1080/13621025.2015.1110280.
Lee, Elizabeth, and Geraldine Pratt. 2012. "The Spectacular and the Mundane: Racialised State Violence, Filipino Migrant Workers, and Their Families." *Environment and Planning A* 44 (4): 889–904.
Lenard, Patti Tamara, and Christine Straehle, eds. 2012. *Legislated Inequality. Temporary Labour Migration in Canada*. Montreal: McGill-Queens University Press.
Levey, Geoffrey Brahm. 2014. "Liberal Nationalism and the Australian Citizenship Tests." *Citizenship Studies* 18 (2): 175–189.
Lewis, Gail, and Sarah Neal. 2005. "Introduction: Contemporary Political Contexts, Changing Terrains and Revisited Discourses." *Ethnic and Racial Studies* 28 (3): 423–444.
Maksay, Arpad. 2007. "Japanese Working Holiday Makers in Australia: Subculture and Resistance." *Tourism Review International* 11 (1): 33–43.
Mares, Peter. 2013a. "Temporary Migration is a Permanent Thing." *Inside Story*. Accessed June 19, 2014. http://inside.org.au/temporary-migration-is-a-permanent-thing/
Mares, Peter. 2013b. Falling between the Cracks of Temporary Migration. *Inside Story*. Accessed January 17, 2014. http://inside.org.au/falling-between-the-cracks-of-temporary-migration/
McGregor, Joann. 2011. "Contestations and Consequences of Deportability: Hunger Strikes and the Political Agency of Non-citizens." *Citizenship Studies* 15 (5): 597–611.
McNamara, Tim, and Kerry Ryan. 2011. "Fairness versus Justice in Language Testing: The Place of English Literacy in the Australian Citizenship Test." *Language Assessment Quarterly* 8 (2): 161–178.
McNevin, Anne. 2006. "Political Belonging in a Neoliberal Era: The Struggle of the Sans-Papiers." *Citizenship Studies* 10 (2): 135–151.
McNevin, Anne. 2007. "Irregular Migrants, Neoliberal Geographies and Spatial Frontiers of 'The Political'." *Review of International Studies* 33 (4): 655–674.
Mountz, Alison, Richard Wright, Ines Miyares, and Adrian J. Bailey. 2002. "Lives in Limbo: Temporary Protected Status and Immigrant Identities." *Global Networks* 2 (4): 335–356. doi:10.1111/1471-0374.00044.
Nagel, Caroline R., and Lynn A. Staeheli. 2004. "Citizenship, Identity and Transnational Migration: Arab Immigrants to the United States." *Space and Polity* 8 (1): 3–23.

Ong, Aihwa. 1999. *Flexible Citizenship: The Cultural Logics of Transnationality*. Durham: Duke University Press.
Ong, Aihwa. 2006. "Mutations in Citizenship." *Theory, Culture and Society* 23 (2–3): 499–505.
Ongley, Patrick, and David Pearson. 1995. "Post-1945 International Migration: New Zealand, Australia and Canada Compared." *International Migration Review* 29 (3): 765–793.
Parreñas, Rhacel Salazar. 2010. "Homeward Bound: The Circular Migration of Entertainers between Japan and the Philippines." *Global Networks* 10 (3): 301–323.
Peterson, Nicolas, and Will Sanders, eds. 1998. *Citizenship and Indigenous Australians: Changing Conceptions and Possibilities*. Cambridge: Cambridge University Press.
Rajkumar, Deepa, Laurel Berkowitz, Leah F. Vosko, Valerie Preston, and Robert Latham. 2012. "At the Temporary–Permanent Divide: How Canada Produces Temporariness and Makes Citizens through Its Security, Work, and Settlement Policies." *Citizenship Studies* 16 (3–4): 483–510.
Robertson, Shanthi. 2011. "Cash Cows, Backdoor Migrants, or Activist Citizens? International Students, Citizenship, and Rights in Australia." *Ethnic and Racial Studies* 34 (12): 2192–2211.
Robertson, Shanthi. 2013. *Transnational Student-migrants and the State*. Basingstoke: Palgrave Macmillan.
Robertson, Shanthi. 2014. "Time and Temporary Migration: The Case of Temporary Graduate Workers and Working Holiday Makers in Australia." *Journal of Ethnic and Migration Studies* 40 (12): 1915–1933.
Robertson, Shanthi, and Anjena Runganaikaloo. 2014. "Lives in Limbo: Migration Experiences in Australia's Education-migration Nexus." *Ethnicities* 14 (2): 208–226.
Rosenblum, Nancy L., and Andrea Tivig. 2014. "Political Incorporation in America: Immigrant Partisans." *Citizenship Studies* 18 (2): 125–140. doi:10.1080/13621025.2014.886390.
Schuster, Liza. 2005. "The Continuing Mobility of Migrants in Italy: Shifting between Places and Statuses." *Journal of Ethnic and Migration Studies* 31 (4): 757–774.
Shachar, Ayelet. 2014. "Introduction: Citizenship and the 'Right to Have Rights.'" *Citizenship Studies* 18 (2): 114–124.
Silvey, Rachel. 2004. "Transnational Domestication: State Power and Indonesian Migrant Women in Saudi Arabia." *Political Geography* 23 (3): 245–264.
Simpson, Kate. 2005. "Dropping out or Signing up? The Professionalisation of Youth Travel." *Antipode* 37 (3): 447–469.
Singh, Supriya, and Anuja Cabraal. 2010. "Indian Student Migrants in Australia: Issues of Community Sustainability." *People and Place* 18 (1): 19–30.
Somers, Margaret R. 2008. *Genealogies of Citizenship: Markets, Statelessness, and the Right to Have Rights*. Cambridge: Cambridge University Press.
Tan, Yan, Sue Richardson, Laurence Lester, Tracy Bai, and Lulu Sun. 2009. *Evaluation of Australia's Working Holiday Maker (WHM) Program*. Adelaide: National Institute of Labour Studies, Flinders University.
Velayutham, S. 2013. "Precarious Experiences of Indians in Australia on 457 Temporary Work Visas." *The Economic and Labour Relations Review* 24 (3): 340–361.
Verma, Sanmati. 2013. "Pathways to Illegality, or 'What Happened to the International Students?'" *Mutinyzine*. Accessed August 5, 2014. http://mutinyzine.blog.com/2013/07/11/pathways-to-illegality/
Walters, William. 2008. "Acts of Demonstration: Mapping the Territory of (Non-) Citizenship." In *Acts of Citizenship*, edited by Engin Isin and Greg Neilson, 182–206. London: Zed Books.
Xiang, Biao. 2001. "Structuration of Indian Information Technology Professionals' Migration to Australia: An Ethnographic Study." *International Migration* 39 (5): 73–90.
Žižek, Slavoj. 2008. *Violence: Six Sideways Reflections*. New York: Picador.

These fine lines: locating noncitizenship in political protest in Europe

Heather L. Johnson

School of Politics, International Studies and Philosophy, Queen's University, Belfast, Northern Ireland

ABSTRACT
Since 2012, refugee protest camps and occupations have been established throughout Europe that contest the exclusion of refugees and asylum seekers, but that also make concrete demands for better living conditions and basic rights. It is a movement that is led by migrants as noncitizens, and so reveals new ways of thinking of the political agency and status of noncitizenship not as simply reactive to an absence of citizenship, but as a powerful and transgressive subjectivity in its own right. This paper argues that we should resist collapsing analysis back into the frameworks of citizenship, and instead be attentive to the politics of presence and solidarity manifest in these protest camps as a way of understanding, and engaging, noncitizen activism.

> Take a strong painkiller. Then turn the front two oven rings of your oven on and wait until they are red hot. Then lay four fingers of your right hand on the right oven ring and the four fingers of the left on the left ring.
>
> Why you are doing this?
>
> … 'The borders that exclude me from elementary human rights, from leading a good life, lay beyond barbed wire. The border which separates people from unworthy people: these are the fine lines on my fingers.' This is what you say before you press your hand on the oven. (excerpted from Leisch February 19, 2013)

The fine lines of border politics as they are lived and experienced by irregular migrants are the lines of geographical borders crossed, of fences and walls that mark immigration reception centres and of the social borders between legal and illegal, allowed and disallowed. They are the lines of the fingerprints that are stored in the Eurodac database. They are the fine lines between citizens and noncitizens and, fundamentally, they are political. They mark legitimate participation, and what might be considered threatening or troubling agency. Any discussion of migrant and noncitizen political agency grapples with these lines, and how they might be, and are, transgressed. This paper begins from such transgression, defining noncitizenship as a political status that is not simply the absence of citizenship, but that has political content in itself. Rather than seeking an enactment of citizenship in order to understand migrant agency, the refugee protest camp movements in Europe are examples of transgressive, situated solidarity as noncitizens give us clues about how we can rethink activism and political agency within the border politics of mobility.

The following paper begins with an examination of refugee and migrant protest across Europe, questioning the utility of citizenship as a guiding framework and engaging with manifestations of presence and solidarity within the politics of noncitizenship. Recent years have witnessed an expanding trend of refugee protest camps across Europe. It began in Würzburg, Germany, in March 2012 and is reflected in ongoing refugee strikes and occupations in Austria, Denmark, Turkey, Bulgaria, Greece, France and the Netherlands (Gržinić 2013). In that the protests are directly engaging the state, the movement speaks in familiar terms, making demands for legal status and for better living conditions. It has roots back through the 'no borders' protests that have persisted in Europe for over 10 years as citizen-activists agitate on behalf of irregular migrants and asylum seekers moving within the evermore restrictive European border regime. However, these emergent protests are not citizen-activist-led social movements but migrant noncitizen-led practices of resistance. In the words of Refugee Camp Berlin (January 1, 2013), the protesters 'call for the recognition of the refugee movement as a political institution.' I take this call seriously here, asking in what ways the resistive politics of noncitizens are producing new practices of presence and solidarity that enact political claims which transgress borders and establish noncitizenship as a political subjectivity. In doing so, I am not arguing for a homogenous or unambiguous understanding of the protests; to do so would be to disregard the multiple tensions, disagreements, and differences within and between each individual protest camp. Rather, I am highlighting perceptible and emergent trends of similarity that are consciously advanced by protesters themselves to open new avenues of thinking about political agency and action. I draw on the Refugee Protest Camp Vienna and the Refugee Camp Berlin in particular, using media and public outreach material drawn largely from the movements' websites, to ask how the self-representation of the protests reveals a politics of noncitizenship that resists a simple collapse back into the frameworks of citizenship, populating the politics of migration and mobility with multiple subjectivities.

The year 2012 marked the emergence of the refugee protest camps across Europe, most notably in Germany and Austria. In both cases, the protest is based on a tactic of occupation and the establishment of 'camps', founded in public places following organized marches from state immigration reception centres. In Germany, the protests were sparked in the spring of 2012 by the suicide of a 26-year-old Iranian migrant, Mohammad R., in one of the *Lagers* (asylum camps) in Würzburg (Hansen, Falkentoft, and Rode 2014, 28). Following his death, 80 fellow residents staged a spontaneous demonstration outside of the City Hall – an action which sparked protests across the country (McGuaran and Hudig 2014, 30). A massive protest march from Würzburg to Berlin was organized, ending in an encampment in Oranienplatz. Dubbing the protest a refugee strike, the protesters in Germany have undertaken rallies, marches, and hunger strikes in major cities across the country. In the fall of that year, the Refugee Protest Camp Vienna (RPCV) began with similar events. A march of over 100 refugees and supporters left from Traiskirchen reception centre, demanding freedom of movement and better living conditions for refugees and migrants, and ultimately established an encampment in the Sigmund Freud Park in front of the Votive Church, close to the University of Vienna. The occupation lasted for a month before it was forcibly cleared by police on the night of December 28, whereupon the refugees moved into the church itself. Inside, the occupation continued, and 45 refugees embarked on a hunger strike which lasted until February 2013, with one pause in January when the refugees' health deteriorated markedly. As with the camp in Berlin, the refugee occupation has been supported by widespread action, including a march of 2500 refugees and supporters. In the spring of 2013, the RPCV was moved to an old monastery (Gržinić 2013). The protest camp has since left the monastery, and has been located in different places throughout the city. It remains a palpable force, however, as protesters have continued to engage in a multitude of strategies and practices of protest: marches, occupations, solidarity rallies, discussion roundtables, film screenings, political speakers and public information campaigns have numbered amongst other efforts.

The protests in Germany and Austria are echoed and reflected in similar events across Europe. They are each important in their own contexts; they are the movements of non-citizens who are claiming rights and making demands on the state that are tied directly to not only their living conditions, but to the quality of their political lives. In doing so, the protestors are asserting the legitimacy of their political voice as noncitizens. However, the movements are also explicitly and consciously connected to one another in strategy, demands, and political discourse and, I argue, they are revelatory of an understanding of political action that asserts noncitizenship as an autonomous and independent subjectivity rather than simply as an absence of citizenship. The politics of noncitizenship are thus more than an appeal to citizenship, and a demand for inclusion in its frameworks. Rather, noncitizenship is not in opposition to citizenship, but alongside it as a status that embodies powerful, transgressive political agency and new ways of interrelating in political action. In the following, I examine the tensions and temptations of collapsing noncitizen action back into citizenship frameworks, and then trace two key dimensions of migrant protest that reveal pathways towards a different understanding: the assertion of presence by breaking the isolation of refugees; and the politics of solidarity premised upon mutual responsibility. It is navigating these 'fine lines' that noncitizen activism generates new political imaginations.

Noncitizen citizenship?

> We ourselves, the refugees, make the demonstration and we are the ones who want it. It is our fight. We thank everybody for their help, but we don't allow anybody to use us. This is a self-organized struggle of and by refugees, one that needs your support, your presence on the street on Saturday. (RPCV February 13, 2013g)

The protests and actions we are witnessing across Europe are unprecedented in their scale, and also in the form they are taking (McGuaran and Hudig 2014, 28). They are led by non-citizens, and are engaging in strategies and demands that contest citizenship as the only framework for understanding political action. Understanding this contestation requires that we resist collapsing back into a renewed emphasis on citizenship as the defining framework for political agency and participation, a challenge that has thus far proven difficult to meet in either theory or in practice.

A questioning of political subjectivity is, at its core, a struggle to define who an agent is, and how an agency itself might be recognized. Citizenship, as a status, is well established as the identity that embodies legitimate (and allowable) political agency and power (Nyers 2006). Grounded in understandings of democratic or representative politics, and the bond between the 'nation' and the 'state', it is a legal status that is bounded by territory and that is clearly defined, exclusive and exclusionary. In locating the capacity for political action in the citizen, an assumption of equivalency between 'Citizen' and 'Agent' is produced. The result is that political action or agency from outside of citizenship, by noncitizens, is seen as illegitimate, and troubling, where it is acknowledged at all (Nyers 2006). The argument about noncitizen politics ultimately becomes that noncitizens do not, or perhaps cannot, exercise political agency until they have achieved citizenship. Such a framework implies that the political work and action migrants undertake must be, and is always, expressed in terms of an aspiration to citizenship status, and that only once this status is attained can other politics occur.

I propose that the protests across Europe demand a different understanding of noncitizen political action. Noncitizenship is less grounded in territory. Instead, noncitizenship is transnational and multiple, a flexible subjectivity that embraces multiple 'categories' which are defined within shifting political contexts. It is reflective not only of assumptions and expectations laid out in state law and discourse, but of the self-representation of noncitizens themselves as they contest and use the frameworks that shape their lives and experiences. The protesters across Europe are asylum seekers, refugees and (often undocumented) migrants, categories that may have clear definition in law, but that in practice are overlapping, simultaneous and interchanged. Throughout the discourses that shape and represent the politics of migration, there is often an easy slippage between 'asylum seeker', 'refugee', and 'migrant' – and this is particularly the case in the language and practices of the protesters themselves. Here, individuals self-identify as one category or another at different times and places according to political context. Most often, the term 'refugee' is used in political statements, in a conscious use of and appeal to the moral and legal rights and entitlements that this category lays claim to. At other moments, 'migrant' is used to call upon a solidarity based in experiences of mobility. These self-representations are conscious, and politically savvy. They make use of the discursive content of each category in political ways to advance key demands; the categories are not simply given, nor are they always imposed. They are also taken, expressed and used to advance claims from a transnational subject position of 'noncitizen'. Although each manifestation of protest is grounded in a specific context, the frameworks and assumptions that they contest are much wider. The protester's demands target not only national policy but also the European Union (McGuaran and Hudig 2014, 28). There is a keen awareness of the ways in which migration policies and practices, such as the Dublin II Treaty and the Eurodac (the biometric database that enables the tracking of migrants via their fingerprints), operate to control the movement of migrants throughout Europe at levels beyond the nation-state. This awareness permeates the protests and contestations of noncitizens, and requires that our understandings resist a collapse back into the frameworks of citizenship and instead engage with multiple and fractured political subjectivities.

Moving beyond citizenship as the guiding framework for understanding political agency, in theory or in practice, is difficult. In many ways, this difficulty reflects a recognition that noncitizens live in difficult and marginalized circumstances which render them particularly vulnerable to the often violent impositions of sovereign power; citizen political action, by contrast, is legitimized and validated and so is reasonably safely enacted (Johnson 2014). The vulnerability of noncitizens is particularly clear in the condition of deportability; ultimately, the noncitizen can be evicted (Oberprantacher 2014), while freedom from deportation is one of the 'few remaining privileges' of citizens (Anderson, Gibney, and Paoletti 2011, 548). Deportability 'robs individuals, particularly those without lawful migration status, of the practical ability to claim even the most basic of rights lest they bring themselves to the attention of immigration authorities' (Anderson, Gibney, and Paoletti 2011, 552). This dynamic is starkly visible in the European protests, and a central demand for most movements is an end to deportations. The demands of the refugees in Vienna are particularly focused on this in response to a state crackdown on protesters in the wake of the occupation. Since 2013, Austria has undertaken a concerted campaign that focuses on the criminalization of the refugees, accusing several prominent protesters of being human traffickers and arresting, detaining and removing them on this basis. The protest has become oriented firmly around contradicting these controlling moves of the state: '[t]he Refugee Protest Movement Vienna insists on no further deportations of refugees and no criminalization of politically active refugees who draw attention to human rights violations in their home countries' (Platzer 2013). Stopping the deportations is a clear strategy for making visibility less risky and thus creating political space for noncitizen action; without this minimal protection, so the argument goes, action simply is not taken. The recognition of vulnerability can quickly become an assumption that agency itself is never enacted – or cannot be enacted – because it is too dangerous. Agency becomes unexpected (Oliveri 2012, 799). The 'fine lines' that distinguish differences between political statuses constrain what kind of politics can legitimately occur, or even be seen and heard.

It is very clear that migrants, noncitizens, do undertake political action. Their ongoing participation and engagement is well documented and described throughout critical literature (cf. De Genova 2010; Johnson 2014; McNevin 2006; Nyers 2006; Rygiel 2011). Reflecting on circumstances in Italy, Oliveri sees migrant protest as potentially re-inventing the premises and conditions of being political (2012, 795). Protesters in Italy, he writes, 'collectively demonstrated that it is possible to stand up and ask for respect even when you live under the continuous risk of being deported' (Oliveri 2012, 794). These politics break the citizen-agent assumption. Nevertheless, efforts to understand this break, and to engage with noncitizens as agents, often return to citizenship itself as a framework, and utilize its ideas and norms to understand agency in other forms. Rygiel writes:

> It is useful, I think, to theorize migrant struggles in terms of citizenship because the language of citizenship invokes agency with respect to subjects who are frequently depicted in the popular imagination, media, and government policy as being something other than political beings. (2011, 6)

In this, she draws attention to the ways in which migrants assert themselves as political subjects by making claims against certain perceived injustices and inequalities and through collective action (Rygiel 2011, 6). Citizens are not the agents here, but citizenship remains the discourse and framework through which agency and voice are understood.

One of the most effective examples of this rethinking of political agency is Isin's 'acts of citizenship' (2008). Isin argues that an 'act' is distinct from 'action' in that it represents a challenge to 'habitus' – the ways of thought and conduct internalized by members of society over the long term (2008, 15). It is a rupture in the given (25), and produces actors who both create and effect change as 'activist citizens' (38). The 'citizen' is thus redefined away from a legal status to a conceptualization driven by action as subjects actively constitute themselves. Citizenship becomes something other than an exclusive, bounded identity, and is rendered emergent, accessible (in theory) to anyone regardless of actual legal status. This analysis is easily applied to the migrant protests. The demands of the protesters are articulated in terms of rights, which they claim entitlement to despite legal refusals and a lack of status. They are thus demands for recognition that disrupt assumptions about citizens as the only figures able to enact or claim rights, and so as the only form of political agent. Such demands are 'acts' that shift the normal political order to include a subjectivity found outside of formal citizenship.

Isin's 'acts of citizenship' emphasize the act rather than the actor and displace status categories as the determinant of potential agency. As Oliveri (2012, 799–800) argues, this framework focuses on the self-constitution of an actor provided with autonomous political agency. Self-constitution is significant, as it enables an understanding of agency that emanates not from the state, but from the individual; state-defined status is no longer the necessary criterion for political action. However, even if citizenship is defined in this way through participation and contestation, the political content of agency remains framed by citizenship. There remains an assumption that the achievement of citizenship, even an 'activist citizenship' enacted by unauthorized agents, is the goal. Citizenship is a difficult paradigm to escape, even if it is stretched and adapted.

As much as scholars struggle to escape from citizenship as the defining framework for action, so too do the protesters themselves. The noncitizen protests are always already navigating a tense and contradictory relationship with citizenship (Oliveri 2012). Within the articulated demands of the migrants themselves, citizenship is simultaneously contested in fundamental ways, while also demanded as a right in itself. For Tyler and Marciniak '[c]itizenship is a site of struggle within these protests: it is both the goal which many immigrant protestors are striving to achieve and the regime of exclusion which they are protesting against' (2013, 153). They write: 'inevitably, one of the main strategies of migrants and pro-migrant activists is to demand the rights of citizenship, however, problematic or precarious this citizenship may have become' (2013, 146). As an exclusive identity, citizenship represents, and in many ways defines, the rigid system of bordered nation-states that creates the conditions of exclusion that the protests are contesting. However, in relating demands for rights to citizenship status, or in making appeals for protection to the state, this system is (potentially) legitimized (Hansen, Falkentoft, and Rode 2014, 53). Many of the protester's demands are for membership, for inclusion, and for recognition, all of which in one way or another are an appeal to and for citizenship. Many of the public statements of the Berlin refugee protesters are key illustrations of this simultaneous repudiation of citizenship frameworks and an appeal to the state that invokes membership. In a statement from the hunger strikers in November 2014, for example, they appeal to human rights as universal rights exceeding state restrictions: 'we will strike till we reach our freedom. We want to have basic human rights, we are not only demanding a secure life, we are demanding to be treated as humans, to have rights as free persons' (Berlin Refugee Strike November 2014). In the same statement, however, they make a direct appeal to state representatives *as representatives*, in an appeal to membership:

> [i]f you, Emilia Müller, minister of social affairs, and you, Joachim Heuman, minister for inner affairs think the Lager-system is human, we are asking from you to bring all German society to the Lagers we have to live in, or bring us into this society. (Berlin Refugee Strike November 2014)

It is clear that in both theory and practice – in both scholarly engagements with migrant politics, and in actual migrant political movements – there is a tension between a desire to contest the equivalence of the citizen–agent, and the pragmatic use of the frameworks and concepts of citizenship to express key political demands. It is an open question whether migrant protest should be interpreted as a re-imagining of citizenship away from a state-based paradigm towards something like 'global citizenship', or whether these protests enable forms of politics that 'exceed or refuse to be a politics of citizenship at all' (Tyler and Marciniak 2013, 154). As Hindess (2004) argues, it is not at all clear whether a return or reinvigoration of citizenship is a productive way of accessing emergent forms of political agency. Hindess puts out a clear call to unsettle the valourization of citizenship as a divisive regime built upon exclusivity which, he argues, embeds a negative view of other ways of life (2004, 306). For Papadopoulos and Tsianos, '[t]he more one tries to support rights and representation through citizenship, the more one contributes to the restriction of movement' (2013, 187). To apply the framework of citizenship to noncitizen action risks missing key elements of the politics that are being articulated within noncitizen protest and engagement. Within such 'acts', migrants find a voice on their own terms, demanding an equality of place that is excessive of a return to citizenship and that requires new frameworks for political action. As Papadopoulos and Tsianos argue,

> Migrants' politics develop their own codes, their own practices, their own logics which are almost imperceptible from the perspective of existing political action: firstly, because we are not trained to perceive them as 'proper' politics and, secondly, because they create an excess that *cannot* be addressed *in* the existing system of political representation. (Papadopolous and Tsianos 2013, 188)

In the somewhat dry words of Clifford Aghator (7 December 2012), a refugee protester in Refugee Protest Camp Vienna, '[t]he refugees and asylum seekers alike are not entirely idiots or illiterates who do not know their rights, or who do not recognize when their rights are being infringed upon.' Gržinić (2013) argues: '[t]he refugees broke the predetermined space of politics in which only predetermined actors – let's say citizens – have visibility and are taken seriously when asking for democratic rights.' They have, in her words, 'repoliticized' and 'rearticulated' the space of Europe in a way that forces the citizen-based organizations and individuals who support them to reorganize their own struggles, adapting and responding to the refugees as active subjects rather than as objects of activism. The refugees are themselves activists, and not simply the issue/object around which citizen-activists organize. They are not simply citizens in another guise; they are subjects in themselves, outside of the 'normal' framework. Citizenship is a paradigm that is built fundamentally on exclusion and othering, upon the lines that divide. In translating noncitizen agency into a framework that remains described by citizenship, we lose the capacity to understand and engage noncitizenship as a political subjectivity that exists in an autonomous way. In the remainder of this paper, I examine two dynamics perceptible in the European protest movements which reveal potential ways to engage with noncitizenship as subjectivity in itself: the assertion of presence; and the active practice of a politics of solidarity.

Presence

> We refugees are fleeing from different reasons from our homecountries (*sic*). We are forced to leave so much loved behind: Our home land, our culture, our businesses and normal lives. We miss our families. We miss our children. Our friends. And we also miss those streets in which we played in our childhood. We lost a lot of family members in war, and also them, we miss so much.

> Every refugee leaving the homecountry (*sic*) is thinking the same: How can I get a legal status and start a normal and safe life in another country? (RPCV February 24, 2014b)

At the centre of the protests that are emerging across Europe is the very specific tactic of occupation. The establishment of protest 'camps' situates the protest in a local context in ways that are highly visible, fixing the excluded noncitizen as quite firmly 'here'. In contesting the isolating and exclusionary policies of states, which require that migrants live in immigration reception centres or in remote, pre-selected housing, the protest camps directly engage a politics of fixity and location, contesting the monopoly citizenship seemingly exercises over presence, over being 'here'.

Citizenship, grounded in territory, links being 'here' – or, importantly, being 'allowed' to be here – with being a political subject. In doing so, the framework of citizenship equates legal status with belonging, and interposes these as the necessary criteria for being present – and so for being seen, heard and recognized. In contesting the isolation of detention and reception centres, in asserting the camp space as a place 'here' and not as a place apart, the refugee protesters are challenging these criteria and re-taking presence. They are contesting citizenship as the necessary qualification for being 'here', and so for speaking and participating. In doing so, they are relocating a different subjectivity in presence, populating the 'space' of society with subjects that are in addition to the citizen.

A spatial analysis of occupation draws attention to the ways in which migrants and refugees coming together in a particular place is manifested politically. Occupation as a political strategy of resistance is about the subversion of public space, and its re-appropriation. As Bassett argues, it creates 'in-between' spaces that are never entirely outside of the police space, but that materialize people power through subverting the 'normal distribution' of police spaces (2014, 893). The protest camps are manifested in direct contestation to the state-built 'asylum camps' and immigration reception centres that are designed to isolate and contain migrants. These state camps are spaces designed to control and limit noncitizen political agency, and to exclude migrants from the body politic; they are spaces of exception, in the theories of Giorgio Agamben (1998), which render individuals as 'bare life' without political meaning. The protest camps challenge this exclusion through the assertion of a political voice that is manifest not in an appeal to citizenship, but in a visible presence.

Expressions of migrant or noncitizen agency within a camp space are described and engaged with most clearly through the literature which addresses 'autonomous migration.' Scholars in this tradition emphasize not an integrationist agenda (where noncitizens are advocating for inclusion as citizens) but the agency of migrants themselves as it is manifested through cross-border mobility. Agency is thus founded not in an appeal to citizenship but in mobility itself. Mezzadra argues that autonomy means 'looking at migratory movements and conflicts in terms that prioritize the subjective practices, the desires, the expectations and the behaviours of migrants themselves' (Mezzadra 2011, 121). This means that there is an attempt to see migration not simply as a response to necessities, be they political, economic or social, but as a constituent force in the formation of the polity that has the capacity to develop its own logics, motivations and trajectories (Papadopolous and Tsianos 2013, 184; Papadopolous and Tsianos 2008).

The analysis undertaken by autonomous migration scholars who investigate border camps is helpful in our understanding of the role the protest camps play in expressions of noncitizen agency. Mountz argues that they are spaces where people wait, but that they are also spaces where migrants organize, network, and speak out (2011, 383). The camp can therefore be seen as a space of community (Rygiel 2011), and so they directly challenge the abjection presented in the camp-as-exception formulation. Crucially, however, Rygiel also points out that an important component of the political action encompassed by these camps is that individuals *ultimately leave* (2011, 15). Noncitizens remain in motion.

The focus on mobility in this literature thus privileges movement over presence, which does not effectively capture one of the key logics of the European protest camps: an assertion of occupation of space. These protests, while grounded in a politics of mobility, are about staying, and about using situatedness and location as resources for enacting political subjectivity. One element that distinguishes the protest camps from the border camps is that they are not simply staging areas for further mobility. They are instead active claims against the state that assert a presence which, inasmuch as it is unauthorized, is also incontrovertible. As De Genova (2010, 103) observes about the undocumented migrant protests in the United States, such claims to presence, to being 'here', are not demands as much as they are audacious statements of fact that assert a radical, open-ended migrant agency.

Presence is asserted by the protest camps first and foremost in the contestation of the isolation imposed upon asylum seekers by European states. As one migrant in Vienna declared during a press conference in March 2013, marking the move from the Votive Church to the Servite Monastery, the protesters were determined that their new home would not be a small 'Traiskirchen' (a 'refugee camp') that isolates refugees from society (RPCV March 4, 2013a). Rather, the refugees in Vienna placed visibility at the centre of action – despite the heightened risks of deportation such exposure was likely to produce. Hansen, Falkentoft and Rode argue that by using '*visibility* and *political agency* in itself, [the camp] is a strategy breaking with the security problem of *exclusion* and *otherness*' (Hansen, Falkentoft, and Rode 2014, 64). Similarly, Nair argues that the protest camps are a 'performance of resistance to oppression through the bodily occupation in, and passage through, public spaces, in defiance of the political invisibility that legal and state structures impose on them' (2012, 784). Moreover, this visibility is understood to actually counter the heightened vulnerability that migrants experience. As a refugee in Vienna stated on 'Refugee Support Day', November 4, 2013, 'it is essential for us to stay public and visible, otherwise our movement will die and we will be deported' (RPCV November 2, 2013f). The summer of 2013 saw the deliberate practice of visibility applied beyond the occupations themselves. 'From July till August 2013, we will go out to public places, show ourselves and call everyone, including representative people from Austrian politics and civil society, to come and listen to our demands for solutions' (RPCV July 12, 2013c; see also RPCV 2013e). Occupation as a political technique of resistance is about fixing the noncitizen inside and here, and their continued presence depends upon the claiming and use of space.

As in Vienna, breaking the isolation of refugees is a key political stake in the German actions. At the core of the movement is the campaign against the policy of mandatory residence, *Residenzpflict*, which bans asylum seekers from travel within Germany. Other demands focused on the shutdown of the *Lagers*, an end to deportations, and the granting of residence permits for asylum seekers (Hansen, Falkentoft, Rode 2014, 28). The protesters stated:

> We, refugees from various camps in Germany, united our local actions and set off to Berlin. Starting from Würzburg, we covered the distance of 600 km in about a month. Because of our visits to the refugee camps along the route, we were able to expose the isolation of the refugees, and invited them to leave their camps and join our march … We declare that we intend to fight the laws and policies that violate our freedom and dignity. (Refugeecamp Berlin, January 1, 2013)

The statement issued on the occasion of the hunger strike in Munich in November 2014 asserted:

> Lagers/camps are prisons for us. Residenzpflicht/residential obligation is a sign of slavery. Restrictions of work and study are made to divide us from society and to force us to be in inhuman situations. Deportations by Dublin regulations are a sign of political organized policy from EU countries.
>
> At this point we want to say we are not poor refugees, OUR RIGHTS HAVE BEEN STOLEN. (November 23, 2014)

Again, in presence a political right is claimed: the right to be seen, to be here.

In the protest camps, the assertion of being 'here' grounds claims of rights and political voice not in citizenship, but in physical presence. To contest isolation, and to claim belonging in this sense is not a claim to citizenship as 'the' territorially relevant identity, but to bypass citizenship and to claim political agency on the basis of being located, present, and *here.*

Solidarity

> Our position is very clear: We do not talk about facilities, about own places, but about legal status and about our struggle. This is the time to share responsibilities. You do your job, outside, on your side, and I do my job, inside. You provide a table, I talk to the prime minister, to the chancellor. This is the European Union. They say they work for a peaceful world, we support this! Because we are also part of this world, and our role is very important. (RPCV May 3, 2013b)

While asserting presence bypasses citizenship as the defining mediator for expressing political agency, the politics of solidarity that are found in and across the refugee protest camps express important ways of thinking through political relations not simply apart from citizenship, but between citizen and noncitizen subjectivities. These relations are a conscious goal of the protests, which have actively adopted 'noncitizen' as a meaningful identity. In March 2013, the Refugee Struggle Congress was organized by the *Aktionskries unabhängig protestierender Flüchtlinge* (Action group of independently protesting refugees), in Germany. Throughout the conference, the concept of noncitizen was debated at length and was consciously used as a political identification, as a way of asserting the political subjectivity of the protesters, and as a denial of their position as recipients of charity (McGuaran and Hudig 2014, 31). Rather than seeking a solidarity which asserts the 'right' of the citizen to use her privilege to speak on behalf of the refugee or to create a space for the refugee – both marking the citizen as the active subject – citizen/noncitizen solidarity in the refugee protest camps has emerged as both a demand, and as a mutual responsibility within the politics of resistance. Noncitizens are outside of the traditional solidarity and community that is at the normative heart of citizenship (Kofman 1995, 123); in the present-day migrant protests, the response of protesters has been to redefine and reinvent solidarity rather than to demand inclusion in already existing, but seemingly inadequate, citizenship relations.

This redefinition of solidarity and political relations rests within a rethinking of how representation operates, and so of where demands are directed and to whom they are articulated. As Papadopoulos and Tsianos note, it is citizenship that regulates the relation between rights and representation (2013, 181). It is citizens who are entitled to representation, and this is the mechanism through which rights claims are made. As Arendt (1951) has convincingly argued, rights are meaningless without the 'right to have rights', which is activated through the mechanisms of citizenship that enable individuals to makes demands upon a state. However, within the migrant protests, rights claims are being made by non-citizens, and in ways that are meaningful and are shifting political relations; the connection Arendt asserts between citizenship and the 'right to have rights' is being contested, but it has yet to be fundamentally broken. A puzzle emerges about how noncitizens can advance rights claims without making appeals to citizenship. In the relations of solidarity that are articulated throughout the protest movement, a partial answer can be found: the relationship between citizens and noncitizens is founded upon a mutual responsibility that makes use of citizenship without making it a precondition for all political action.

This understanding of solidarity requires a sustained, ongoing and dynamic interaction across the fine lines of status that demarcate the boundaries of citizenship. Franke writes,

> At stake is not access to recognition and protection but, instead, access to debate and the willingness to receive the challenges of others. At stake is the *right to be political, not governed.* (2011, 51, emphasis added)

Such solidarity is rooted first and foremost in direct contact and conversation. As one refugee in Vienna states, '[i]t is important to be in contact with normal people' (RPCV May 3, 2013b). Through this contact, the relations between citizens and noncitizens are understood to also comprise obligations. In response to a series of deportations in December 2013, for example, an article was released by Refugee Protest Camp Vienna stating:

> To bring this inhumane system to an end and to stop deportations, we have to organize and to take to the streets. We have to put pressure on those in power, but at the same time get active ourselves. We are all responsible. (RPCV December 14, 2013d)

The article is signed with the statement: '[t]he authors of this article have different statuses in Austria, we are people with and without papers, some have refugee-background and some don't' (RPCV December 14, 2013d). In many of the press releases and reports released by the collectives in all locations, this sense of locating the struggle across legal status categories is explicit: 'it's not about the victims – it's against all of us, against the repression of political protest' (RPCV June 17, 2014a). The refugees in this way understand themselves not as simply asserting their own rights to political agency and participation, but as protecting this space of resistance for all people – noncitizens, but also citizens. Further, the roles of 'refugee' and 'supporter' are blurred. A refugee being interviewed during the occupation of the Votive Church in Vienna was clear that he identified himself as both a refugee and a supporter – that his work in the protest and in the occupation was also about standing in support of other refugees and other noncitizens, in Vienna and elsewhere. This introduces a multiplicity of identities in the political subjectivity of the noncitizen, a plurality that destabilizes otherwise fixed 'roles' in activism. Solidarity, as it emerges from a practice of politics that asserts noncitizenship as an independent, and not contingent, subjectivity places at its heart a responsibility to act for both the noncitizen *and for the citizen*, expanding the normative political community to include multiple categories.

The efforts in the protest movement to organize across the divide between citizens and noncitizens are clear, and it is important to note that they are noncitizen led. In June 2014, a post on the Refugee Protest Camp Vienna website announced:

> As it became rather quiet around refugee and anti-deportation protests in the last months, it is high time for people who want to act against the European border regime and the Austrian asylum system to connect. Thus, we want to meet regularly again, in order to get to know

> each other and act together for freedom of movement and equal political and social rights for everybody. (RPCV June 20, 2014c)

Similarly, the protesters in Berlin called a meeting in November 2014 'to create the structure we need to give efficiency to our struggle' (CISPM, November 2014). The proposed topics for the meeting included bringing groups together into a common strategy, establishing a regular and permanent assembly of all refugee groups in Berlin, and communication strategies amongst the group, and with the wider society (CISPM, November 2014). The work that is being done locates the practice of solidarity in the everyday lives of participants, both citizens and noncitizens, and is as much about relations within the community as it is about relations with the state.

This founding of solidarity in relations of mutual responsibility rejects traditional, often paternalistic, interactions across the citizenship divide. Instead, solidarity is a demand. During a public speech following the Refugee Protest Camp Vienna's symbolic rejection of the Ute Bock Prize for Moral Courage in January 2013, one of the refugees sent out a challenge: 'You are citizens that support our demands. Therefore, why don't you demand that your political representatives – who you, as citizens, have elected – change this unbearable situation?!' (Gržinić 2013, 3). This statement is powerful. It expresses a desire for solidarity that positions noncitizens as capable of making demands not only of the state, but of one another and of their citizen supporters. This is therefore also a call for a relationship of equality that recognizes the different political positions of power and of vulnerability. It recognizes that citizens have the power to operate within traditional politics of representation, but also that with this power comes a responsibility to use it in support of noncitizens, who, despite their vulnerability, nevertheless have the capacity to articulate their own demands and to be seen and heard. The call is widespread: '[e]veryone living in the "western world" is responsible for not looking away and showing solidarity', declared the Refugee Protest Camp Vienna in December (2013d), in response to a series of deportations. Such statements are not simply rhetorical, and the collective has not hesitated to be critical of actions (or failures to act) that are understood to contravene their expectations of support.

> We call for active resistance against Austrian authorities who threaten refugees with deportation! And we want to criticize sharply the role of Caritas which is running a lot of the refugee houses in Vorarlberg and other areas from where refugees are picked for deportation and doesn't show any visible protest or practical solidarity with the victims of deportation. (RPCV December 14, 2013d)

In standing up to be heard, the refugees have exposed themselves to state and police crackdown that may have serious consequences. The solidarity called for is a solidarity that recognizes and respects their action as political participation, and as a radical demand for change. It enables a relationship of mutual support and protection that uses the security of the citizen, but does not reduce or subordinate the power of the migrant. Such solidarity is not easy; it requires a rethinking of protection, equality and of protest itself.

Fine lines

> The borders that exclude me from elementary human rights, from leading a good life, lay beyond barbed wire. The border which separates people from unworthy people: these are the fine lines on my fingers. (Leisch February 19, 2013)

Tyler and Marcianiak, write: '[t]he radical potential of immigrant protests precisely resides in the ways in which migrants organize and act despite their lack of access to the rights and protections of citizenship' (2013, 149–150). The refugee and migrant protests that have emerged in Europe, and that continue to contest both state and European policies and frameworks are significant in their durability, and their visibility. The protesters are demanding a reconfiguration of not only the migration frameworks of the borders of Europe, but also of the ways in which the nation–citizen–state nexus determines our notions of political agency and action. In asserting presence out of mobility, and in shaping a demanding solidarity that entails a relationship of mutual responsibility across the citizenship divide, the protesters are exhibiting a noncitizenship that is a political subjectivity in its own right, and that opens up possibilities for rethinking and reimagining political action. It asserts noncitizenship as autonomous and independent rather than simply a status marking an absence of citizenship. The politics of noncitizenship are more than a demand for inclusion in citizenship frameworks, and instead represent a powerful political agency that calls upon new and dynamic political relations across multiple lines that divide.

'Why you are doing this?' asks the poem with which this paper began. Such a question is worth asking beyond the act of the burning of fingerprints, a violent and embodied act of resistance against the border regimes of Europe. The answer lies in the relationships across geographical boundaries, and across the fine lines between citizens and noncitizens. In recognizing political action and actors that are beyond our current citizenship-based framework for understanding agency, borders are being crossed in ways that are both present and in solidarity, and are powerful in their imagination of a coming politics.

Acknowledgements

I would like to gratefully thank Katherine Tonkiss, Tendayi Bloom and the anonymous reviewers for very helpful comments. I would also like to thank members of Refugee Protest Camp Vienna for giving of their time and stories. All errors are my own.

Disclosure statement

No potential conflict of interest was reported by the author.

References

Agamben, Giorgio. 1998. *Homo Sacer*. Stanford, CA. Stanford University Press.
Aghator, Clifford. 2012. "Asylwerber Am Wort: Wie Es Uns So Geht [A Statement of Clarification Coming from the Camp]." December 10. http://refugeecampvienna.noblogs.org/post/2012/12/10/asylwerber-am-wort/
Anderson, Bridget, Matthew J. Gibney, and Emanuela Paoletti. 2011. "Citizenship, Deportation and the Boundaries of Belonging." *Citizenship Studies* 15 (5): 547–563.
Arendt, Hannah. 1951. *The Origins of Totalitarianism*. New York: Harvest.
Bassett, Keith. 2014. "Rancière, Politics, and the Occupy Movement." *Environment and Planning D: Society and Space* 32: 886–901.
Berlin Refugee Strike. 2014. "Hungerstrike of Refugees in Munich." November 23. http://oplatz.net/2014/11/23/hungerstrike-of-refugees-in-munich/#more-5601.
CISPM (International Coalition of Undocumented, Migrants, Refugees and Asylum Seekers). 2014. "'Declaration by International Coalition of Undocumented, #Migrants, #Refugees and

#Asylum Seekers', The VOICE Refugee Forum Germany". November 26. http://thevoiceforum.org/node/3790.
De Genova, Nicholas. 2010. "The Queer Politics of Migration: Reflections on 'Illegality' and Incorrigibility." *Studies in Social Justice* 4 (2): 101–126.
Franke, Mark F. N. 2011. "The Unbearable Rightfulness of Being Human: Citizenship, Displacement, and the Right to Not Have Rights." *Citizenship Studies* 15 (1): 39–56.
Gržinić, Marina. 2013. "A Refugee Protest Camp in Vienna and the European Union's Processes of Racialization, Seclusion and Discrimination." *e-flux Journal* 43 (Mar.).
Hansen, Nanna Kathrine, Maja Felicia Falkentoft, and Carsten Baltzer Rode. 2014. *"Desecuritizing Migration: The Case of the Berlin Refugee Strike" Special Project*. Roskilde: Roskilde Universitet. Institut for Samfund og Globalisering.
Hindess, Barry. 2004. "Citizenship for All." *Citizenship Studies* 8 (3): 305–315.
Isin, Engin. 2008. "Theorizing Acts of Citizenship." In *Acts of Citizenship*, edited by Engin Isin and Greg Nielson, 15–43. London: Zed Books.
Johnson, Heather L. 2014. *Borders, Asylum and Global Noncitizenship: The Other Side of the Fence*. Cambridge: Cambridge University Press.
Kofman, Eleonore. 1995. "Citizenship for Some but Not for Others: Spaces of Citizenship in Contemporary Europe." *Political Geography* 14 (2): 121–137.
Leisch, Tina. 2013. "Stellen Sie Sich Vor, Sie Wären Flüchtling [Imagine Being a Refugee]." February 19. http://refugeecampvienna.noblogs.org/post/2013/02/19/imagine-being-a-refugee-stellen-sie-sich-vor-sie-waren-fluchtling/.
McGuaran, Katrin, and Kees Hudig. 2014. "Refugee Protests in Europe: Fighting for the Right to Stay." *Statewatch Journal: Reflections on the State and Civil Liberties in Europe* 23 (3/4): 28–32.
McNevin, Anne. 2006. "Political Belonging in a Neoliberal Era: The Struggles of the *Sans-papiers*." *Citizenship Studies* 10 (2): 135–151.
Mezzadra, Sandro (trans. Rodrigo Nunes). 2011. "The Gaze of Autonomy: Capitalism, Migration and Social Struggles." In *The Contested Politics of Mobility: Borderzones and Irregularity*, edited by Vicki Squire, 121–142. London: Routledge.
Mountz, Alison. 2011. "Where Asylum-seekers Wait: Feminist Counter-topographies of Sites between States." *Gender, Place and Culture: A Journal of Feminist Geography* 18 (3): 381–399.
Nair, Parvati. 2012. "The Body Politic of Dissent: The Paperless and the Indignant." *Citizenship Studies* 16 (5–6): 783–792.
Nyers, Peter. 2006. *Rethinking Refugees: Beyond States of Emergency*. New York: Routledge.
Oberprantacher, Andreas. 2014. "Holey Union: Contested European Frontier Zones." *Journal of Conflictology* 5 (2): 72–80.
Oliveri, Federico. 2012. "Migrants as Activist Citizens in Italy: Understanding the New Cycles of Struggles." *Citizenship Studies* 16 (5–6): 793–806.
Papadopolous, Dimitris, and Vassilis Tsianos. 2008. *Escape Routes: Control and Subversion in the 21st Century*. London: Pluto Press.
Papadopolous, Dimitris, and Vassilis Tsianos. 2013. "After Citizenship: Autonomy of Migration, Organisational Ontology and Mobile Commons." *Citizenship Studies* 17 (2): 178–196.
Platzer, Michael. 2013. *Report to the United Nations: Deportation of Protestors against Inhumane Conditions in Refugee Camps and Asylum Procedures in Austria* [online]. http://refugeecampvienna.noblogs.org/post/2013/08/25/report-to-the-un-deportation-of-protestors-against-inhumane-conditions-in-refugee-camps-and-asylum-procedures-in-austria/.
Refugeecamp Berlin Info. 2013. "Why We Marched to Berlin and Why We Continue Our Resistance." January 1. http://refugeecampberlininfo.tumblr.com/.
RPCV (Refugee Protest Camp Vienna) 2013a. "AUDIO: [Own Words] Striking Refugees Now at Servite Monastery: Press Conference by Refugees, church and Caritas on March 4, 2013." March 4. http://refugeecampvienna.noblogs.org/post/2013/03/04/audio-o-ton-protestierende-refugees-nun-im-servitenkloster-pressekonferenz-von-refugee-kirche-und-caritas-am-4-marz-2013/.
RPCV (Refugee Protest Camp Vienna) 2013b. "Interview: Die Forderung Nach Eirem Normalen Leben ... – The Demand for a Normal Life ...." May 3. http://refugeecampvienna.noblogs.org/

post/2013/05/03/interview-die-forderung-nach-einem-normalen-leben-the-demand-for-a-normal-life/.
RPCV (Refugee Protest Camp Vienna) 2013c. "Month of Visibility – We Still Demand Our Rights! We Need a Solution!." July 12. http://refugeecampvienna.noblogs.org/post/2013/07/12/month-of-visibility-we-still-demand-our-rights-we-need-a-solution/.
RPCV (Refugee Protest Camp Vienna) 2013d. "New Wave of Deportations from Austria – Get Active for Concrete Solidarity to Stop Deportations." December. http://refugeecampvienna.noblogs.org/post/2013/12/14/new-wave-of-deportations-from-austria-get-active-for-concrete-solidarity-to-stop-deportations/.
RPCV (Refugee Protest Camp Vienna) 2013e. "Open Doors at the Refugee Protest." October 16. http://refugeecampvienna.noblogs.org/post/2013/10/16/willkommen-im-refugee-protest-wien-welcome-to-the-refugee-protest-vienna/.
RPCV (Refugee Protest Camp Vienna) 2013f. "Refugee Support Day: Monday, 4/11/2013." November 2. http://refugeecampvienna.noblogs.org/post/2013/11/02/refugee-support-day-monday-4112013/.
RPCV (Refugee Protest Camp Vienna) 2013g. "Speech on Occasion of the Protest Songcontest at the Theatre Rabenhof." February 13. http://refugeecampvienna.noblogs.org/post/2013/02/13/speach-on-occasion-of-the-protestsongcontest-at-the-theatre-rabenhof/.
RPCV (Refugee Protest Camp Vienna) 2014a. "Podiumsdiskussion Und Soli-Party." June 17. http://refugeecampvienna.noblogs.org/post/2014/06/12/podiumsdiskussion-und-soli-party-its-not-about-the-victims-its-against-all-of-us-against-the-repression-of-political-protest-17-06-2014/.
RPCV (Refugee Protest Camp Vienna) 2014b. "Solidaritätserklärung Gegen Die Kriminalisieming Von Migrantinnen Und Refugees [Solidarity Statement against the Criminalisation of Migrants and Refugees]." February 24. http://refugeecampvienna.noblogs.org/post/2014/02/24/solidaritatserklarung-gegen-die-kriminalisierung-von-migrantinnen-und-refugees/.
RPCV (Refugee Protest Camp Vienna) 2014c. "Saturday, 21/06/2014: Votivpark-Gathering." June 20. http://refugeecampvienna.noblogs.org/post/2014/06/20/saturday-21062014-votivpark-gathering/.
Rygiel, Kim. 2011. "Bordering Solidarities: Migrant Activism and the Politics of Movement and Camps at Calais." *Citizenship Studies* 15 (1): 1–19.
Tyler, Imogen, and Katarzyna Marciniak. 2013. "Immigrant Protest: An Introduction." *Citizenship Studies* 17 (2): 143–156.

Index

abuse 24–5, 42–4, 46–9
access to human rights 18, 34–55
acquiring nationality 43–5
activism 116–17, 119–20
'acts of citizenship' 19–20, 109–110, 119–20
'acts of demonstration' 95–6
affluence 4
Agamben, Giorgio 111, 122
ageing out 106
Aghator, Clifford 121
AI *see* Amnesty International
Alien Migrant Interdiction Program 40
American Convention on Human Rights 36, 40
Amnesty International 44
analytical category of noncitizenship 86–99
Ancient Greece 2–3
Andersson, Ruben 64
anticipation of justice to come 89
arbitrary detention 36, 43, 46–7
Arendt, Hannah 2, 5–7, 38, 72, 75–6, 81, 86–7, 124–5
assembling noncitizenship 17–33; conceptualising noncitizenship 18–22; conclusion 27–9; introduction 17–18; migration narratives 22–7
assimilation 38–9
assuming citizenship 1–16; citizen–noncitizen binary 2–6; emerging noncitizenship studies 6–8; future agenda for theorising noncitizenship. 11–14; interdisciplinary approaches 8–11; introduction 1–2
asylum seekers 22, 26, 34–41, 45, 74–5, 117–18, 123–4
attributes of citizenship 2–6, 17–18
Australia 100–114; *see also* contractualisation
Australian Industrial Relations Commission 106
autonomous migration 122

Bahamas 71–85
Bailey, Adrian J. 106–7
Ballesteros, Enrique 65
bare humanity 86–7, 103, 106, 122
Bassett, Keith 122
Beech, Nic 75
being here 122
belonging among stateless people 71–85
Benhabib, Seyla 89–90
Bentham, Jeremy 7
Bertram, Christopher 6
bidoon jinsaya 5
'boat people' 39
border politics 115–17
Bosniak, Linda 66, 73
breaching noncitizen human rights 107–9
bribery 43–4
Brodie, Janine 63
business of noncitizenship 56–70; commodifying noncitizenship 63–5; conclusion 67; introduction 56–7; limits of privatisation 65–7; migration business 57–9; peculiar sort of privatisation 59–63

Carens, Joseph 66
categories of noncitizenship 17–18, 34–55
CERD *see* Committee on the Elimination of Racial Discrimination
character of global migration 17–18
children 44–5
churning 19–20, 106
citizenisation 10, 90–97
citizen–noncitizen binary 2–6, 87, 93–7
citizens-in-waiting 106–7
citizenship and inclusion 86–99
civic citizenship 104
coercion 43–4, 61–2
cold war 60
COLLECTIVE LIFE 11
colonialism 7, 101–4
'Commerce of Migration' 57
Committee on the Elimination of Racial Discrimination 43, 45–6
Committee of the Protection of the Rights of All Migrant Workers... 35, 42–3
commodifying noncitizenship construction 63–5
conceptualising noncitizenship 18–22; as assemblage 20–21; noncitizen conditionality 21–2

condition of statelessness 37–8
conditionality 17–33; migration narratives 22–7
confiscation of passports 38, 46
consular intervention 35
consumption 104–7
contemporary Australia 100–114; *see also* contractualisation
contingency 20, 26–7
contractualisation 100–114; conclusion 110–111; depoliticisation of noncitizens 107–9; intimacies of state power 104–7; introduction 100–101; limits of solidarity 109–110; staggered pathways 101–4
Convention on the Reduction of Statelessness 38
Convention on the Rights of the Child 38, 44–5
corruption 43–4, 105
criminal detention 62
CRISPP see Critical Review of International Social and Political Philosophy
Critical Review of International Social and Political Philosophy 6–7
CSC 58
Culic, Irina 105–6

Dauvergne, Catherine 107
De Genova, Nicholas 123
de Graauw, Els, 7
debt bondage 43–4, 46
decision-making 65–7
defining noncitizenship 1–2
degradation 36, 48
Deguis Pierre, Juliana 79
Deleuze, Gilles 20
democratisation 90–91
denizenship 4–6, 93–7
Department of Homeland Security 47
depoliticisation 100–114
deportability 19, 118–19
deportation 19, 38, 46–8, 118–19, 123–4
derivative rights 34–5
deservingness 18–21, 25–8
destitution 94
determination of asylum status 40–41
dhimmi 4
diplomacy 49–50
discretion 18–21, 26–8
disenfranchisement 34–5
displacement 71–85
displaying solidarity 124–6
dissociation 96
Dolce, Harry 78
domination 6
Dominican Republic 71–85
Doty, Roxanne 61–2
Dublin II Treaty 118

ECtHR *see* European Court of Human Rights
Eichmann in Jerusalem 38
Eisenhower, Dwight 60
emerging noncitizenship studies 6–8
employment discrimination 45–6
enacting citizenship 90
entitlement 18–19, 22–7
equality 36–7
equivalency 118
ethnic lobbying 108–9
Eurodac database 115, 118
Europe 115–29
European Convention on Human Rights 36
European Court of Human Rights 36
European Union 2–3
exclusion 39–40, 59, 87–93, 95
explicit delegation 59
exploitation 100–101, 106–7
expulsion 46–7
extermination 38
extreme statelessness 80–81

F.A. v Norway 45–6
facilitation of migration 57–8
Falkentoft, Maja Felicia 123
Featherstone, David 109
female migrants 48–9
Fernandez, Deepa 60
Final Solution 38
fine lines 115–29
Fine, Sarah 6–7
fingerprint tracking 118, 126–7
for-profit entities and noncitizenship 56–7
force 65–7
forced displacement 72–4
Foucault, Michel 96
457 temporary skilled worker programme 100, 102–3, 106, 108
fragmented citizenship 110
Franke, Mark F.N. 125
fraud 43–4
Free National Movement 78
freedom of movement 36–7, 61
freeloading 41
friction between human rights law and citizenship 34–5
Friedman, Milton 60–61, 63
future agenda for theorising noncitizenship 11–14

G4/G5 movement 109
G4S 58
gatekeeping 19–21, 26–7, 34–5, 57–8
Geneva Convention Relating to the Status of Refugees 38–9
genocide 38
Gerry's 58
global connectivity 57–8
global migration 17–18
Golash-Boza, Tanya 60
Goldring, Luin 102
grassroots organisations 109–110
Gržinić, Marina 121

Guantánamo Bay 40
Guardia Civil 65

H&C *see* humanitarian and compassionate grounds
habitus 119
Hansen, Nanna Kathrine 123
Harney, Robert 57–8
Hawthorne, Lesleyanne 105
Hewitt, Claire 105
high-risk travel 47–8
Hindess, Barry 121
Hischnjakow, Civolani 77
Holocaust 86–7
Honahan, Iseult 6–7
housing discrimination 45–6
Hovdal-Moan, Marit 6–7
Howard, John 39
human rights, access to 34–55
Human Rights Committee 35
humanitarian and compassionate grounds 23–5

IACHR *see* Inter-American Court of Human Rights
illegalisation 19–20, 27, 64, 105
ILO *see* International Labour Organization
IMF *see* International Monetary Fund
implementation of human rights 35–6
implications of commodification 63–5
implicit delegation 59
imposed nationality position 78–80
'in-between' categories of migrant 104, 122
In-Simon, Natacha 72
incarceration 62
inclusion 86–99; citizenship vs. noncitizenship 87–93; conclusion 97; introduction 86–7; rethinking noncitizenship 93–7
indefinite detention 46–7, 77
indigenous Australians 101–4
inequality 17–18, 21–2, 43–4, 94
injustice 94
inner exclusion 88–9
insecurity of presence 103
inside–outside divide 88–9
integration conditions 104
Inter-American Court of Human Rights 36, 43, 76, 80
interdisciplinary approaches 8–11
International Bill of Human Rights 36, 42
International Covenant on Civil and Political Rights 35–7
International Labour Organization 42–3, 46, 49
international migration 3
International Monetary Fund 60
intersectionalism 103
intimacies of state power 104–7
intimidation 43–4
invisibility 110
'Involuntary Immobility' 73
irregular movement 36–7, 47–8
Isin, Engen 64, 119–20
issues of national security *see* terrorism

Jacobson, David 73
'Jewish Question' 38
jus sanguinis citizenship 35, 37
jus soli citizenship 35, 37, 45, 79

key life projects 73–4, 76
Knight Review 107
Krahmann, Elke 60

Landolt, Patricia 102
LCP *see* Live-in Caregiver Program
Lee, Elizabeth 105–6
legitimacy 57–9
liminality 74–8
limits of justice 3
limits of privatisation 65–7
limits of solidarity 100–114
Lister, Ruth 91
Live-in Caregiver Program 23, 25–6
locating noncitizenship 115–29; fine lines 126–7; introduction 115–17; noncitizen citizenship 117–21; presence 121–4; solidarity 124–6
Louis, Gillard 71
Lubkemann, Stephen C. 73

Marciniak, Katarzyna 120, 127
Mares, Peter 102
marginalisation 90–91, 93–7
marketisation 59–61
Marsden, Sarah 107
Marshall, Thomas H. 3, 88
Martelly, Michel 78
mediating noncitizenship 56–70
Mezzadra, Sandro 122
middling noncitizens 101–4
migrant agency 17–21
migrant workers 34–5, 45–9; abuse 46; arbitrary detention/expulsion 46–7; housing/employment discrimination 45–6; irregular movement/high-risk travel 47–8; plight of women migrants 48–9
migration business 3–4, 57–9
migration control activities 57, 67
migration narratives 22–7; assembling noncitizenship 24–7
Mountz, Alison 122
MS Tampa 39
mutations in sovereignty 110

Nair, Parvati 123
natural disasters 48–9, 108
Nazism 38, 86–7
neoliberalism 63
neuropolitics 64
NGOs *see* nongovernment organisations

'no borders' protest 116
noncitizen citizenship 117–21
noncitizen conditionality 21–2
noncitizen immobility 9–10
noncitizen insiders 71–2
noncitizen workers 42–3
noncitizenship as assemblage 20–21
noncrisis situations 80–81
nondiscrimination 36–7, 43
nonexistence 71–2
nongovernment organisations 74
'nonsense on stilts' 7

occupation 116–17, 121–2
official noncitizenship 57
OHCHR 65
Oliveri, Federico 119–20
organised crime 43–4
Origins of Totalitarianism 86–7
Other anxiety 64
outer exclusion 88–9
Owen, David 7

pale of the law 72
Papadopoulos, Dimitris 121, 124
papering process 19
paradox of belonging among stateless people 71–85
patchwork belongings 101–4
peculiar sort of privatisation 59–63
perimeter fences 6–7, 19
permanent residency 22–6, 42, 102
Petit-Homme, Bernard 77–8
plight of women migrants 48–9
Plotke, David 6–8
pluralism 87–90
Pogge, Thomas 7
political protest 115–29
Politics and Society 6–8
possibilities of solidarity 109–110
post-colonialism 101–4
post-traumatic stress disorder 44
potential agency 120, 127
Pratt, Geraldine 105–6
prescribed rights 37–45
presence 121–4
privacy 48
privatisation 56–7, 59–63
problematisation of legimacy 59
promise of citizenship 110
proscription of rights 34–5
Prosegur 58
prostitution 43–4
protecting human rights 49
protest 94–5, 109–110, 116–19
Protocol Relating to the Status of Refugees 39–41
pseudo privatisation 59, 61
PTSD *see* post-traumatic stress disorder

racial discrimination 43–4
racism 34–5, 38–9, 43
rape 43–4, 46
Rawls, John 3
Redclift, Victoria 73
refoulement 40
Refugee Board of Canada 22
Refugee Convention *see* Geneva Convention Relating to the Status of Refugees
refugee determination process 22–7
Refugee Protest Camp Berlin 116–17, 120, 126
Refugee Protest Camp Vienna 116, 119, 121, 123–6
Refugee Support Day 123
refugees 38–41
relational quality of noncitizenship 24–7
Relph, Edward 81
remote control 65
renationalisation 104
Residenzpflicht 123–4
resistance 101–2
retaking presence 122
rethinking noncitizenship 86–99
'right to have rights' 2, 5–7, 86–7, 124–5
Rights of Man 6–7
rites of passage 107
Rode, Carsten Baltzer 123
Rodrigue, Antonio 79
rooted displacement 71–85; conclusion 80–81; imposed nationality position 78–80; introduction 71–2; liminality position 74–8; statelessness as forced displacement 72–4
Rosario, Roberto 80
Rosenblum, Nancy L. 109
RPCB *see* Refugee Protest Camp Berlin
RPCV *see* Refugee Protest Camp Vienna
Rygiel, Kim 123

St. Cecile, Marie 71
Sale v Haitian Centers Council 40
Salt, John 57–8
sanctions 59–60, 62
Sanctuary City policy 25
sans papiers 5
Saward, Michael 96–7
scapegoating 45–6
'scum of the earth' 75–6
season labour 42–3
segregated cultural spaces 108
self-constitution 120
self-identity 118
self-reliance 108
self-representation 118
September 11, 2001 41, 46
settlement infrastructure 22, 47
sex trafficking 37–8, 43–4
Shachar, Ayelet 101, 103–4
Sigmund Freud Park 116
silent suffering 19

sin papeles 5
sites of belonging 7
slavery 35, 37, 43–4
smuggling 48
social learning 22
sojourner-consumers 107
solidarity 100–116, 126–7
sort of privatisation 59–63
sovereignty 49, 63, 66, 92, 110
Soysal, Yasemin 73
staggered pathways 101–4, 106, 110
state power 104–7
state-constructed illegality 64
statelessness 71–85; as forced displacement 72–4
Statelessness and Citizenship 73
status of conquered people 4
substantive settlement 25
systemic contingency 20, 26–8
systemic violence 106

taking liminality position 74–8
Taliban 39
telos of politicisation 95
temporary migration schemes 102, 107–111
terrorism 46–7
Tivig, Andrea 109
Toronto 17–33
trafficking 34–7, 43–4, 48
trajectory of inclusion 97
transgressive situated solidarity 116
travellers 72–3
treaty protection 49
Tsianos, Vassilis 121, 124
Tully, James 93, 96
Turner, Victor 75
Tyler, Imogen 120, 127
types of noncitizen 34–45; children 44–5; noncitizen workers 42–3; refugees/asylum seekers 38–41; stateless people 37–8; victims of trafficking 43–4

understanding social life 27–9
unequal access to human rights 34–55; categories of noncitizens 37–45; conclusion 49; equality/nondiscrimination 36–7; implementation of human rights 35–6; introduction 34–5; migrant workers 45–9
UNHCR 39–41
United Nations Charter 49
Universal Declaration of Human Rights 38–40, 76
US Coast Guard 40
Ute Bock Prize for Moral Courage 126

valorisation of citizenship 121
Vargas, Tahira 76
Velayutham, S. 108
Verma, Sanmati 105
Vfs Global 58
victims of trafficking 34–5, 43–4
Vienna Convention on Consular Relations 35
'Vindaloo against Violence' 109
violation of human rights 46, 48, 80–81
vulnerability 49–50, 61

Walters, William 95
Wannsee Conference 38
Wheatley, Elizabeth 61–2
White Australia Policy 104
Wirayuda, Hasan 39
work of conditionality 17–33
World Bank 60
World War II 38, 63, 72
WorldBridge Services 58
worthiness 105–6, 110

xenophobia 28–9, 34–5, 41
Xiang, Biao 108
XL Airways 65

Žižek, Slavoj 106–7
Zolberg, Aristide 62

For Product Safety Concerns and Information please contact our EU
representative GPSR@taylorandfrancis.com
Taylor & Francis Verlag GmbH, Kaufingerstraße 24, 80331 München, Germany

www.ingramcontent.com/pod-product-compliance
Ingram Content Group UK Ltd.
Pitfield, Milton Keynes, MK11 3LW, UK
UKHW050054200926
475702UK00019B/2840
9780367030087